R.K. Singh's Mind and Art
A Symphony of Expressions

R. K. Singh's Mind and Art

A Symphony of Expressions

Edited By

Rajni Singh

ADHYAYAN

ADHYAYAN PUBLISHERS & DISTRIBUTORS

NEW DELHI (INDIA)

Published by
ADHYAYAN PUBLISHERS & DISTRIBUTORS
4378/4B, 105, J.M.D. House, Murari Lal Street
Ansari Road Darya Ganj, New Delhi - 110002
Ph.: 011-23263018, 011-23277156, Fax: 011-23280028
Email: adhyayanpublishers@yahoo.com

R. K. Singh's Mind and Art *A Symphony of Expressions*

Edition 2011
ISBN 978-81-8435-296-2

Printed in India

Published by Harish Chandra Yadav for Adhyayan Publishers & Distributors, Laser Typeseting at A.V. Rao and Printed at Tarun Offset Printers, Delhi

PREFACE

I began work on this anthology of critical essays on the poetry of R. K. Singh on the premise that critical writings on Indian English poetry are still confined to the appreciation of the canon, or the already established names of the Pre- Independence era and its successive three decades.

I am highly indebted to all the scholars who readily participated in making the book. I register my gratitude to the poet professor, R.K. Singh for his help in collecting his books and other reference materials. I am no less grateful to Harish Chandra Yadav, proprietor of Adhyayan Publishers and Distributors, New Delhi for readily agreeing to publish the study. I place on record my regards to Prof. Asha Viswas (Retired Prof., B.H.U, Varanasi), Prof. I.K. Sharma (Retired Prof., University of Rajasthan), Prof. Charu Sheel Singh (Mahatma Gandhi Kashi Vidyapeeth), Varanasi for inspiring me to concentrate on Indian English poetry after 1980s. I also express my regards to my mother Asha, father Shri Gajendra Singh and attest my love to all my friends, my husband Rajeev, daughter Anika and son Raghvendra for being my strength.

March 2011 **Rajni Singh**
Dhanbad

List of Contributors

Asha Viswas, formerly Professor of English, Banaras Hindu University, Varanasi, (U.P.) India.

D. C. Chambial, Editor, Poetcrit, Maranda, Himachal Pradesh, India. He has six books of poetry and three of criticism to his credit.

G.D. Barche, formerly Reader at SSVPS Arts & MFMA Commerce College, Dhule (Maharastra). He has published three books and several articles in leading journals.

Jayshree Goswami, Research Scholar in the Dept. of HSS, Indian School of Mines, Dhanbad, India.

Jindgai Kumari, Research Scholar in the Department of HSS, Indian School of Mines, Dhanbad, India.

K. V. Dominic, Editor of *Indian Journal of Postcolonial Literatures* (IJPCL). He is faculty member of the PG & Research Department of English, Newman College, Thodupuzha, Kerala, India.

Mahendra Singh, Varanasi (U.P.). He has authored two volumes on Phenomenology and Existentialism and three volumes on Post Colonialism.

Md. Mojibur Rahman, Associate Professor, Department of HSS, Indian School of Mines, Dhanbad, India.

P. C. K. Prem (P. C. Katoch), IAS (Retd), poet, novelist, short story writer and critic from Malkher Garh, Palampur, Kangra, Himachal Pradesh, India.

Patricia Prime, poet and critic from 8 Te Atatu South, Auckland, New Zealand.

Rajni Singh, Associate Professor of English, Department of HSS, Indian School of Mines, Dhanbad, India.

Ram Sharma, senior lecturer in English, J.V. College, Baraut, Baghpat, U.P.; writes poetry and reviews.

Raghuvanshmani Tripathi, Associate Professor, Department of English, Shivharsh Kisan P.G. College, Basti, U.P., writes poetry.

Sudhir K. Arora, Department of English, Maharaja Harishchandra P. G. College, Moradabad (M. J. P. Rohilkhand University, Bareilly) UP, India.

V. V. B. Rama Rao, formerly Reader at the Maharaja's College, Vizianagaram; he is an ELT Specialist, creative writer, literary translator and biographer.

Yana Atanasova Rowland, Senior lecturer in English Literature, English Department, Plovdiv University, Bulgaria.

Contents

INTRODUCTION

I

The history of Indian English poetry reveals that from the time of Rabindra Nath Tagore and Sri Aurobindo to the present day there has been no dearth of poets who through their levels of poetic consciousness have contributed their bit in shaping the genre. But if one goes through the poetry anthologies and literary journals, particularly those published till the turn of the last century as also while browsing the syllabuses and stacks of research sections of universities, one encounters the acknowledgement of a dozen of names that have been repeatedly discussed and studied, suggesting that the Indian English poetic creativity, if not the tradition, is exhausted. Moreover, there is no paucity of critics who take pride in claiming/ asserting their critical venture as off-beat even though it harps on those names that possess celebrity status. This hostility or aversion for the less known, or the relatively unknown but competent writers, without excluding the regional writers, and the way they are relegated to anonymity, is an indication of a section of academia and media believing in the blind acceptance of a canon which gives credence to merely churning and recycling of the past with little or no consideration for the recent or contemporary.

The entire scenario leads the common readers to a conviction that genuine Indian English poetry is grounded in the poetic consciousness of only a handful of so called recognised /established writers and the others' creative output is simply trash and worthy of rejection.

Furthermore, the criteria adopted for the selection of readable and not so readable poetry are based on without reading the works or the popularity index of poets are set by publishers, prejudiced reviewers, popular columnists, critics, and award-giving agencies. The same manoeuvring and manipulation is visible in the critical writings of poetry where mindless full-throated praises are made, at times followed by unjustified, mismatched, abnormal comparisons between poets and their works, or complete rejection of their works. Was it not

Dr Samuel Johnson who said, he who praises everyone praises no one? This practice of selection-rejection, or calling ones favourites great, has put forth a great challenge before the new writers, who cannot find good readership for their works or fair critical attention. Most of them publish spending their own resources and end up virtually unknown!

The politics of acclaiming the already acclaimed and subtly streamlining the others can never be a part of healthy literary culture. It is to be remembered here that history has never been a full circle and neither can it be so; it has to look forward and embrace the present open-mindedly and whole- heartedly in order to maintain its historicity. For any literary tradition it is vital to continue to discover continuities for its enrichment and growth. It is this continuity that has the capacity to strengthen its tradition and hence forth it puts the literary scholars, critics and connoisseurs to a task which calls for a serious, consistent and balanced examination of the ongoing trends in contemporary Indian English poetry.

The present anthology is a humble attempt in this direction as it intends to explore the poetic corpus of Ram Krishna Singh (b. 1950), who has not only shown consistency in his writing but has also demonstrated in his verses the sound and sense of good poetry and has tried to remain Indian and at the same time international in his approach while assimilating the traditional with the modern sensibility.

II

As a poet, critic and editor R.K. Singh has shown his merit both in quantity and quality. He has authored more than 150 articles, 160 book reviews and 35 books, including, 13 collections of poems. His poetry volumes include *My Silence* (1985*), Memories Unmemoried* (1988), *Music Must Sound* (1990), *Flight of Phoenix* (1990), *I Do Not Question* (1994), *My Silence and Other Selected Poems:1974-1994* (1996), *Above the Earth's Green* (1997), *Every Stone Drop Pebble* (1999), *The Face in All Seasons* (2002), *Peddling Dream* (2003), *The River Returns: A Collection of Tanka and Haiku* (2006), *Sexless Solitude and Other Poems* (2009), and *Sense and Silence: Collected Poems* (2010). Some of his poems have been translated into French, Spanish, Romanian, Chinese, Serbian, Croatian, Slovene,

Japanese, Bulgarian, German, Italian, Portuguese, Greek, Esperanto, Albanian, Hindi, Punjabi, Kannada, Tamil, and Bangla, and his poetry has been studied by several critics through articles and anthologies just as it has been explored for a couple of academic degrees.

The early years of one's life are the formative period that shape up one's mind. Eliot once said that "a writer's art must be based on the accumulated sensations of the first twenty one years." This applies to the poet as well. R. K. Singh was born, brought up and educated in Varanasi. Both the place and home atmosphere laid the seeds of creativity in him. He has been a voracious reader since childhood and this practice of reading ignites his creative impetus. He started writing short stories and poems for the local newspapers at a very young age and this practice of writing continues till date.

As a professor of English language and a practitioner of ESP at the Indian School of Mines, Dhanbad, R.K. Singh takes seriously his poetic expressions. Like a merchant of words, he chisels his verses, brushes each word with utmost solicitude and fits it in the right place, thus, making every word stand by itself. On the surface level the equation of words appears simple but his poems almost always mean much more than the sum of his words, challenging the readers to untangle the complex connections, and possibly due to this reason even the best critical interpretation is not able to provide full satisfaction by dissipating the entire complexity which yet remains clinging to his poems.

Another noteworthy feature of Singh's poetry is its style. The poet keeps experimenting with his long and short verses (haiku and tanka). Some of his poems have titles while in majority of his poems he avoids providing titles, letting his readers to surcharge their imagination. There is very little use of punctuation marks in his poetry. (In fact, the poet's latest volume, *Sense and Silence: Collected Poems* contains no title or punctuations in any section). The poet also distances himself from the use of lazy or colourful adjectives, repetitions and jingling effect that conventional poetry contains, and prefers speech rhythm over rhyme. Singh's poetry contains bare minimum embellishment or tapestry of any kind, yet the pulchritude of his verses never lessen. Thus, all the conventional norms of poetry writing are tailored and refashioned into a new style which is exclusively R.K. Singh's.

Singh not only advocates economy of expression through his verses but also gives significance to poetic diction, particularly to imagery and striking metaphors. Most of the images in Singh's long poems are conventional, drawn from myth, ritual and religion, nature and literature, and urban settings, with a small infusion of images and symbols, which are synthetical or compounds of the conventional and the fabricated. Generally, his images are morbid and dark in nature, especially the animal images and the images that present squalor but the images that emerge from his haiku and tanka are crystal clear and refreshing. Moreover, Singh's verses with the use of enjambment add richness of meaning to the images and metaphors. He demonstrates an increasing mastery over the difficult form of the brief personal lyric. Above all, he has a good musical ear, modesty enough to permit the subject to find its proper voice, and an inner vision with sensuous accuracy, as his American poet-professor friend Lyle Glazier would say.

If R.K. Singh's poetry is marked for its crafting and scintillating style, it is also noted for its boldness and conceptual daring. Woman is seminal in Singh's poetry. The female body becomes the tool, in fact, source of inspiration through which the poet renders his states of feelings about love, sex, beauty and art. For him:

> Woman
> is the measure
> of all things: body, truth
> love, spirit, God, society, peace....
>
> (*Above the Earth's Green*, Poem 57)

And in the poet's vision howsoever she (woman) is strange, she is:

> ...ever new:
> pierce like diamond
> or thread like pearl
> to weld in her depth
> her nudity
> ...her mystery
> (she is)...perfect poetry
> beyond the sky (*Above the Earth's Green*, Poem 60)

Through the metaphor of woman, Singh presents his ideology of poetry. In fact, in his verses the two amplify into a whole to stand as an epitome of pleasure, pain and ecstasy. Some of Singh's verses may appear naked portrayal of sexuality but the poet stands for man and woman in deep synchronicity: the harmony between them is basic to physical, emotional, sexual and social existence. The poet's attitude, in fact, is in keeping with the Rig Vedic "first fruit of the intellect," which sex or love essentially is. Thus, love is the fulcrum of his poetry and one can notice all its facets, from the physical to metaphysical, in his poetry.

R.K. Singh's verses not only lyrically celebrate love and glorify the female body but also render the anguish and yearning of life in a powerful and original voice. Along with existential and ecological concerns and sociopolitical issues, one finds traces of subtle and ironical insights into the fallibility of human nature. Some of his verses might appear as if these have stemmed from his immediate world or appear like the poet's diary where the poet pens down his ramblings, too personal in tone.

In a nutshell, the poetry of R.K. Singh spans a wide range of experience. He dwells on simple daily emotions and transports them to his readers with an awesome power of sight. His poetry has the power to draw the attention of the commoner as well as to satisfy the intellectual appetite of a serious reader. The immense contribution that Singh has made to Indian English poetry in particular and Indian English writing in general, and the sense that his poetic expressions possess generate a compulsion to dive deep and seek for newer/ final meaning from his verses.

III

The twenty one critical essays in the book set out to explore the myriad shades of R.K. Singh's poetry and in the process unravel his poetic mind and art.

The first essay is a comprehensive presentation of Singh's creativity. It demonstrates the multifarious dimensions of his poetic artistry and also sets a background to the reading of the other essays.

Jindagi Kumari and Rajni Singh's article explores the poet's concept of art and the way it finds expression in his verses. They find the poet's aesthetic consciousness oriented towards beauty and self-harmony.

Yana Rowland's revealing paper discusses monotony of existence which is one of the major concerns in Singh. She figures out the causes of anxiety which is due to ageing, the failing sense of tradition, the failure in evaluating the self, aligned with time where there is sterility, materialism and moral degeneration. The discussion is developed in the light of Existentialism as conceived by Heidegger, Levinas and Bakhtin.

G. D. Barche's article is a stylistic interpretation of the poem "Sexless Solitude." Through his analysis the writer brings forth Singh's poetic craftsmanship.

D. C. Chambial concentrates on a single poem, "Karmic Credit," to explore the text and technique of the poem.

Mahendra Singh's article makes a close analysis of R. K. Singh's poetry in the light of the philosophy of David Hume, Kierkegaard, Hegel, Nietzsche, Kant, Husserl, Heidegger, Descartes, Sartre and Ponty. The article primarily rests on existential concerns, anxiety and quest for being and truth in Singh's poetry.

G. D. Barche in his article, '"Sanjaya" and "Dhrutrashtra" Reconstructed in the Capsule Poems of R. K. Singh', inquires into the poetic mind of Singh in order to unmask the private and personal, the social and scriptural elements.

Rajni Singh's article examines death motif in the poetry of Singh. She finds the metaphor of death as a positive presence in the poet because it is indicative of search for life and meaning in existence.

P.C.K. Prem's article is a profound study on the social issues and anxieties in Singh's verses.

V.V.B. Rama Rao assesses the poetry of Singh in the light of the poet's statements given in an interview pertaining to art, his poetry and the creative process. He finds no dissimilitude between the mind that thinks/ advocates and the mind that performs.

'Poetry is both personal and social criticism'. Jayshree Goswami's article rests on this idea. She makes a comparative study of R. K. Singh and P. Raja in terms of culture and society.

Jindagi Kumari in her incisive paper argues that Singh's erotic poems are sensuous, embodied with carnal yearnings and is deeply rooted in the Indian philosophy of *prakriti-purush*, and the idea of harmony in duality.

Raghuvanshmani Tripathi's paper dwells upon the subject of sex in Singh. He is of the opinion that the idea of sex in Singh's poetry is deceptive. To him the sex expressions seem asexual as through it the poet explores the society in an unconventional manner.

Jindagi Kumari and Rajni Singh's article deals with the use of myths in the poems of Shiv K. Kumar and R.K. Singh. They draw similarities and dissimilarities in the two poets in their mythic treatment.

Ram Sharma in his article discusses the major themes of Singh's poetic collection, *Sexless Solitude and Other Poems*. He designates Singh as a poet of modern sensibility and also considers him as the most representative poet of the time.

The remaining six articles of the anthology deal with the haiku and tanka of R. K. Singh. Rajni Singh's article studies the haiku form in general, and the Indian English haiku in particular, along with special reference to Singh's haiku. The article serves as a background to the latter articles.

Asha Viswas takes into account the three liners of Singh to display his dexterous handling of the poetic form. Similarly, Patricia Prime in her paper studies the haiku of Singh to demonstrate the sense and scintillating effect that the three liners enfold.

K.V.Dominic in his study of Singh's haiku minutely observes the kigo words and the way the poet exploits it to produce the desired meaning.

Sudhir K Arora in his article ranks Singh as a significant poet whose verses are packed with sense, sound and pointedness.

The last article examines R.K. Singh's haiku and tanka sequences, a form which is practised in India probably by the poet only. The writer finds the haiku pieces as complete unit and when hooked together they display a mosaic of expressions as well as reflect relatedness, giving a larger impression.

IV

Though the poet has been explored by researchers and critics here and there, there always remains a possibility of further exploration as the output of Singh's creativity is yet to reach its ebb. Though some of the articles that the book contains explore the dense texture of Singh's poems, aspects such as gender expressions, biblical, and Indian and western mythical allusions, poetic confessionalism, metaphysical consciousness, religion and morality, post modernist idioms, comparative study with other established/ new poets remain unexplored, and thus require detailed evaluation in future by interested scholars and readers.

WORKS CITED

1. Tobin, David Ned. *The Presence of the Past-T.S. Eliot's Victorian Inheritance*. Michigan: UMI Research Press. 1983, 84.
2. Singh, R.K. *Above the Earth's Green.* Calcutta : Writers Workshop. 1997.

1

Journey of Beauty: Nature and Woman in the Poetry of R. K. Singh

— P. C. K. Prem

To understand and appreciate the poetic mind of R. K. Singh, one needs to fully comprehend the fact that nature and woman occupy the centre stage in his philosophical thinking. The poet discovers meaning in passions; and sex is interpreted as a liberating and purifying factor in Singh's poetic scheme. To that extent the poet exhibits anxiety for tradition and heritage. As Singh gives an uninhibited expression to thoughts on love, woman, beauty and nature, and while talking about exploitation and poverty he in reality, shows concerns about the social issues, borrowing images, metaphors, symbols and similes from Nature and sex. He seeks out release from emotional tension discreetly; and cautiously describes man-woman relations and in the process subtly establishes profound emotional ties with the readers. He exposes them to hypocrisy and questions of morality without malice or prejudice. His thematic voyage never deviates from the basic philosophy of love, life, beauty and woman and this, he continues with awful power. His latest collection of poems *Sexless Solitude and Other Poems* opens up certain other interesting areas of his thought process earlier left unvisited.

Singh like any other creative man is deeply worried about the outcome of struggle continuing between the flesh and spirit – an eternal issue that mystifies the existence of man on earth. Singh is also concerned about man's existence and identity: the existential crisis in a multilingual, multicultural, multi-religious, and plural society vis-à-vis the ethos of Indian society and inheritance. It is not so much the tradition of English or Indian English poetry writing but the poet's own thoughts or repetition of emotions and ideas that strengthen his argument in varying contexts, creating a pervasive interest which one would like to redefine and interpret. There is an undercurrent of vibrant struggle as he seeks to extract himself (and all of us) from the enchaining norms and values of the society. He discovers new meanings via images of woman and Nature; he explores life and its purpose, and relationship between the body and the soul through unmitigated passions; from silence to noise unheard, Singh searches for identity.

In Singh's poems from *My Silence* (1985) to *The Face in All Seasons* (2002), we discover the poet's many dimensions: his social awareness in terms of contemporary life and values exposing man's innate instincts, pretense and nakedness; his understanding of myths, legends, history, politics, culture and religion; philosophy of humanity, and interpretation of art and tradition. In *My Silence*, a collection of formative years, written in a long span of ten years from 1974 to 1984, the thread of silence runs through all the poems.

For the poet, silence is a boon and a pillar of strength on which stands the intensity of creativity; and solitude provides him with rare moments to communicate with god. In Nature, the poet finds glimpses of infinity. In autumn tree, looking like 'a young woman', he sees promise of the return of spring 'too lovely to touch' (1). The poet is enamored of the splendor of Nature, incarnating herself into a woman and affords ample opportunities to the tender heart of the poet to dwell on the mystery of life, its reality and pains. To him:

> The best poetry
> is a woman
> concrete, personal, delightful
> greater than all (*My Silence*, Poem7)

Nature, as a woman is all beauty and blessing 'She stands between two parched trees like a sea of beauty' as he sees. His images are superb, at times shocking but earthliness transmits vibrant sensations, tingling heart and intellect. Through the eyes of Nature, the poet makes a long, difficult and meandering journey into meaning of life and its hidden purpose. The realities of life are slowly revealed with electrifying rapidity and the reader is transported to a different world when the poet says, 'To express sex/a crowd is convenient in the bus/ during the Puja he rubs hard/his cock against the ladies, 'bottoms.' There is a terrific insight into man's heart which should stun even a saint out of his subliminal thoughts where everything happens in the name of religion, culture and traditions which unfortunately turn into a national waste.

Singh's razor-sharp and penetrating words shatter the in-built self-conceived idea about ethics in public life, when he says, 'spring's full youth/he unbuttons/her printed skirt/on the red cushion'. (*The Face in All Seasons*, Poem 15) He condemns the inherent frailties, a man nurses. One is coarsely amazed at the revelation of naked realities. The poet is dangerously cute and correct when he talks of Banaras and Lucknow. These two cities become symbols of ills, sins and foul play. There is nothing sacred but total collapse of value system. Here, thoughts of heaven and salvation turn into myths. Words like law and liberty lose meaning, 'they repeat blunders/out of ignorance/or kindness'. It is a society where 'bureaucrats/...politicians and journalists/who appear/in mating season/like dogs in/ October and November/and perpetuate the blur/...of decaying ancestors.' (Poem 38).

The poet discovers that man lives a futile existence amidst proclamation of sanctity and piety. He is in a chaotic state of mind and in search of harmony in disturbed times. He stands:

...like an island
shielding chaos
I hear the serenade
and live my joy (Poem 48)

And this presents an image of self-contradictions and intrinsic dissonance. The poet's harshness and at times vivid crudity reveal a life of disgust and vices, when he observes:

...in cells naked gods nudge
borrowed girls with wealth
uncreate their seeds
for hurried happiness (Poem 54)

There could not be a greater denunciation of relation among men and women. Here love has no meaning. It gets commercial undertones and prostitutes itself opt for it without a feeling of repentance. It is between prayer and passion that meaning is searched. Only emptiness confronts a man even when he realizes a subtle fulfillment.

The poet cannot be blamed for his terseness and slightly unconventional interpretation of nature, woman and beauty in nature, chaos and deceitful harmony among objects of Nature, and frantic search for identity without visible results. Even the confluence of

Ganga and Yamuna/ is a homosexual union/charming but sterile.'(Poem 64) It becomes apparent that personal experience of sickening routine in Dhanbad leads the poet bit by bit to see for himself' the anguished uncertainties of hard lives amidst academic conspiracies where he finds 'fears are real with curses on lips. He says:

> ...fight with the devils desiring
> to procreate christians (Poem 66)

It is an abrupt shift in thought process where religion does create fissures to unsettle man who is already living in dangerous conditions. It is a sense of division within that plays havoc. The poet who started his journey with the flight of fancy and found solace and solitude in nation and woman, unexpectedly faces challenges of life and finds that everything around 'shrink and shrivel everyday/the self waste and wars and cries/reduce man to naught.' (Poem 66)

He seeks answers in prayerful silence. The strength lies in the message that only in struggles and sufferings, whether physical or mental, a man can survive and realize the real purpose of life.

For, in the end he returns to his own cell and brushing aside loneliness, he prays before Ganesh and Luxmi; and thus supreme joy enters the entire being. A sense of calmness prevails within and without when the poet prunes thoughts to write well; to be simply understood. Possibly towards the end of journey, the poet realizes that living peacefully with oneself can guarantee lasting peace in anarchic times.

To incorporate 'multiplicity of modern man' is a challenge that has to be met which shall ultimately lead to self-awareness. In short, *My Silence* is a terrible journey of modern man suffering from agony and intense pain. When the poet at last says that, 'I can't weave/gaudy mess/of dreams any more' (Poem 79) he in reality exhorts man to see within and be at peace.

Singh gives a satisfying account of man's dilemma in *My Silence*. His quest to find happiness and permanence could be easily construed as a struggle of man to find an identity in a consistently changing world without violating impact of culture and traditions and here he conveys a strong message. The pattern of poems of *My Silence* is unique and swings musically from passionate activity to serenity, from puzzles to solutions, from confusion to harmonization. Here, he comes very close to W. B. Yeats. In chaotic surroundings and meaningless pursuits, a man can achieve a lot provided he understands life. Yeats firmly believed that a man truly starts living life when he sincerely moves around the sufferings and agonies of life and here Singh, too, in *My Silence* moves from a disturbed to a peaceful and purposeful life.

Music Must Sound (1990) composed almost during the same period as *My Silence*, carries the thought content and emotional load of the poems of first collection. Here the poet is calm, serene and provocative and a kind of confidence can be observed in his expression. Through an inner search the poet attempts to create a poetic world out of real life experiences. He celebrates poetry and its latent strength. A poem, in the very beginning, seems to him 'like life' with sound and silence, movement and stillness, fragment and wholeness. It is imagination that lifts him to eerie heights of creation through 'lotus and mud.' His experiential imagination elevates, shocks, surprises and also raises curiosity. In a poem, he finds native virtues and vices too. It is a flight into the depths of life's mysteries. It lights up dark chambers of an individual and fills life with fragrance.

However, there is consistent and inevitable sullen strangeness in the poet's shifting thoughts. There are small poems talking of intense worldly activities, nirvana, and mind-boggling flashes such as 'hidden between thighs/is the spring music/beyond birth' and 'while he neared the coital bliss/the little child woke up/with erect penis cried/ to spoil sex she slipped aside/and put out her breast to feed him' (*Music Must Sound*, Poem 11). Here images and metaphors intermingle and play prominent roles to communicate subtle meaning. Strangely enough, the poet glorifies the role of flesh and body which could be misunderstood.

Underneath, the poet tries to establish synthesis between body and soul. His words create a tremendous pressure of uncertainty in belief. Breaking all norms, at times, the 80 odd poems give birth to startling images of sizzling sex and tantalizing beauty. It is celebration of sex and passion, of woman's beauty and body, of physical needs of body and sincere desire to purify soul. For example:

> The dress hides
> undress
> and you look beautiful (*Music Must Sound*, Poem 13)

And

A stray sperm
grows in the ovum
blooms as a puffball (Poem 14)

And

...under a bloody roof
my tattered trousers remind
the bedsheets love stained
before light shone (Poem 16)

This is not a usual culmination. The poet is perturbed about the vital anxiety that raises questions of man's life. He is wholly conscious of the limitations of body and soul. The concerns and worries are genuine. Not for a moment, the poet is incapable of running away from the mental grooves which speak of utter helplessness and self-collapse and there the mental degeneracy plays its fatal role. Along with the man's deception and hypocrisy, he keeps alive his fertile imagination and yet bemoans the destiny of modern man's obsession with physical pleasures. Whenever thoughts crowd the mind, he runs wild and finds even 'Darkness a whore/Isleep with/ cross legged/without copulation.' (Music Must Sound, Poem 23) And abruptly, a strong desire takes roots to 'maneuver to kill a poet/ learning the secret of/the first menstrual flow'(Poem. 24). The irony is: before he could even begin, he faces the end' 'with the best of motives'.

The poet uses sex imagery copiously with subtle hints and sometimes he is obvious. Each image explains the mental obsessions and aberrations of a man caught up in the vicious rather thrilling for him, cesspool of sex- or meaning of sex. The words like 'milky silence' 'skin shrinks' 'wet bare backs' 'tow white moons' 'monkey, snakes, and night impart sensuous meanings to each description and constitute a big force as:

The night drips
from their faces
like the rains

assails my vision
I fail to distinguish
man from beast (*Music Must Sound*, Poem 34)

Even religious fanatics dancing on the top of tower 'plan to erect/ Shiva's phallus as token of love.' A definite and weird current continues to flow in all the poems which are devoid of any title but demonstrate tangible unity in various fragments. It appears Singh is unsympathetic and partially negative towards life but down deep an impression sustains of his being entirely realistic to the purpose of life-a positive and hopeful attitude. Imparting an innovative and fresh perspective he is continuously exploring, inventing new ways to lead a life of peace, to 'work out salvation' and earn fruitfully 'the bread of life.'

Whatever might be the challenges in ambiguities, the poet avers, man must wade 'through the maze of rootlessness/fragmented memories and finger prints' in order to rise again before extinction. He throws sufficient hints of a life wasted which needs to be redeemed from the pit of vice and guilt. It is loss of human values and morality that disturbs the poet. He is aware of the socio-political situation and fully knows the rotten conditions to which society is moving ahead, suffocating man without pity. The sufferings are not one-sided but multidimensional. Conflicts and dilemmas are many but the escape route is equally visible among impossibilities. It is a different matter that Singh does not want to stick to one thought or stay at one place. It is a personal dilemma permeated with a sense of in-born anxiety and misery. It is a movement from one thought to another, a journey in time through variable impressions, many situations, thought of a moment - part hazy, part confused; and jumbled thoughts in a horde of moments.

The poet bewails and weeps when he observes:

> He walks through the high walled narrow lanes
> where children play with dead or dying dogs
> that eat their own stinking flesh
> he sees them sitting over the running wheels
> murdered innocence peep out from windows
> but no one bothers the tragic turn
>
> (*Music Must Sound*, Poem 56)

It is burden of the modern life persistently choking man but he is wide awake. The modern metros don't provide solace and contentment but kill man with ear-splitting noise and pollution. Many insidious and unholy deeds keep man occupied and he cares little for the excellent and pleasant things of life. Even rouged faces of working girls show hidden frustration and nobody is really in a position to run away from the miseries of inane, meaningless and frantic search for identity. Many a time, it looks as if the poet is lost in the predicaments of life and fails to find a solid base. In flash of a moment, he finds life pulsating and stimulating but next minute, it is darkness before the eyes. In all sincerity, in total failure and vacuity of thought, in a spirit of helplessness and loss of faith, the poet who impersonates himself as a protagonist of modern man finally decides to '...swallow pills/ to live in a safer tomb.' (64)

It is the failure to set right 'the rotten state of man' that agitate; and distress the soul:

> ...missing all turbulence
> so necessary to wash out
> the ills of ages it seems
> it's lifeless now
> impotent to set right
> the rotten state of man (*Music Must Sound*, Poem 66)

The poet points to the pathetic state of mind and human affairs and glimpses of depressing times ahead. This age, the poet laments, is beset with fears, vices and uncertainties. Here love or sex is a hoax. These sublimes sentiments get a severe beating when confronted with selfishness and depravity of modern times. In fact, the poet is blunt and outspoken and to him such gentle and lofty thoughts have no value and meaning and there appears genuine self-contradiction to accept such situations. Again, the man in the poet struggles hard to search concrete moorings where he would elevate himself and thus a firm faith is born that all is not lost and salvation is possible. (Poem 73)

This long poem in the totality of its fragments and wholeness, elevation and enrichment, is slow where it shows man suffering acutely the savage assaults of times and human nature. The poet now tries to salvage himself and the man at large. He gives voice to inherent anguish and pains and subsequent contempt for weakness and frailty among human beings for a life of easy virtues. 'Love without clothes/ without bone has/a joy within...' (*Flight of Phoenix*, Poem 9) And without knowing, that it shall create instability and madness. He is enlightening and challenging at the same time and there lies its true significance.

Singh appears sharp, sensitive, imaginatively devastating, perceptive and accurate while turning to woman who continues to remain a strong fulcrum of his poetic strength; and here he is quizzically insightful in creating word pictures.

In *Flight of Phoenix* (1990), a distinct progress in his poetic journey is visible and he seems to look out for an unconventional path. After writing a number of woman-centered poems, either he lands up with a coherent message or puzzles the reader with a question. He is in the habit of living estranged from the readers and yet guardedly establishes intimate relations with them which can only be described as interesting, ironic and unpredictable. His poems are short, very short indeed but convey meaning of love and beauty. It looks at times that the entire philosophy of life hovers around woman and Singh feels several times a kind of long distance from wholeness that he looks out so assiduously in women and precisely this feeling disturbs his mind.

Singh may be violating sensibility of a man at certain moments but in reality he opens up those new grounds of facts and truths which are intentionally ignored by men and women while living in the contemporary world. To me certain pieces of short poems appear fragile and foreign to the major theme connecting all poems but still a surprising continuity appears on the surface. For example:

I make myself man
each time I create
setting, character, tone
in a poem (*Flight of Phoenix*, Poem 1)

In the first poem, he speaks of poetic sense in a man. It is the poetry of self that will save man according to Singh. Immediately, he recollects a song lying dormant in memory. The journey, from a man in poet to a poem itself, makes an amazing shift. He calls a poem madness 'inverting the safe existence'. He meanders in a terrible lane of secluded uncertainty of thought and emotion. His emotions become thoughts and thoughts melt into emotions and here, the mysterious poet Singh must be caught even when he is trying to visualize:

...sleepless poetry
fails to negotiate night
I wait for white dreams (*Flight of Phoenix*, Poem 4)

He appears to set up his own parameters of writing poems. Then he comes to another thought –

Love is my prison
... to be everything
her shiva and
shakti a dual- single
me and she, one (*Flight of Phoenix,* Poem 6)

Next moment, love is something which leads him to beauty and vision with perfection. A few lines on love and life are innovative and refreshing in description and design:

It hangs like a drop
any moment evaporate
love is gullible (*Flight of Phoenix,* Poem 10)

And suddenly an idea enters the physical joy of love, when he says:

When I inhale in
your mouth and exhale stroking
hairs or caressing
I ride you into joy and
make you hail the morning like earth
(*Flight of Phoenix*,Poem 11)

His flights take swift turns from earthly existence to terrestrial life and even back. Sometime, it looks, the poet who is genuinely concerned about man's destiny and fate, falls into the trap of his own ideas and feelings which to a simple mind appear confused and intertwined and also detrimental to the concept of man's life. Here emphasis is on a highly intellectual and imaginative poetry and the apparent meaning that it purports to furnish.

Music Must Sound and *My Silence* carry in them life's 'enigmas and mysteries' and a similar strain is witnessed in *Flight of Phoenix*. The changes in thoughts and emotions take place with terrific rapidity.

If there are efforts to shield 'some dumb myths', there is also an attempt to ward off 'Moments of Truth'. Truths can be uncomfortable when 'winter is caughtin waves of narrow discussions/under the blanket/fingers move by nipples erect/without sensing consummation.' (Poem 16) Here the poet harps back on the theme of bodily pleasures.

It is stark materialism that destroys man and soul as he comments elsewhere while stretching the thought. Even sexual overtures do not afford satisfaction. This leads to total loneliness in spite of desires that a man carries around.

Another unique feature of Singh's poetry is that in short poems he constructs a new scene every time with recurring thoughts, new tilts and contents. In the midst of turmoil, the poet feels forlorn and vulnerable and the satanic forces work to dupe him again and again. It is noise within he wants to escape. In total vacuity of mind, he wants to forget everything. In different objects of Nature, he wishes to find comforts but fails wretchedly. Singh shows preference for Nature and its wildness. He turns meditative and sad. His imagery is startling like Andrew Marvell's as he is full of satire and metaphysical conceits. It happens many a time he tries to bring together discordant and self-contradictory thoughts. Strange comparisons take place. For him even 'stony breaches' give birth to 'wild plants and creepers'.

The river walks without shoes, the frog in mirror steps by damp towel and the stunning lines like 'growing hair on soul/man longs for known grooves of death/safe in sterile womb' (Poem 36) create word painting that require intellectual and emotional efforts to understand.

Again, he speaks of crazy people who know not what to do, for he calls all:

> We are a nation
> of cowards worshipping dumb
> images can't stand
> a full- fleshed person speaking
> nude in God's home like in bed
>
> performing love with
> wife or self in dark alone
>
> (*Flight of Phoenix,* Poem 41)

And the same restrained thought imbued with dark and parched emotions runs in these lines also:

> Apple, snake and three-fifth of me
> in bed manipulates man
> inside selfish rubbles (*Flight of Phoenix*, Poem 35)

It can be easily inferred that the poet while philosophizing over the fate of man engaged in worldly pursuits talks of inner despair and agony of man, who, again and again, finds consolation in physical pleasures though transient and yet ever ignorant, 'moralizing/hell of fear/with legs tucked up/posing brave.

As a reader moves from poem forty two, he is transported to a new world of sex, love and joy. It is clear in all thoughts and philosophical broodings that woman is important for Singh. She is predictably present in each word he writes. Each part of a woman's body speaks out a different language, conveys a fresh meaning, gives purpose to an empty man and lastly infuses a spirit to live life either to waste it willingly or without guilt. A sensitive man enjoys this deeply passionate and dangerous poetry and a discerning lover of poetry finds new meaning and purpose as he goes through such pieces right from poem forty two onward. He finds woman exciting in many ways. Women submit to men to make them cheerful and comfortable. They elevate and teach men the art of love and life. The poet makes it clear that woman possesses a wonderful quality of head and heart.

She is the only gift of God to man who serves man well through her beauty, body and intellect. The poet might appear highly erotic and sex-possessed but he makes it clear that when a reader shall penetrate within, he would not be different.

Poems such as 'Woman is the flesh/and spirit of poetry/eternal love thirst/growing younger as /one grows older day by day/perfecting the body.' (Poem 49) And 'call it Yin and Yang/our basic sex, *lingam* and *yoni*/harmonise' (Poem 52) and 'like a woman's mind/resides between her thighs joys/and satisfaction' (Poem 56) are boisterous and amusing celebration of woman, her beauty, mind and wantonness. Wantonness of a woman is also handled with superb grace and decency and there lies the strength of the poet. But one comes to face reality with a jerk when he observes –

> A meanest moment
> of eternity it was
> when I was conceived (*Flight of Phoenix*, Poem 65)

It is thought of sin and guilt in a sacred act of procreation in which a man and woman are involved and here host of moral issues crop up. It is an act, noble and purely transcendent and to create is a blessing to mankind and it can't be termed as sin. But the poet wants to shatter the belief for a minute when adds:

after 40 years
I see same degeneration
my mother saw first (*Flight of Phoenix*, Poem 65)

Singh in all seriousness, is concerned and worried about the fate of man, life and the world, 'always puny grave/and also man's place in the entire spectrum. It is definitely not a religious impact but faith in man is evident. It is the sweep of intellect that ensnares and chases frequently. In another way, poetic journey has been quite undisturbed, giving space for new rejuvenated thoughts and feelings infused with fresh zest for life and Singh never stops.

A collection of poems *Some Recent Poems* (1990-1994), covers a span of about five years. Maturity and depth of personal experiences extend perhaps beyond the boundaries of intellect and emotions. Here Singh is authentic and assertive. From abstract thoughts, he returns to facts and reality of life but hardly achieves his objective in concrete stipulations and thus the struggles continue in terms of religious and metaphysical tension.

The poet at the outset raises questions of life and death. A few streaks of metaphysical thoughts continue to flow with images and metaphors. The first poem 'I do not question' is a difficult poem with immense metaphysical conceits. It gives many meanings and yet defies a definite intellectual interpretation. In 'I don't fear Death, he is worried about life. In a few words he tells us that without/fortuity/ of birth and continuance' life would be meaningless. It is a far better proposition, the poet avers, to tie up with nature with its weeds and flowers than to depend upon 'covenant and prophets.' The poet's anxiety and search for communion and unity with soul is infinite. It remains unending and unrelenting with knowledge of inherent failures. At another moment as in 'I seek the roots' he proclaims a sense of rootlessness. In a single moment, he thinks of various religions. Here, unlike others poems, a stream of religious thoughts flows and he remembers Abdul Baha. To him, Baha's thoughts are unique and noble in sweep. It is recognition of the oneness of mankind and equality of sexes. In Baha's teaching, one finds the 'real spirit of Christ, hope instead of condemnation, 'love, unity and 'a great assurance for all men.' One must admit frankly that in many poems, notwithstanding simple style and straight forward method of saying, Singh remains highly intellectual. In emotional outbursts, he is puzzling and explosive. His images are obfuscating on the surface but deep down he provides intimations to anxieties about the import of life and its disenchantments.

'I must resurrect symbols of authority and take off afresh to find new haven'

The poet appears optimistic with a slow awakening even as the questions of love and search for identity continue to haunt the poet in nearly all the poems. He is in search of some mysterious power and poetic idiom where he could find vigorous expression. Here the grammar of silence looks as if imperative. A strong feeling indicates that in love only self-identity is possible. Elsewhere the poet confounds and frightens with a different interpretation of love and pleasure. In 'The Tempest' the sun appears erotic to the poetic vision and the winds turn tempestuous-a trivial hint at a probable incident in an epic. It is an eerie walk into physical joys where one crosses continents of 'body, fate and psyche'; and forays into the world of physical pleasures that enchants poets' imagination. The images stir finer sensibilities and create disturbing mental storms. Look at the images: Slums of sleep, time floated in our echoes, orbit of love, asthmatic wheezing, yellow Sun, breathing pipe, and the words that instill a vivid sense of pleasure and 'when I fail to sleep I seek/solace in her soft moist thighs/and pray to god to bless my passion.' It is a terrible sense of passionate longing, for he wants to run away or forget 'the cares of a crazy world' and again 'rains revive memories/ shattering emotions/in solitude.

In 'Burial of Warmth', 'Bulli', 'Erection Can't Create', 'End of the Season', 'Love Yields', 'Aloneness', 'Fount of Poetry', 'Finale of Love', 'We had a Pact', 'Love Moods' and 'Invitation', a reader confronts innovative twists in images and similes. A few poems disturb, others horrify and some alarm. In simple words, the impact is effective. A new angle to man's thoughts and emotions is given and one is surprised at the world of happiness and obvious fright, the poet generates. One ought to concentrate deeply to fathom meaning of terms like 'burial of warmth in water smell, mocking compromise of living, a famine of love/menopausal silence/erection can't create, peel their image/in mirror, the rains cry to meet earth, boys jog/in women's tents/ ejaculate/continue sorties, neutral itch, on tip of grass/the dance of Shiva, and expressions like 'she kept fiddling with her reticule- offer adequate hints of fervent, passionate love and celebration of pleasure. It is through the intimate love of a woman that the poet wants to establish identity. Woman appears frequently in his poems to infuse new vigour, to create impulsive love and passion and to inspire man to perform well and derive meaningful identity.

Again a twist in thought imparts a grave meaning to life like 'On Platform 13', 'Leaf by Leaf, 'Nature' and 'My Goddess and I', totally new patterns emerge:

> Time stands still
> in November chill
> I fill emptiness
> with words paint season
> on your face. ('On Platform 13' p. 39)

And

> In the art of living
> let's not look for perfection ('Nature' p. 40)

His search attains and embraces fresh horizons when he accepts obliquely:

> ...rest is reduced
> to orgiastic pain melting down
> into the sea of barren academics
> I search the red tears shed on the Cross
> ('Truth between Dream and Day' p. 46)

Here suffering of humanity is evident and a prayer is offered in solitude for the peace of disturbed souls of men.

In *Above the Earth's Green* (1997), the poet reverts to the scheme of untitled poems in the expected and known vein of earlier poems. Here, poems are short but paint a different portrait. No specific prototype is discerned but one finds here an apparent continuity, a unique coherence in the flow of thoughts, contents and emotions. As observed eisewhere the poet is swayed away by fragment of a thought and then he gives it an exciting visor but emotions are integral to the intrinsic thought process. He has a wild and incorrigible habit to intellectualize emotions and in the ensuing inner struggle within, he derives strength from day to day affairs which are routine and monotonous on the surface but deeply impregnated with meaning. He also extracts inspiration from religions and myths with an extraordinary synthesis.

The poet, as usual picks up the pen and the flow of emotions and ideas get converted into plain words. In the above collection, there are hundred and nine poems, each separate but affording an integrated meaning. The first poem tells that 'poetry is prayer' in the humdrum of life and a 'saving grace' in the chaotic world; and then he attempts to control himself 'to breathe a pure breath without passion/and discover essence of beauty' (Poem 2) which shall in the end bring harmony, perfection and peace for life to be lived in full.

The poet conjures up varied images and experiences within and confuses him at times but he knows to live through the 'silence of shore'. In Nature, he is in search of union when he observes that 'river has no sex/so it dried up/trapped in its own banks' (Poem 5). And soon he turns to an island where in the moonlight ghost rise to mate creating granite sensation'.

The imagery simply amazes a sensitive mind. The poet's sense of curiosity grows among different shadows, during the night that rise up amidst 'whispering darkness', enlarging moments of happiness. This happiness is short lived as the contemporary agonies multiply and the poet witnesses many scams around and hints at the prevalent corruption making life polluted. To him then 'God seems irrelevant and/altruism is preposterous.' (Poem 14) Another little poem opens up inner anguish and helplessness as the poet feels homeless and so seeks refuge in the cage of beloved's heart –a loving shelter he always seeks as a woman remains a permanent source of peace. At this stage, a personal experience tends to encompass a feeling of vacuity and then follows the prayer to Mother, for the man in poet fears 'diseases/born from within' (Poem 19)

Time and age have miserably destroyed body and the injured man asks a genuine question. His body is totally contaminated and so he requests beloved to marry soul. Emerging out of the loving and passionate shadows of woman, he shows awareness of the sufferings of man in general and so all words and expressions appeal; the poet successfully establishes deep relation with the reader. Personal miseries for the poet don't end despite the fact that he finds deep and warm affinity with the people around. Now contemporary issues disturb him as he finds in the world outside that politics plays an extremely destructive role in life.

He fails to understand 'why dogs defecate' around on the one hand and on the other, his mental miseries increase 'in the name of faith/ and god/politics fuels bigotry/strips the prophets/corrupts clarity'. (Poem 27) In politics, he finds all the ills that cripple man and soul. In terse words, he says 'politics is based/neither on knowledge/nor principles but scams' (Poem 29). Again, he makes a point, 'the criminal dies/and his followers extort/sums for *samadhi'* (Poem 30). A tragically comic conclusion he obtains. The modern man has to exist and live in such circumstances with no reprieve. In this world, villains shall continue to threaten and then demolish huts of the helpless. In such pitiable conditions, no salvation is possible and the man shall pride 'in snares of deceits/buries his own peace' (Poem 31). To the poet, fate of man is important. He is worried about the present and future and there is no escape. The wild apparitions continue to torture and haunt him. The chaos, disorder and turmoil born out of ego, anger and fanaticism prove too strong and powerful. The poet refuses to act alone and live in isolation. In his preoccupations with intellectualized sentiments, he says:

I can't suffer the crises I haven't authored even in thought
I can't endure aches of incompletion, dark void that sounds aloud
In my sleep I can't see my innocence afflicted by mirror

eating into my soul, ingesting my own body for something
there is neither consolation nor forgiveness, but negation.
(Poem 34)

Conscious of the modern sufferings, there remains a bitter lamentation in the heart. He, in moments of extreme worry, talks of education, knowledge, repression and dependence. Failure of man is carrying him to a new century without redemption, he understands and at a certain stage, poetry seems painful. He takes up social issues confronting man but fails to find a definite solution in all pervasive pollution and degradation. He is ready to suffer provided a decent death is ensured –impossibility in the present scenario. The culmination of this thought current is reached in poem forty seven, when he observes:

Pseudo, shams, crooks and
politicians pervert: (Poem 47)

and thus man, alas poet, lives through pains and 'alone I suffer sins/I didn't commit'(Poem 49)

From here, the poet returns to the theme close to his heart. He has suffered immensely. The world outside has not given him peace and happiness. He comes back to the dreamland and the lady-love appears again to soothe his wounded body and soul. In poem fifty seven, he frankly admits, 'Woman/is the measure/of all things: body, truth/love, spirit, God, society, peace/and man.' (Poem 57)

Woman is a splendid gift, God has bestowed on man and so man ought to link all happiness to her. If he stops humiliating her, he shall attain the ultimate because –

> It needs less than a drop to procreate
> but months and years of readiness to enjoy
> sex sustains both life and art (Poem 59)

To a sensitive man at peace with himself, like the poet, woman shall be a mystery/perfect poetry /beyond the sky.' (Poem 60) Not for a moment, however, he runs away from the realities of earthy existence. He does not wish to philosophize when simple living can provide joy and happiness. He accepts:

> Philosophy frightens me
> confounds obscurity
> with profundity (Poem 77)

The poet does not want to complicate life which is already cumbersome and difficult. Rather, he seeks to restore love which is ecstasy, prayer; a strong basis for a meaningful life, for love is a sacred thought, a pious relation. This is exactly what poet tries to tell us notwithstanding the feelings of eroticism. Out of these feelings, and art - that is permanent and inspiring, is born:

> I seek in sex
> freedom of nature
> ... and celebrate
> pristine purity
> of Prakriti
> reach ecstasy (Poem 91)

It is a tragedy of times that in materialistic surfeit man is unhappy and in the intensity of activity he is thoughtlessly in need of releasing his tensions and bodily exhaustion. Life of speed and rashness also spells dangers to physical pleasures:

Trucks on GT Road:
invasion of the body
for a quick release (Poem 98)

A terrible thought shatters all goodness that man nurses:

He survives in bones
brittle like hers in forties
it's winter again (Poem 102)

The poet mirrors the facts and truth of life. Between illusions and delusions, hopes and joys these continue to enrich man and he is filled with hopes for the future. There are disillusionments no doubt but joys of life, too, attract and fulfill man. Singh appears to be an inveterate optimist. He loves to roam about in shades and shadows of joys and illusory world and yet he comes back to confront life:

I love rebel rays coming in
shatter narrow illusions
moon is the poem in sky
silence sounds in brevity (Poem 106)

A cursory reading of Singh's poem doesn't provide any clue to his intellect and social anxieties, to life's mysteries and facts and truths about life. It is only after a careful reading that depths of emotions and thoughts can be understood. Singh makes subtle but powerful poetic observations on life, love and woman. Social awareness stirs his mind and heart touching sensitivity. There are ample political comments with evocative imagery and brevity. He wastes nothing, neither words nor emotions. Sublimity at certain moments enthralls. The sophistication of tiny words surprises. He is a poet of contemporary world if one goes by simple words, small and trivial experiences of life, language and idiom.

In *The Face in All Seasons* (2002) the poet comes closer to the common man's experiences. Each moment that he lives, is full of meaning. He permits nothing to go waste or possibly nothing moves unnoticed. A keen observer may forget even routine movements of time, man and nature but not so it happens with the poet. Certain emotions and thoughts have been present in the mind of man since time immemorial and it requires a great mind to catch hold of each fraction of a second and examine the impact. For a sensitive mind like Singh, each second is important. It can be visualized and described in simple words. Yet he knows limitations. He understands the wastes of world in which he lives. He envisions a situation when even emptiness provides a meaningful interpretation of life. He knows that today's man is living in a world which is divided and afflicted with immense uncertainties. Man can't run away from the inner sufferings, outer pressures, inherent contradictions and inconsistencies and continuing self-created maladies where to assert an identity is a big issue. Problems of inter-related equations and entities are bound to arise.

Today, man is disillusioned and sad. He wastes a life time in search of a fraction of a minute for happiness and he knows that life is all joy. Life is struggle, conflict and suffering; and full of contradictions and there is hidden a meaning. This is the message of 'The Face in all Seasons.' Like earlier poems, here also he leaves the poems untitled. Reason: He is happy when no restriction is imposed on the poems. He loves freedom of expression and uses his own methods and syntax, including lack of punctuation marks to transmit delicate feelings and ideas. Each of the eighty poems gives a separate and beautiful image. While reading, a scene arises before the eyes, it starts taking shape and when words try to make a scene complete, everything is dissolved and another image takes birth with another scene – lazy yet clear and loud - a kind of motion in stillness. In the first five-liner, he makes it clear that like a river, he can't merge with the sea, for he is not a river. As such, he has to find a path. It is a search in strange places among unknowns. It is impossible to understand everything. It is the limitation of human intellect that he can't fill meanings in the blanks that are left between men and emotions, between speech and words.

It is only through acts and motives that soul can be known and valued. This world is a riddle and to know it in its entirety is just not possible. Nobody knows what it is that creates a state of mourning and what one wants to conceal. But the poet can paint a marvelous picture.

It is left to the imagination of the reader to explore, for example, those 'nightmares' guarded by the 'colours of the rainbow' (*The Face in All Seasons*, Poem 5).In the next scene, helplessness keeps people disturbed because they 'bargain small pleasures in smallness. And suddenly a picture emerges where exploitation is shown its real face while remembering 'Taj in Grains.' To strengthen the same thought, a sordid and horrible scene is described. The poet paints a disgusting picture of a woman and children being beheaded in the name of God. He reminds us of the acts of barbarity committed in the array of social justice. In a split moment, another scene is created showing worship amidst sex acts and mantras. Words like 'nail parings; pubic hairs, lion-penises, cock's testicles and genital enthusiasm vividly paint a scene that benumbs the reader. In different poems, nature appears silently to beat the tortured man who had seen the barbarians committing rapes and murders. The poet is sufficiently clear when he admits his limitation and says:

> I'm no god or godfather to sacrifice
> ...nor any gods of love visit my house (Poem 12)

Pervading pollution disturbs and he observes 'the morning in Banaras/along the Ganges/is no longer fresh'. Here sin, lust, vice and unlawful sex-relations dominate various word-paintings which follow. He takes note of the miserable plight of children and environmental pollution and this disturb a sensitive mind. It is unfortunate that man wants to live in improved conditions of life but it is not possible. The narrator's troubles continue to multiply even if he changes religion. For earlier low caste stood to condemn. In the new religion, he fights his battle alone in the hope of a sun (Poem 24). This automatically leads to serious and deep thinking about the country smoldering in obscenities and dishonest rule. Even after a half century of self rule, democracy has not given peace to the citizens, and for this rampant disease reasons are quite visible:

> ...country is dying
> with too little democracy
> too much Hindu and Muslim
> too much rich and poor (Poem 25)

Truth is revealed about the fateful situations through which the country passes amidst plenty of parochial feelings, religious chauvinism and awful self-interests.

Social responsibilities awaken the poet but he can do nothing positive and in moments of failure, he escapes to the original theme of sex and body to which he imparts a certain degree of soul and spirit and these provide him shelter away from the worldly inferno. There is a vast presence of Gods and Goddesses in his room in the shape of paintings and prints on paper. There is Christ on the cross who continues to watch sex, prayers and restlessness each night' (Poem

30) Sex obsession gives a jolt to the theme the poet wishes to elaborate but then perhaps somewhere he tells that modern times find truth and meaning in sex-like orgies. Truths are so bitter. The poet is worried about every Indian home and attempts to expose the hypocrisy that people exhibit while suppressing feelings of sex and love residing side by side with the Holy Spirit and soul. One finds a swelling of passions and the chasing commitment to moral values reigning in the wild feelings and a sad fact in man's life surfaces when he finds his woman not responding to hidden desires (of sex).

The consummation remains a dream and then the narrator seeks to 'redefine/her feminine hold/I lonely sun' (Poem 36). It is a poetic tribute to woman's body and soul with an effort to give new meanings. (Poem 20)

Poetry for him is a religion, a passion and food for thought. Not a word releases without sounds of music and rhythm. He is transcendent, lyrical and tender poetically. Singh's strain of thoughts and philosophical mind-set continues in his latest collection of poems *Sexless Solitude and Other Poems* (2009).

To him, words come straight from the heart, quite raw, chaste and unsullied. If the reader travels along with the words, he enjoys and gets uniquely blessed with inspired will to live life freely as if in a Garden of Eden. He takes the reader to the verdant and, at times, dreary fields of life and leaves him there to extract meaning and purpose of life. He is neither modern nor puritan in approach but is definitely a poet of love, romance and woman:

> Ending with lewd joke
> with sensation between thighs
> his morning discourse
> arouses the disciples
> to dance in groups groping sex

where the exercise is to:

> realize consciousness
> through multiple copulation
> bliss of heaven
> in the evening practice
> kundalini meditation

(*Sexless Solitude and Other Poems*, 'Group Dance')

and body for liberation, yoga and meditation. Here words dance and sing.

Nervous anxiety of mundane life with immense vacuum and loneliness disturb but still he gets meaning out of it. Darkness has light and hope he avers. For him pollution is pervasive and so he says:

I wish I could clean the cobwebs of legends
that veil the vision, moralizing future
with doubtful glories urge us to move backward

echoes of the dead reverberate; no use
setting the alarm to go off 2010

(*Sexless Solitude and OtherPoems*, 'Conclusion')

Choking stoically within, struggling for breath, he feels pains and agonies of life but knows:

I am no Jesus
but I can feel the pains
of crucifixion

as a common man
suffer all what he suffered –
play the same refrains

(*Sexless Solitude and Other Poems*, 'I am no Jesus')

God and belief in God is now alien to him. Contrary to eloquent tributes to peace and harmony and its lasting impact, fear and insecurity is a truth that terrorism has brought and so it is a painful experience:

Each day ends in fear
of one or the other kind:
living in uncertainties
it's life in death..

(*Sexless Solitude and Other Poems,* 'Terrorism')

It is poet's strength that he awakens men to the facts and truths of life but does not sermonize. Singh's poetry is simple but conveys subtle meaning and truth of life in the contemporary scenario and it deals with theme of sensuality and sensuousness in poetry with a razor sharp intellect and stirs and disturbs every one, for in truth man wishes to hide feelings of sex like vicarious pleasures while putting up a brave moralistic face. To poet's intellect nothing is lost and still many aspects are left untouched. Through the beauty of the body of woman the poet kids us to face various problems of life. Sufferings, whether mental or spiritual or materialistic, political or social, religious or moral continue to challenge man. Return to Nature and woman ultimately makes the poet comfortable. Singh is blunt, sharp and happy while unbuttoning love for beauty and body and in the process reveals hidden emotions and thoughts with total sincerity of purposes.

Out of disgust and unripe understandings of sex, woman, beauty and Nature, one may condemn Singh's glorification of physical pleasures but in the end, finding his own unspoken truths and genuine passions revealed in right perspective, one may find in the poems a moral strength to grow up. Possibly, Singh is the only poet in Indian English Poetry who has composed lyrics on women with so much furious passion and sensuous intensity. A teacher of linguistics that he is, one finds in him terrific economy of words. As Singh writes about women with marvelous intensity that frightens at times an astute lover of poetry for its dispassionate sensuous delineations of a woman's body I am tempted to observe whether such an obvious depiction of sex and sensuality will help sensitizing readers to ethics and morality. On the other hand, one has to be aware of the poet's dilemmas through which he passed through during the seminal years of seventies and eighties when awful, chaotic and disturbing trends in Indian society had taken shape to influence man's life and when, in him, poetry waited eagerly to sprout. Here he gives ample scope for a debate on whether creativity in any genre of literature should have ethical and moral quality and standards; and there remains a big question. Or is he taking us back to the times of the Pre-Raphaelites and aesthetes who stood for the literary theory of 'Art for Art's Sake?'

Coming back, one finds that Singh is manipulative and inquisitive in the use of words with a variety of twists in meanings and while going through poems one has to cautiously take care of each word with multiple layers and meanings. Singh, underneath it seems, hardly adheres to traditions but continues to travel deeply to fresh pastures of feelings and thoughts. He is a poet of beauty in women but modern-day sufferings, social distortions, disparity and prejudice around disturb him. Like Shiv K. Kumar, K. N. Daruwalla, I. K. Sharma, O. P. Bhatnagar and I. H. Rizvi, he understands the intensity of sufferings in modern living without any sense of reprieve. One is meanderingly led to believe, perhaps as one begins to enjoy each verse with eagerness and passion that the poet finds absolute peace and harmony in the beauty of woman and for him, there is hidden a real redemption.

WORKS CITED

1. Singh, R. K. *My Silence*, Madras: Poets Press India, 1985.
2. __________. *Memories Unmemoried*, Berhampur: Poetry Time Publications, 1988.
3. ______________. *Flight of Phoenix*, Berhampur: Poetry Time Publications, 1990.
4. __________. *Music Must Sound*, Dhanbad: Author, 1990.
5. __________. *I Do Not Question* (Two Poets), New Delhi: Bahri Publications, 1994.
6. _______________. *Above the Earth's Green*, Calcutta: Writers Workshop, 1997.
7. ______________.*Every Stone Drop Pebble*, New Delhi : Bahri Publication,1999.
8. _________.*Cover to Cover, A Collection of Poems* (jointly with Ujjal Singh Bahri). New Delhi: Bahri Publications, 2002.
9. __________.*Pacem in Terris,* (a trilogy collection with Myriam Pierri and Giovanni Campisi, 2003.
10. __________.*The River Returns*, Bareilly: Prakash Book Depot, 2006.
11. _________.*Sexless Solitude and Other Poems*, Bareilly: Prakash Book Depot, 2009.

2

The Poetics of R. K. Singh

— Jindagi Kumari & Rajni Singh

The best poetry
is a woman
concrete, personal, delightful
greater than all (*My Silence*, p.139)

R. K. Singh considers best poetry as a woman. 'Woman' is a metaphor that the poet has used for poetry. His concept of poetry and woman is so merged that poetry seems to be dissolved in woman, and woman appears as poetry personified, concrete, personal and delightful.

Both poetry and woman, for the poet, are most treasured entities because they are real. Both can be experienced by the senses; both incite passion, both are intimate; and, above all, both have the power to delight and elevate. Poetry and woman are, thus, conceived as accessories to the higher levels of consciousness. The greatness of poetry, therefore, lies in its power to transcend the physical through physical. For example:

Woman is the flesh
and spirit of poetry
eternal love thirst

growing younger as
one grows older day by day
perfecting the body (*Flight of Phoenix*, p.70)

Perfecting the body of poetry and woman is the crux of the argument of the poem. The same idea is reiterated in the following lines:

A woman
in poet's vision
howsoever strange
is ever new;
pierce like diamond

or thread like pearl
to weld in her depth
her nudity

I love for
all her mystery
perfect poetry
beyond the sky (*Above the Earth's Green*, p.72)

Again, in poem number 57 of the same collection, the poet says that woman is "the measure/of all things: body, truth/love, spirit, God, society, peace /and man" (*Above the Earth's Green*, p.69).

The poet's basic ideology of art and poetry is expounded in his idea of woman who is all encompassing and constitutes the major content of his poetry. The other significant themes such as love and sex are but different facets of his core ideology with different manifestations. In one of his interviews given to Kanwar Dinesh Singh in *New Indian English Poetry: An Alternative Voice,* the poet says: "Woman in my poetry…is a universal woman, the invisible part of the primordial pairs we know as Purush – Prakriti, or Yin-Yang, unchanging over time and culture".

In the above statement the poet relates 'woman' with the basic principle of life and creation. The following poem is an expression of the universal principle of creation:

The split in cypress
is vulva I know the roots
purush – prakriti

call it Yin and Yang
our basic sex, *lingam* and
yoni harmonise

like lotus rising
from the depths of lake through mud
crossing existence (*My Silence*, p.71)

When the poet mentions purush and prakriti in harmony or as one, he emphasizes the presence of maleness and femaleness in each individual. Each person is naturally endowed with both male and female energy or quality and this needs to be harmoniously nurtured to make unadulterated expression of life, celebration and delight, or to feel innocent joy, or to be perfect or whole. Creation is not possible in the absence of feminine principle or prakriti. Therefore, for creation masculine and feminine principles need to be harmonized into a single whole. The same idea is illustrated in the following lines:

The fig of life with
roots above and branches below
man and woman one (*Flight of Phoenix*, p.71)

The poet appreciates that with their pragmatism and ability to cope with reality, women are earth bound: man leans towards the sky and woman is rooted in the earth; the deeper the roots of a tree go the higher the branches rise. The poet stands for man and woman in deep synchronicity: woman provides the roots and man provides the flowers. The harmony between the two is basic to physical, emotional, sexual and social existence. Here, the idea is akin to what one finds in verse 20 of the *Brihadaranyank Upanisad*: "Then he embraces her, (saying), 'I am the vital breath and you are the speech; you are speech and I am the vital breath: I am the *Saman* and you are the *Rg*, I am heaven and you are the earth. Come let us strive together...."

This verse signifies the union of man and woman in the act of creation. For life and existence, the union of the two elements of feminine and masculine, prakriti- purush or yoni and lingam is essential:

Love is my prison
and freedom both
in her presence
my wish her wish

to be everything
her shiva and
shakti a dual- single
me and she, one (*Flight of Phoenix*, p.54)

Similarly, the reference to Shiva and Shakti as 'dual- single' in the poem again links the poet's inspiration to the Classical Hindu Mythology. Mitali De Sarkar, too, in her article, "Harmony in Duality: Indianess in R.K.Singh's Poetry", avers: "According to the Svetasvatara Upanisad, Iswar and Sakti are regarded as the parents of the universe: *"only when united with Shakti has Siva power to manifest; but without her the god cannot stir*".

This principle of harmony of the two opposite elements in fact evinces the poet's craving for union in all the spheres of life. Since most of the problems originate due to discordance of ideas, modern world is full of elements of disintegration and destruction threatening existence of humanity as well as of creativity.

Poetry, like a woman, conceals beauty in its form, which provides emotional pleasure and spiritual calm, leading to creativity. This creativity is the result of the amalgamation of the two poetic elements: the form and the content that unite to make an inseparable whole. This view is beautifully brought out by the poet in the following lines:

> A poem is
> like life
> sound
> and silence
> movement
> and stillness
> fragment
> and wholeness
> Avibhiktam
> Vibhakteshu
> like Shiva
> and Shakti
> lotus
> and mud (*Music Must Sound*, p.100)

More importantly, the ideology of union as professed by R. K. Singh, is not something alien, rather it is essentially rooted in Indian tradition and culture, as clear from his use of 'Shiva and Shakti', 'dual- single' and 'purush- prakriti'.

In addition, R.S. Tiwary in his scholarly article, '"Secret of the First Menstrual Flow": R. K. Singh's Commitment to Fleshly Reality' in *New Indian English Poetry: An Alternative Voice*, opines that the poet frequently alludes to purush-prakriti -- the celebrated formulation of Sankhya Philosophy. Purusha is the counterpart of the Brahman of the Advaita darshana that remains inactive but when he comes in contact with prakriti,that is, the feminine principle, he gets agitated and their union eventually leads to creation. To quote R.S. Tiwary: "This integration of twin principles of Masculinity and Femininity has its roots in the Vedic provision that the 'Paramatman' the Supreme being, divided himself into two, man and woman, to enjoy himself, becoming bored by solitariness."

Reference to "Avibhiktam Vibhakteshu", too, is made to present the philosophy of the *Bhagvat Gita* in a nutshell by the poet. The idea is interpreted in the *Bhagvat Gita* as "Even when it is fragment, even in that fragment the whole world resides." Thus, it can be understood that the poet's ideology is developed around some of the fundamentals of the Vedic philosophy.

Woman: The Source of Love

Love is the guiding of emotion that leads to unity as well as harmony. This love springs from charm and beauty. R. K. Singh's concept of love facilitates the exploration of various related aspects of his ideology. The poet advocates physical love and glorifies it without any reticence, as a reinforcer of emotional and spiritual bond. Physical love, for the poet, is in no way demeaning, because it is a fact of life. Inhibition or hideousness in the matter, therefore, underlies hypocrisy. It is in this form that sex becomes instrumental in exposing the pretensions imbued in all walks of modern life.

Elaborating the poet's ideal of love one finds that it is connected with his ideal of beauty and pleasure. Since woman and poetry are considered as the chief sources possessing eternal beauty and eternal pleasure, intimacy with them leads to physical as well as spiritual comfort, as in the poem:

> She is the tree
> green and wide
> abundantly dressed
> overflowing
> spreading her sleeves
> blesses all
> in her cool shade...
> I feel
> nearer God (*My Silenee*, p.137)

Here, the tree imagery used for woman indicates her physical glories, as she is "abundantly dressed". This bodily charm and all-encompassing love make her a source of enduring comfort and the speaker feels "nearer God" in her company. She is so overpowering that her presence cannot be resisted. In the following poem the speaker helplessly submits to her original charms and cherishes a dream to reach "the pavilion of eternity" with her assistance:

Blind
I see her beauty
deaf
I hear her melody
ignorant
I partake of her knowledge
poor
I share her wealth
in - drawn
her vision reigns my heart (*My Silence*, p.139)

In another poem the speaker is found looking forward to his progress in the movement of woman:

I seek new strides
in each of your moves
new dreams in your eyes and thighs

nude lyrics in lips
shape the night's sway
set my heart afire

I seek the lingering fragrance
the rhythm that frenzies the soul
the timeless joy you conceal

I seek the hues that blaze being
and shade the nest I rest in:
your chains renew my freedom

each time I look at you
I see natural woman
the fount of poetry (*Some Recent Poems*, p.33)

The poem represents an analogy between woman and poetry. Moreover, the idea suggested in the poem gets illustration when we examine the poet's statement from an interview given to K. D. Singh: "I see woman (and her nudity) as the mainspring of our being (and art) as "the major incident in man's life," shaping the psyche and constituting the sensory experience. She is eternal and there is no poetry possible without her." R. S. Tiwary's remark also seems apt when he says; "Woman is the chief source of his (R .K. Singh's) creative afflatus; woman not as an imaginary angel but woman in her all corporeal riches...." It is on this account that Tiwary studies the poet's frequent references to sexual imagery and symbols like "eyes", "thighs" and "breast", as part of the influence of ancient Indian erotic poetry.

The poet himself admits this association when he says in an interview defending his interpretation of physical love in his poetry: "Our ancient erotic manuals, *Kamsutra*, *Kokashastra*, and *Ratirahasya* treat love as a matter of giving and receiving pleasure. The aesthetics of erotica, the sexual metaphor makes it possible to convey what it feels like to be filled with desire; such a state, in our classics, has been valued highly, as sexual love is seen as a means of access to the realm where human and divine meet."

It is perceived that the poet's treatment of love reinforces his fundamental idea related to unity. This unity, however, is not limited to bodily union but touches one's consciousness. It results in the evolution of a harmonious society. The following poem hints at the poet's effort to preserve the humanity *within* man by means of poetry:

I make myself man
each time I create
setting, character, tone
in a poem
create poetic sense
disclose my natural being
playing five senses
my distortions and inversions
evolve in history and society
to save the man in me
through poetry of self (*Flight of Phoenix*,p.53)

Here, poetry is conceived as a play with dramatic elements like setting, character, tone and poetic sense and may present a sensuous drama involving five senses but its purpose ultimately lies in safeguarding values and humanity. Thus, poetry is a platform for the poet to expose the distortions and deformities of self and society. The following poem also contains an identical thought, but the attention, here, can be transferred to the technical part of poetry:

A poem is madness
unique fascination
liberating language
re-creates, re-symbolises

disfiguring the known
secured norms
inverting the safe
existence (*Flight of Phoenix*, p.53)

A poem is, hence, a camouflage, because it means something different from what it appears to be suggesting. This multiplicity fascinates and is equated to madness. The logic behind the liberation of language is to "re-create", "re-symbolise" and "disfigure" the conventional norms to refresh them and ensure safe existence.

Commenting on Singh's manipulation of the medium, R. S. Tiwary opines: "Language is exceedingly malleable in his hands. Like Keats, he takes delight in coining phrases, such as, 'fractured faith', 'drugged sleep', 'rituals of flesh', 'dark combats', 'that icy sun' etc. Although there are few purple patches in his poetry, yet the similes and metaphors employed by him are always delightful, carrying a pregnancy of meanings."

For the poet, poetry is not "…just functional/ like brief-case" (*Memories Unmemoried*), it is an extension of his self. R. K. Singh advocates subjectivity in poetry. He approves personal poetry because it can serve as an instrument of self- exploration. In the following statement he stresses the same idea:"I think, I often talk about myself, withdrawn into my personal world, to me, perhaps, it is a means of defying the disgusting socio-political world outside…By writing brief personal lyrics...I make my life a work of art or enlarge myself to the universal sameness of human feeling." The following lines sum up the poet's thought:

Poetry is prayer
in life's vicissitude:
a saving grace against
manipulated or
unmanifested odds
overwhelming without
warrant or patterning (*Above the Earth's Green*, p.13)

Some poems by the poet give clue to his sources of inspiration which lie mainly in his past experiences and memories, as the construct of the given poems suggests: "What I write shows/my past…." (*Memories Unmemoried*) and "Oasis in memories/of desert rhythm of wilderness/ sound is the poetry" (*Memories Unmemoried*).

The word 'memory' has been used as a metaphor, which stands for creative process, or imagination where past experiences get synthesized and work as awareness for the present. Also, the poet, names one of his poetic collection as *Memories Unmemoried*. Memory, therefore, is a vision device to collect a timeless frame to express the consciousness. It is free and can make illusion of a truth as well as truth of an illusion. What is being unmemoried is the expression, which is the visible aspect of awareness.

Thus, by expressing the memories, the poet relives them and soothes the agitated mind undergoing the conflict of sweet bitter impressions. The poet's consciousness guides him towards the realization and acceptance of differences and thus manifests his broad and unconventional outlook, as in the following poem:

> A poem
> elusive like a butterfly
> is the dynamics
> of a culture
> a process of exchange
> a cultural artifact
> fascinating
> stimulating
> reshaping
> reader and creator
> it incorporates
> multiplicity
> of modern man
> fluid, mobile
> multicultural
> manipulating
> matrix of tongues
> and patterns of languages
> into a stable whole
> of self awareness

(*My Silence*, p.169)

The poet advocates brevity of expression. His belief in precision is proved by his own poems, which are mostly brief in structure. As he articulates in one of his poems: "moon is the poem in sky/silence sounds in brevity" (*Above the Earth's Green*).He compares poetry to the moon, which occupies a small space in the vast sky, but its smallness becomes significant with the effect it casts. The poet practices brevity by following the imagistic and symbolic patterns.

Irony is another remarkable feature of R. K. Singh's poetic style. He employs subtle irony in his poems by means of symbols and images. For example: "A monkey turned the coat/to let off snakes/ hidden in velvet lining" (*Music Must Sound*)

Another important aspect of R. K. Singh's poetics is that he does not give titles to his poems nor does he use punctuation marks; thereby he individualizes his style availing himself of poetic freedom. Moreover, the poet has not used a period in the first four collections, viz. *My Silence* (1985), *Memories Unmemoried* (1988), *Music Must Sound* (1990), *Flight of Phoenix* (1990), but one can find semicolon, colon and dashes in some of his poems. The same style appears in *Above the Earth's Green*, *Cover to Cover*, and *The River Returns*. By not using punctuation, such as a comma at the end of the line or a period at the end of the sentence, the poet frequently ends up using enjambment. As a result, the meaning flows as the lines progress. The reader has the freedom to understand one or more meanings from the poem. The instances of this kind of verse can be found in e. e. cummings who created enjambment combined with the use of punctuation as an art form.

Regarding the poems without titles I. K. Sharma's remark calls for one's attention, when he says: "To a common reader a title is a big help that makes a poem accessible". Obviously, a common reader cannot be assumed an expert of the nuances of poetic language. So, there remain chances of misinterpretation. This even increases when the content of poetry is as unconventional as sex. However, the poet believes that poems without titles and punctuation marks allow greater freedom to the reader to imagine and interpret the meaning. Even if "titles tell too much", as R. K. Singh believes, they limit the meaning and lessen the effect of the poem.

The poet also evinces interest in alliterative device as a means to generate musical effect in his verses. For example:

> Love leads to beauty
> and vision with perfection
> pillar of dust or
> fleeting shadow can

turn into light reveling
pure songs wrought out of

the clay blending joys
in naked passion seek signs
of self- discovery

roving with delight
and perfume of fellowship
in vaiiey of peace (*Flight of Phoenix*, p.55)

Formal Features

R. K. Singh adopts Japanese form of three-line seventeen syllables haiku and uses it as stanza unit in many of his poems. Although he does not always conform to the traditional pattern of haiku (5-7-5 syllable) and tanka (5-7-5-7-7), he has uses three- line stanza pattern that appear haiku-like and thus seems to nativize the foreign form in his style. In addition, one finds two- line, four- line, five- line stanza patterns but they have an occasional occurrence. Haiku in different beats, 3-5-3, 4-6-4, 5-7-5 or in free form, are individually composed by the poet in his haiku collections as well as in stanza form in his longer poems. His poems are without rhyme but there is always some or the other sort of rhythm that the poet creatively develops.

R. K. Singh does not believe in conforming to the conventional or the outmoded but wishes to 'shatter' them by creating, what he calls 'rebel rays' in plain unadorned ıanguage. He also discards the high sounding or philosophical issues and rejoices giving vent to the ordinary or personal impressions because these are true to one's experiences:

Philosophy frightens me
confounds obscurity
with profundity:

I don't reflect time and space
or probe metaphysics
to construct Everest

I love to climb the peak and
search the best route without
high minded debate

that affronts simplicity

symmetry, nudity
a poet's beauty (*Above the Earth's Green*, p.89)

The poetics of R. K. Singh echoes what Wordsworth talks about a perfect woman:

She was a phantom of delight
A perfect woman, nobly planned,
To warn, to comfort, and command;
And yet a spirit still, and bright
With something of angelic light ('Perfect Woman')

R. K. Singh's poetics, thus, signifies the new momentum Indian English Poetry has now gained. He not only sings love lyrics and glorifies human body but also talks about existential issues and ecological and social environment. His verses with the use of enjambment add richness of meaning to the images and metaphors that he uses in typical Indian contexts. The chief aim of his poetry is to:

...discover essence of beauty
spring a move toward self harmony
perfection and peace, prelude to nude
enlightenment to carve life in full -

(*Above the Earth's Green*, p.14)

To sum up, R. K. Singh's poetic belief is oriented towards Beauty, Self- Harmony, and Peace, with its base in Indian thought and culture which considers search for beauty or truth as the chief aim of life.

WORKS CITED

1. Singh, R. K. *My Silence and Other Selected Poems*. Bareilly: Prakash Book Depot, 1994.
2. Singh, R.K. *Above the Earth's Green*. Calcutta: Writers Workshop, 1997.
3. Sharma, I.K. ed. *New Indian English Poetry: An Alternative Voice.* Jaipur: Book enclove, 2004, p.277.
4. Radhakrishnan, S. ed. *The Principal Upanisads*, New York: Harpe Collins Publishers, 1953.
5. Hayden, John O.ed. *William Wordsworth: The Poems*, Vol. I, Penguin Books, 1990.

3

"I seek freedom from myself": Existential Restlessness in R.K. Singh's *Sexless Solitude and Other Poems*

— *Yana Atanasova Rowland*

A poignant appeal towards ontological partiality, R. K. Singh's collection *Sexless Solitude and Other Poems* seeks to awaken our sensitivity towards a wide variety of issues of ethical validity, such as: a world falling apart amidst global technocratic nonchalance; post-modern unconcern towards the organic role of religious dialogue; the notion of the futility of academic humanitarian aspirations of one of a "*hanging generation*" paralysed by inner spiritual angst and troubled by physiological inconsistencies; the universality of the condition of alienation which transgresses the conceptual boundaries of gender and of national identity; the devaluation of the human potential and society's overall neglect towards artistic creativity. In melancholically meditative yet vehemently self-critical overtones, R.K. Singh's lyrical speaker questions the integrity of his own identity and that of his Time, claiming the necessity of acknowledging existence in historical perspective. The poet gives us an individuality tending to close up for lack of external spiritual resource. Also prioritised are: ageing and dying; the failing sense of tradition; the difficulty of one's political self-evaluation; the meticulous, almost medically precise examination of the sense of internal disease; the secret hope of reaching a realm impervious to the need of self-definition. Those stem from the author's perceptiveness towards the hyper-ordinate problems of *Time, Memory* and *the Past,* and could be seen to demonstrate his hermeneutic vigilance within a literary space prepared to examine personal worth against observable acts of communal experiential cultural awareness – in actuality and in historical research.

What unites the melancholic yet vehemently argumentative lyrical speakers of all the poems in R. K. Singh's collection *Sexless Solitude and Other Poems (2009)* is a common confession as to man's generic inability to relate to Time and Space other than through negation of complacency, of self-content and of any possible feeling of superiority over those who are no more. A typically alienated post-modern researcher, the poet here seems ambiguously composed of a variety of manifested concerns for history, physical integrity, mental well-being, social nonchalance and humanitarian reticence. The fate of such a meditative scholar could be defined as outliving and memorialising. He tends to codify the meaningful excerpts of a multi-cultural global consciousness, being analytically active and partial to the ethically formative value of the notion of existing for the sake of posterity, in the name of an *Other* in respect of whom man holds the obligation of sharing: sharing knowledge by remembering. From the point of view of linguistic coherence, striking is the intensity of: the continuous flow of words (some of which very much ingrained in local Hindu culture and therefore challenging for the eyes of an external examiner); the subverted patterns of traditional English syntax; the abandoned traditional regulated iambic rhyme-pattern; the tendency for resorting to enjambment; the episodicity of narration. The poet's endeavours to verify his own Poetic Self are seemingly dramatically monologic yet the quantity of particularized memories of actual events (communal or strictly private) hint at an overtly confessed need to dialogise, to share, to be heard and responded to, to live in heteronomy[1]. Reciprocally, the poet wants to impart knowledge to an *Other* and to thus protect that *Other* from the self's general proclivity to privatise, subjugate and deform Life. In *Sexless Solitude and Other Poems* we are gradually taught that Life ought to be at all times regarded as Cathartic continuous interaction between mutually related meaningful parts of existence of individual contributions of temporal validity. And also, that, ironically enough, Survivor and Dead, Author and Interpreter, Including and Included, or at last Present and Past, alternate all the time. Such hermeneutically fruitful alternation could be called the Eucharistic *Eventness* of *Co-Being*[2].

---

[1] Cf Levinas 2000: 298, 301.

[2] Cf Derrida 1998: 93-4.

The prevalent self-reflective tone of voice in R. K. Singh's collection whereby author and hero merge seems to give evidence of one variety of what Bakhtin, in his fundamental contribution to literary anthropology and ontology called "*Author and hero in Aesthetic Activity*", defines as "*crisis of authorship*"[3]. That is, when the poet's rescuing *transgredience* (aesthetically mirroring the attitude between the "I" and the Other in reality where the "I" is in the capacity of externalising, objectifying and completing the Other by virtue of the extra knowledge its possesses over what is "Not-I") is weak and he finds himself unable to control the lyrical persona's domination who is himself thus left on his own – to toil over the riddle of the purpose of his being in this world and gradually turns into a non-finalizable hero. The author's reflex concerning the hero is thus internalised within the hero's own intentionality. If the lyrical speaker's representations here could be argued to be numberless and discontinuous, so appears to be the ambience of whole named *Sexless Solitude and Other Poems (2008)*. Yet at the core there seems to lie the argument that the Self, taken in isolation, proves to be insufficient a tool for understanding and conceptualising the whole of Life since every concrete Self's existence is an entity temporarily accommodating the existence of a range of Other individuals whose centre the Self could never actually be (Cf Bakhtin 2003: 180).

When the speaker "[*seeks*] *freedom from [himself],*"[4] as in *Valley of Self*, he could be said to search for a communally trustworthy milieu of sharing his lifetime knowledge in a way which maintains, rather than severs, the sense of tradition and social belonging. He is looking for an appropriate technique of preserving and expressing, or externalising in contributions to Life as an organic whole, rather than denying, the many cultural variables that foster his rather contemporary perception of "*sensory overload*" (*Overload*). In *Aloof* we read that "*Unlinked to the trees/ he doesn't know his family/ stands aloof, questions// ancestors don't change/ the mood of the weather:/ the leaf reads his name/ nature's wonder on the edge/ .../ thousands of lights/ twinkle in colours like stars—/seat belt fastened*". There stands

[3] Cf Bakhtin 2003: 240.

[4] All excerpts from, and references to, R. K. Singh's poetry have been supported by the author's kind permission to quote from the original Prakash 2009 edition.

out the image of a crestfallen rootless traveller in space and time – at odds with its surrounding natural environment which cares not for his particular internal anguish. The selected excerpt also suggests that one could not possibly change one's origin, one's past, one's predecessors; but also that one's previous history of human trace, meaningful and dear as it may be to the individual, matters not within the multitudinous cadences of Nature which healthily passes by, rather than takes notice of, this solitary pilgrim. This orphaned despair is, to rephrase Terry Eagleton, "*both infinite merit and absolute ruin, a sickness which it is the greatest ill-fortune never to have contracted. For we can arrive at the truth, tragically, only by way of negativity (...)*"[5] It is by way of acknowledging one's orphanhood, of one's involuntary untraceability, of one's "*I can't*" that the poet proposed the idea that the *I* is but the condition of the possibility of the *I*'s life but never its valued hero (Cf Bakhtin 2003: 180). It seems that the poet takes an attitude of hermeneutic vigilance when he writes: "*I may create space/ for you to stand but I can't/ become the legs/.../*" (*On Her Birthday*). He declares that he may be taken as the condition of (very possibly) his child's life, but that the active ingredient lies outside his strong intention to explore the purpose of *Being*. If in the poem just referred to it is a child whom the speaker addresses, it is intriguing to note that this heir is also described as an amalgam of the symbolic marriage between two celestial bodies (the planets Mars and Moon, written with lower-case initials – a sign of the generic repetition of their internal characteristics of, respectively, heat/ activity and cold/ tranquillity). Would we be right in concluding that the poet here is carrying out his ontological research over the meaning of *Being* in Time? And if so, he quite probably hints that temporality (alluded to by the reference to the limited capacities/ lifetime of a parent/ predecessor) is the actual condition of the existence of historicity. We may be able to perceive R. K. Singh's idiosyncratic engagement with the phenomenology of Presence which is also hermeneutics per se: it implies interpretation by way of recognizing the mutually enriching dependence between part & whole, or Self & Other, or Heir & Predecessor, or Present & Past.[6]

---

[5] Eagleton 2003: 51-2.

[6] Cf Heidegger 1997: 19, 21, 37, 197.

In "*Ignite Minds With Flickers*" man is again condemned for his "*smallness of mind*": his existence is likened to that of a short-last piece of news which flickers and then dies in the media, echoless. Pettiness and spiritual starvation appear to be constant characteristics of man's life which is but a repeated "*surfing channels with coffee*." Yet the symbolic oblivion of a piece of news (or a lifetime forgotten), quite in reverse formation, yet again builds to the effect of proposing some organic, or communal, milieu amidst which meaning soars up and is then quieted by the doldrums of the steady technocratic mundane. Tennyson sighs: "*Death is the end of life; ah, why/ Should life all labour be? /.../ all hath suffer'd change/ .../ Our sons inherit us: our looks are strange: / And we should come like ghosts to trouble joy. /.../ We have had enough of action, and of motion me. /.../ Surely, surely, slumber is more sweet than toil, the shore/ Than labour in the deep mid-ocean, /.../*" (*The Lotos-Eaters, 1832*). "*Standing still/ among the ungodly*", R. K. Singh hopes for rest, but where – "*in dust? Or in the light/ of living*?" Or maybe he ought to "*bear without regret/ the burdens of the world/ loss of love, or even hope/ to live like a lotus leaf...*" To expose oneself to the outside and be made doubly vulnerable, or to curl and protect oneself like a leaf rolled up and let one's potential die in? In any case, the vegetable imagery in both poets in effect produces a sense of continuity and growth, a sense of dependence, and social relation, of a thwarted attempt to get lost, rather than a sense of starved and irredeemable alienation. Similarly, in "*Portraits We Fear To See,*" we have an emphasized image of accumulation, of growth and generational amelioration: "*culture is not repression/ but sublimation through expression.*" The movement is always in the direction of externalised verification, in the presence of more than one participants, to the outside, even though in essence mostly of man's inside is chanted. Temporality and merciless indiscriminate chance variability are essential components of existence: "*there's no forever/ in the cocoon life that bursts/ in the thin air in moments/ most unexpected*" (*An Unfinished Psalm*). Reciprocal appears to be an Almighty's benign intervention (ibid.), yet since unceasing motion is implied at all times, sense is maintained as a lasting ingredient. So that in *Holi,* difference is finally revealed to mean "*freedom*": difference in the sense of comparability of, or dialogic interaction between, a number of "I-s" and "Not-I-s" that, taken together as a whole, make sense and so claim spatial definition. Or, to remind ourselves of Heidegger yet again, the world of presence (i.e. of interactive dutifulness) is a world of compatibility, of exchange: between *own* and *other* which both co-constitute Space and make Time matter (Cf Heidegger 1997: 113, 118). The poet warns us: "*living in isolation/ builds islands*" (*A New Life*). Or, "*non-suffering is no key to nirvana:*" since "*island existence*" is "*degeneration*" and "*life only freezes*" (*Nirvana – II*). Or, do we perhaps hear Donne preach: "*No man is an Iland, intire of itselfe; every man is a peece of the Continent, a part of the maine; if a Clod bee washed away by the Sea, Europe is the lesse, as well as if a Promontorie were, as well as if a Manor of thy friends or of thine owne were; any mans death diminishes me, because I am involved in Mankinde; And therefore never send to know for whom the bell tolls; It tolls for thee.*"[7]

R. K. Singh's collection reads, too, like a subtly constructed elegy on the death of humanitarianism traditionally embedded in literature- and language-teaching – on an academic level. Once again, the speaker in *Abusing in Sleep* suffocates amidst pervasive mediocrity which washes away his aspirations towards bringing salvation to the modern technocrat's mind. His head is "*an abyss*," indented by "*the drugged/ wholes of the mind.*" The very self-conscious image of the "*poet-professor/ unable to redress/ his inner balances*" rises, victimized by "*academia that care/ a tuppence for native/ geniuses*" that he apparently perceives to be the core of a particular national range of talents from which he himself is but a solitary outcast. The consciousness of national identity, which stands behind self-definition for the speaker, could be argued to be one expression of the poet-professor's interest and *care* for a multitude of youthful minds (those of his students?). Such *care*, viewed form the point of view of Emmanuel Levinas' existential ethics, also manifests that limitless responsibility for an *Other*: that defines as apostolic apprenticeship in service of protecting Life.[8] That is, when the subject's subjectivity is directed at negating the Self as entirely independent

---

7 John Donne, MEDITATION XVII (*Devotions upon Emergent Occasions,* 1624). The text of the poem is quoted from: http://isu.indstate.edu/ilnprof/ENG451/ISLAND/text.html. Date of access: 26th April 2010.

8 Cf Levinas 1997 (b): 91. See also: Levinas, Emmanuel 1997 (a): 79.

and therefore admitting its uniqueness when achieved as one of, and thanks to, the many. Intentionality is preceded by answerability. We are then able to detect R. K. Singh's overall hermeneutic orientation in yet another dichotomic unity of his poetic identity: *death & creativity*. As in *Creation:*

> 'To create is to die:
> die to love, to time
> to memory, to god
> to everything we know
> do or experience'

The excerpt cited clearly implies motion, activity (even though the second stanza maintains "*stillness [...] within and without*"). And it also suggests that creativity and death (which extends, for example, to one's ability to create) are interchangeable: both phenomena leave a trail behind – if only in the memory of those who survive, or inherit a lifetime baggage now completed. In addition, it underlines the terminus each occasion of birth automatically issues: by being born one is guaranteed death. Yet Death – as the expected boundary of one's self-conscious *Being*, creates a perspective, a horizon for man to spread one's potential within. For, in Death, which deprives the living of everything which could be said to last, is still inscribed the possibility of every *Dasein*. One's loss, or the loss of that One – those are the two opposites side of the same phenomenon – man, once born, is automatically guaranteed some limits and relations, and those make one open to the meaning of Being, which is exactly how one becomes unique (Cf Derrida 1998: 79, 103). When R. K. Singh writes "*to create is to die*" we may also read that aesthetic, or poetic, creativity and existential vigilance, go always hand in hand: for, the life of a poet cannot be cut loose from that of the real man who has suffered those pains (social adjustment, personal love, memory, cognition). There is one life: a poet is a man and vice versa, one could not be freed from the other and this syncretism nourishes the imagination of a true humanitarian: *I write in order to be & to give, and I am & am given to this world in order to write.*[9] "*To create is to die*" suggests man gradually growing awareness of his delimited capacity to know because of his restricted time the earth. As opposed, for instance, to

[9] Cf Bakhtin: *Toward a Philosophy of the Act*. In: Bakhtin 2003: 120.

an animal which, deprived of the semiotics of human languages which memorialise and breathe eternally by rendering existence in written accounts available to posterity, is blessed with lack of conscientious awaiting its own end. We are tempted to recall Yeats on this matter: "*Nor dread nor hope attend/ A dying animal; / A man awaits his end/ Dreading and hoping all; / Many times he died, / Many times rose again./ .../ He knows death to the bone – / Man has created death*" (*Death*, from *The Winding Stair and Other Poems, 1933*, William Butler Yeats).[10] Man indeed dies all the time whilst living because he knows there is an end coming up. Ironically, that certainty is also one's ultimate opportunity to reach self-identity – in relation to Time, which means in effect to others – before and after one (Cf Heidegger 1997: 251-2).

The lyrical speaker of *Leeches* is burdened with accumulated knowledge, wisdom and insight. There is a general sense of resting unused, unwanted, unclaimed and therefore unrelated to the outside world he is supposed to enlighten with this amassed wisdom which is bound to thaw amidst his own ageing generation. He is "*rusting with ageing colleagues.*" Making empty sounds "*in the hollow/ of a hallowed pond /.../*" is his symbolic regret over the futility of his humanitarian aspirations. This hollowness, or vacuity of existence could alternatively be discerned in the expression "*the bees won't return / to naked trees*" (*The Bees Won't Return*). There the naked trees could be perceived to signify the emptiness of human imagination, confessed by a professor of poetry famished by the spiritless mechanics of calculated living that today's global technocratic nonchalance has created. Ideas won't, from now on, be perching all that often on the tree of human knowledge: it offers them no steady abode because it has become a polished skeleton of quick-thinking ignorance. Gone are the times when a poet like Emily Dickinson might have said that "*to make a prairie it takes a clover and one bee, /...// And revery. / The revery alone will do, / If bees are*

---

[10] The poem is quoted from: Yeats, W. B. *The Major Works: Poems, Plays and Critical Prose. Edited by Edward Larrissy*. OUP, 2001, pp. 121-122. In R. K. Singh's *God* we, peculiarly enough, read: "*The word is not God/ but the mind creates it/ after its own image/.../*" The word "*word*" appears italicised in the original.

few" (Poem No 1755, "*To make a prairie it takes a clover and one bee*").[11] There simply are no reveries left for the poet...

R. K. Singh demonstrates a conviction that the process of self-definition inevitably requires certain theological awareness of one's native environment. And again, that is so because the knowledge of religion(s) constituting a self indicates our knowledge of Time. To know Time, as Paul Ricoeur argues, is phenomenologically inevitable. The memory of one's native religious background is one element underlying one's definability in the Present. And that confirms Memory to be a cognitive factor which enhances the individual's behavioural unfolding (Cf Ricoeur 2004 /a/: 41, 86, 136-7). I *Am No Moses* and *I Am No Jesus* quite apparently form what may be called a poetic diptych. In both poems the speaker dismantles a hierarchical understanding of canonized saints ethically superior to the common mortal by the sheer fact of comparing himself to both Moses and Jesus, using the negative construction "*I am no*...". He admits he possesses no unique supernatural talent of being universally well-known, or of perceiving the truth without light (*I Am No Moses*). Yet he is capable of experiencing the agony of mere existence, and that is by simply being a man: "*I am no Jesus/ but I can feel the pains/ of crucifixion// .../ sins I didn't author// I am no Jesus/ but I can smell the poison/ and smoke in the air// feel for humankind/ like him carry the cross/ and relive my dreams/.../*" (*I Am No Jesus*). The two works are a smarting concoction of admitted namelessness, impersonality and defencelessness plus an enviable, if openly erotic, skill of physical self-perception. "*For sins I didn't author*": the Self is a weak, cheap and temporary cowardly copy of the everlasting original, and as such it has so far shown no readiness to act, to be for the sake of the whole lot, or maybe to teach truthfully the humanitarian ideals of poetic art. This self has not really been tempted: today's life is one of lukewarm stillness where no cultural heroes are required to lead the congregation forward. This cultural quasi-hero reminds us so much of T. S. Eliot's self-abnegating speaker of *The Love Song of J. Alfred Prufrock*: "*/.../ I have seen my head (grown slightly bald) brought in upon a platter, / I am no prophet – /.../ I am*

[11] The poem is quoted from: Dickinson, Emily. *The Complete Poems*. Edited by Thomas H. Johnson. London & Boston: Faber & Faber, 1987, p. 710.

not Prince Hamlet, nor was meant to be; / Am an attendant lord /.../ deferential, glad to be of use, / Politic, cautious, and meticulous; /.../ "[12] In both poems the speakers admit to growing old. Eliot's decides "*to wear the bottoms of [his] trousers rolled:*" he has shrunk back child-size and needs to fold up his trousers, which prove too large, or perhaps his memory which is now failing him. R. K. Singh's speaker views with disgust and dismay "*the whitening chest and pubic hair*" which speak of "*the death of [his] potential*" (*I Am No Moses*). Mortality is implied in both cases and in the latter poem that is dressed in the repellent metaphor of "*the cyst on my neck*" – a sign of malformed genius and bodily ugliness. This ugliness comes seems to be related to the self's inability to risk living, to risk testing one's creed and thus strengthening it in real experience. He will never be a prophet, because he lacks readiness to put his faith through a test. He is too introverted to trust an outside resource of help. And in any case, it is unclear whether there is any one definite God implied throughout. For in *Hey Ram* we understand that "*Ram has ceased to be my God.*" In this poem the speaker finds it impossible to separate the ideal of true faith and forgiveness, which a God emblematises, from letting bloodshed and ignorance spread which, too, abound in facts of the history of humankind, in holiness begotten though it may be.

Shiva, or Jesus, or some other God – in any case R. K. Singh's poetry gives certain indications that modern man's epistemological apparatus has been muddled up and that man's cognitive capacity has reached an overall state of globalized polytheistic gloom and capable of phallic deliverance only: "*gods sin against God/ betray creation/ break covenant//.../ worship lingam/ forget Shiva*" (*Shiva's Third Eye*). Hence the grief over seeing man as a piece of "*shit*" for which, quite like for an animal, the wheels of an automobile "*don't care*" (*Man or Animal*). We have invented an insensitive monstrous ogre which would serve right modern man's tendency to abuse the many forms of life around anyway. The lyrical speaker dwells in a condition of hellish unintelligibility because he cannot escape his inclination to research

[12] The poem is quoted from: /ed./ Larkin, Philip. *The Oxford Book of Twentieth-Century English Verse*. Oxford: Clarendon Press, 1974, pp. 228-232.

meaning on his own, in solitude, through reflection, rather than through action – even though he confesses to seeking freedom from himself (*Valley of Self*). And meaning as such could never be in principle one's solitary possession (Cf Eagleton 2003: 64). Just as the physicality of our Life as co-experience suggests, meaning always stands out to be seen, touched, expressed: it is round and has many sides, it is convex and yet covert, mysterious. Just as the protuberant formation round the woman's waist could tell of her "*hubby's love*," as in *Sleeping Light*. Or meaning could be oval: meandering in feminine nudity and nestling in the woman's "*dark womb*," as in *Wit and Soul*. Yet both poems contain references to emptiness, vacancy, "*nudity*" of existence if that be existence for the sake of mere physical well-being. In both poems is sensed the anxiety of unshared desire, of unachieved companionship of spirit and therefore of incomplete meaning – always hoped for but never truly discussed. In *Wit and Soul* an object of unrivalled impressionist art – a Matisse or a Picasso – comes as something much over the top. It thwarts the interpretability of a shared kiss. It could "*only complicate*," rather than alleviate, the search for a reliable common terrain of understanding the purpose of Being as Co-Being. There seems to never be true dialogue, true exchange of confessions, of memories, and therefore of personalities. Nonetheless both poems urge us think that meaning is yet to be born, because it is hidden and preserved – until requested. The trouble is that here, man seems to be afraid of afraid of boundaries, and seeks freedom from any externally applied act of definition which could form, or help him understand himself better in true communion where he would be expected to give, before he asks for, something. All the same, the very fact that the lyrical speaker manifests hyper-sensitivity to the fact of the coexistence of always two centres of vision (e.g. that of the pregnant wife and of her husband, or of the lover and his mistress), indicates that the poet insists that an act of thinking (artistic thinking), or description, is already an act of ontological partiality. For, rephrase Bakhtin, active thinking always has in mind the architectonics of *Being* as *Co-Being* (Cf Bakhtin 2003: 16, 258). By grieving about the psychological, gender, cultural, generational or religious inconsistencies of our age, the poet reveals his predisposition to forgive all those ills. And forgiveness is a gesture of conforming and inscribing *Meaning* into

Being – it is a-historic, it interrupts the sequence of cause and effect (temporally definable) and it incites action: dutiful and responsible action (Cf Kristeva 1999: 213, 219).

R. K. Singh's poetry, with its many cultural references, is poetry where the Self is made to recognize the fact of eternal, indeed a-temporal, mutual obligation amongst the members of a society (Cf Ricoeur 2004 /b/: 319). If a poem of R. K. Singh's rejects singularity of experience and of one-dimensional inter-textual reference, then perhaps we should consider the impossibility of the singularity of authoring experience as such – on the level of ethics. And the poet proves he is at any one moment aware that Being as Co-being has no gate though which one could exit it (Levinas 2000: 39). Similarly, one could not possibly shed off the amassed racial, religious and cultural determinants in a Self's temporal definability. By now, however, those have grown to be seen as: "*sins of races*" flowing into one's blood (*Don't Condemn Me*), or "*the beasts within nurtured for years*" (*The Dead Too Are Restless*). The Self is a "*self-same cocoon,*" where "*fungus of illusions grow/ toadstools of damned tract*" (*Is This All?*). Those excerpts create the image of ritualised imprisonment for which the human mind, burdened with memory, is largely responsible. It is not that we do not remember, but that we tend to remember carelessly: we tend to heap our remembrances and clatter out ability of sharing- existence-in-aiding. Instead, we let ourselves fall into a perception of "*age-wrapped youth,*" of repeated and misinterpreted customs and blindly followed traditions where many Gods flow together into one "*mumbo-jumbo.*" Our psyche has become an abyss of non-differentiated delusional hopes for the future and a variety of vignettes about personalities long gone and by now nonchalantly thrown about as chunks of info about the Past (especially in: *The Dead Too Are Restless*). We have forgotten the ethical merit of our situation in Time: our being in Time is our being amidst others; our historicity is an inter-subjective connection (Cf Levinas 1998: 81).

That existence is motion and interchange from one mode of being into another is something which two especial poems, *Awareness Matters* and *Nude Origin*, suggest. In the latter, the transition from one state to the other is visible in the interplay in colour symbolism: darkness signifies pre-natal gloom whereas light represents our conscientious life on the earth. Awareness is given full colour: or state of embryonic mindlessness is like a silent black-and-white cinematographic film. And it is awareness that matters: "*each death has a passage/ to surprise the dead/ awareness matters*" (*Awareness Matters*). "*/.../ get back to what God gave us/ in love let life shape anew/ from the nude origin*" – these lines imply not only the innocence and helplessness of our naked body at birth, they could also be argued to mean that creativity and novelty depend on loss, on mortality, on extinction. For the dead passing away may be equal to total and final sensory oblivion which could never be fully predicted (i.e. death is always a surprise), but for those who survive it is every time yet another occasion to build knowledge anew, to grow cognitively richer whilst remembering; it indeed *is* life at its most intense.[13] Death is at any one given moment both pre-ordained and contingent. To make matters even more complicated, we ought to say that even though death clearly implies transition from one state to another, i.e. it is motion and it may therefore mean that the dying crosses a certain threshold, no dead person has yet returned from that state of ultimate finality to report back about its happening so that no exact "topography" could be verified.[14] In *Awareness Matters*, the sentence "*each death has a passage / to surprise the dead*" is apparently plagued by the same doubt: that dying, just as well as discussing Death – both of those happen on the borderline between truth and non-truth. And that is most certainly valid especially because doer (i.e. the dying one) and analyser (i.e. surviving) constantly interchange places.[15] In that sense, the metaphor "*hanging generations*" (Hanging Generations) refers not simply restrictively to one particular generation that the lyrical speaker may claim to belong to. It is the universal state of historic definability, of in-between-ness, of temporal dependence that we grow to be part of and which grows into our consciousness too.

---

[13] Cf Derrida 2004: 10.

[14] In that relation, it would be interesting to note the apocalyptic imagery in *I Am Promised A New Sun*, where the "*enormous yacht*" drifting towards a royal mansion over the sea water could be perceived to suggest a rewarding finale and liberation from the curse of historicity which dictates that even after death we still "move," i.e. we still continue to be, but in the memory of survivors only – we are, in other words, never at peace.

[15] Cf Derrida 1998: 40, 95, 110.

Respectively, the "*hanging generations that may never be*" may be taken to suggest the interminability of our lifetime (and posthumous) definition – always in relation to other people and other times. Similar is the collective and organic perception of "*the long trip/ ahead in spirit*" for the lyrical speaker in *Long Trip*. The ashes, or the earth, he would become are elements not of finality, of freedom from dependence, but rather of recuperative fertilization of Life as such. For the dying individual it may be an occasion of "*celebrating life*," good or bad as that life might have been, but for the living that loss intensifies the sense of limit and meaning of their own lives. The latter poem confirms a belief deeply held by Paul Ricoeur. Namely, that above the biological principle of a finality of an organism philosophy teaches that the skill of dying and leaving behind ought to turn – within each single lifetime – into a conscientious conviction that one *ought to die* and thus prolong Life as a chain of unique interrelated opportunities (Cf Ricoeur 2004 /a/: 499-500). Such attitude may be able to help us understand the androgynous format of the body and its death hinted at in *Bliss Through Death*. Male of female, menstruation or phallus, it still feeds life. The lyrical speaker – probably male – is "*fleshed as my daughter,*" himself derived from his mother's womb. The moment of one's conception, just as the moment of one's death, are genderless phenomena. The two sexes merge in creation as well as at expiration. Meaning, too, transcends gender definability: it is sexless in its continuity. Death, which fosters meaning through memory, brings alien and intimate together and dismantles the opposition between fate and freedom (Cf Eagleton 2003: 121).

The care with which the poet examines Man's bodily functions often verges on medically precise description of an internally deceased, rotten, challenged physicality amidst a general feeling of Life's incognizability. The lyrical speaker is prone to self-chastisement and admits to his inability to express himself to the external world ("*I can't turn my inside out*"), to disentangle his "*knotted self.*" He is drifting "*between earth and sky*" – in some kind of interlude named "*life*" (*Shrinking Into Itself*). His hands reflect his genealogical complicatedness, burdensome past, incurable pain and suppressed memories of broken happiness: "*the lines on the palms//*

spiders' network/ gleaming with corpses/ that have no face" (*Dying Light*). He has been unable to achieve harmonious being in life: he therefore awaits "*the coffin/ to reconcile the truths/ [he] could not conceive*" (*Stripped and Naked*). But whilst he rues his own imperfect apparatus of cognition, he sensitively notes that the state of impersonality and delusiveness is a general feature of all humanity, that life is a myriad of copies of an ideal original, or an array of lost "*shadows/ that seek identity*" (*Shadows*). We could hear the confession that the idealism of self-perception in isolation is wrong, is deceit and that true phenomenology of being is the naturalist recognition that an *Other* completes *Me*. Moreover, it turns out that in order to be one ought to remain incomplete, open-for-oneself – at all times, in all the crucial moments of one's life – one ought to always be imminent to one's own self, one ought to not fully coincide with oneself to contain the hope of dialogic co-existence (Cf Bakhtin 2003: 95, 184). What the author may be taken to argue is that self-appropriation cannot get by without the participation of an interlocutor. And in that sense, it seems natural that the *I* is always that which one for oneself cannot see and confirm. Self-consciousness is possible only as experience in contrast (Clark & Holquist 2002: 43, 46, 68).

In view of the above reflections, the lyrical speaker's sickness of "*living among the sick*," of being tormented by "*germs and allergens*" (*I Want to Sleep*), of being "*diseased/ in soul before the devil/ reappears/.../*," of his body being "*loaded with emptiness*" (*I Can't Remedy*), of inherited "*fears and uncertainties*" (*Plastic Flowers Couldn't Keep Time*) – those are all variations of this whetted sense of incompletion, of the need for dialogue, for organic, all-inclusive experience which binds fates together and purges solitude and self-conceit. In *I Hang Nobody's Picture* we meet a "*shipwreck in a void*" whose imagination has been emptied through unattended-to appeals to be heard, to co-exist, to hold on to something steadfast and trustworthy. He is a man who has reached his "*andropausal day*" (*I Can't Remedy* –genderless ageing is implied) and oscillates in a state of perverse mental emptiness. He is "*wandering between two worlds, one dead, / The other powerless to be born*" (See Arnold, Matthew, *Stanzas From the Grande Chartreuse*,

1855).[16] Poetic talent seems a malady, a curse, rather than a blessing – in a world where humanitarian ideals (including teaching poetry) seem a futile strain of mind. Transitoriness seems to be the only unarguable truth worth recognizing in a world colourless and dull, a world of "*beige and indigo shades*" (*Rainbow* – ageing and unimaginativeness is suggested). Writing is an ache, a bodily malfunction: "*I secrete poetry like semen/ in consummation leave smuts/.../*" (*I'm Different*). Can the poet cope with his troubled past: "*I was/ dependent on my father// a self-made man against/ the currents/.../*"? His many complexes of self-perception make him victim to his own physical disabilities: "*caries, cavities/ cyst and myopia haunt/ and sexual anxieties/ disturb sleep.*" To the point where he declares that he "*[resents his] identity*" (*When I Stopped...*). He finally summarizes that living involves a great dose of incidental coming together of people and of discourses which voice out their inclinations, desires and weaknesses – all that happens simultaneously which is why direct learning from one another is virtually impossible. That, it would appear, poses obstacles for teaching as a sphere of human-mediated activity (compare *It Hardly Helps to Teach*). A teacher, or a university professor, like every man, remains but a speck amidst life's variability.

* * *

One is always incomplete and in order to uncover one's origin and purpose, one must look carefully back and also into one's relationship with other individuals – all constituents of interminable Co-Existence. And Co-Existence faces both ways: it is turned to the Past and to the Future. It remembers, or retains, and at the same time it anticipates. Quite like R. K. Singh's *99 poems* – an odd number: incomplete and therefore suggestive of existential incompletion as the most truthful and most humanizing characteristic of *Being*. R. K. Singh's poetry professes self-derision as the basis for self-evaluation which is penitential. Doubting the possibility of self-completion and self-perfection is a sure mark of a desire to exist in heteronomy, or to Co-Exist. The poet obviously cares for Life in the humanitarian sense of the word: by wishing to escape the narrow frets of self-insight. R.

---

[16] The edition of Arnold's works referred to is: Arnold, Matthew, *The Works of ~*. With an introduction by Martin Corner. The Wordsworth Poetry Library, 1995.

K. Singh's poetry confirms Heidegger's belief that the meaning of being *present* is *care*, and that the ontological sense of care is temporality.[17] By seeking freedom from himself, the poet may be seen to actually argue non-definability of personality: or to be more precise, he believes that person-formation is a lifetime process, a rich blend of various spatial, temporal, cultural and ideological oftentimes contraries, which, marrying one another, produce an entity yet refillable. So that, in an intriguing manner, the polymorphous and poly-genealogical grounds of R. K. Singh's authorial activity cherish an ethical need to write in order to exist & make existence possible – by facilitating amassment of meaning – rather than challenge the validity of literary authority, or of feasibility of meaning, in the post-modern world.[18]

WORKS CITED

Bakhtin 2003: In the original: М. М. Бахтин. Собрание сочинений. *Том 1 – Философской эстетика 1920х годов.* Москва: РАН. "Русские словари", 2003.

Clark & Holquist 2002: Катарина Кларк, Майкл Холквист. *Pro et Contra*. Творчество и наследие М. М. Бахтина в контексте мировой культуры. Антология. Том II. Санкт-Петербург: Издательство Российского Христианского Гуманитарного Института, 2002.

Derrida 1998: Derrida, Jacques. *Apories.* In Bulgarian: Дерида Жак. *Апории.* София: ИК "Критика и хуманизъм", 1998.

Derrida 2004: Derrida, Jacques. Interview with Jacques Derrida. In: *Le Monde* on 19/08/2004. In Bulgarian: "*Аз съм във война със себе си*" – разговор на Жан Бирнбом с Жак Дерида. Превод от френски на Любен Каравелов. В: в. Култура, бр. 35, 24.09.2004.

Eagleton 2003: Eagleton, Terry. *Sweet Violence. The Idea of the Tragic*. Blackwell Publishing, 2003.

Heidegger 1997: Heidegger, Martin. *Sein und Zeit*. In Russian: Мартин Хайдегер, *Бытие и Время.* Москва: Ad Marginem, 1997.

---

[17] Consult: Goricheva, Tatiana in: Clark & Holquist 2002: 307; Levinas 2000: 301; Heidegger 1997: 364.

[18] Cf Kolarov 2004: 219.

Kolarov 2004: Коларов, Радосвет. "*За автора – Post-Mortem. Изпитанията на теорията.*" В: *Литературоведски диалози.* София: Издателска къща "Александър Панов", 2004.

Kristeva 1999: Kristeva, Julia. *Black Sun. Depression and Melancholy*. In Bulgarian: Юлия Кръстева. *Черно Слънце. Депресия и Меланхолия.* София: ГАЛ-ИКО, 1999.

Levinas 1997 (a): Levinas, Emmanuel. *Humanism of the Other*. In Bulgarian: Еманюел Левинас. *Хуманизъм към Другия човек.* СОНМ, 1997.

Levinas 1997 (b): Levinas, Emmanuel. *Noms Propres*: In Bulgarian: Еманюел Левинас. *Собствени имена.* СОНМ, 1997.

Levinas 1998: Левинас, Эммануэль. *Le Temps Et L'Autre.* In Russian: Левинас, Эммануэль. *Время и Другой. Гуманизм Другого человека.* Санкт-Петербург: Высшая Религиозно-Философская Школа, 1998.

Levinas 2000: Levinas, Emmanuel. *Totalité et Infini.* In Russian: Еманюэль Левинас, *Тотальность и бесконечное.* Москва & Санкт-Петербург: Университетская книга, 2000.

Ricoeur 2004 /a/: Ricoeur, Paul. *La Memoire, L'Histoire, L'Oubli.* In Russian: Поль Рикер. *Память, История, Забвение.* Москва: Издательство гуманитарной литературы, 2004.

Ricoeur 2004 /b/: Ricoeur, Paul. *Soi-Même Comme Un Autre.* In Bulgarian: Пол Рикьор. *Себе си като някой Друг.* Плевен: "ЕА" АД, 2004.

4

A Stylistic Interpretation of R. K. Singh's Poem 'Sexless Solitude'

— *G.D.Barche*

Needless it is to talk of the heat and height R. K. Singh has acquired in the realm of poetry. Generally he is stamped to be a tough poet. He is also labelled to be a sex proned poet. To me he is like Dronacharya constructing the Poetic Chakravuha and naturally it needs Arjun to deconstruct it and come out safely with the booty. One such chakravuha is his poem '*Sexless Solitude*'. And now let us see how I break it, enter it and come out of it.

Sexless Solitude

I don't seek the stone bowl
Buddha used while here:
she dwells on moon beams

I can see her smiling
with wind-chiselled breast
in sexless solitude

her light is not priced
but gifted to enlighten
the silver-linings

Obviously the poem has a protagonist. He is a seeker in search of 'what type of life should be chosen?' He sees two ways of life before him, viz., the life of detachment (Vairagya, Sanyas) as lived by Buddha with his begging bowl; the other is the life of domesticity with woman as nucleus with her inborn gift of glow and gravitation that stem from her lips, breast, etc. And the seeker opts for the latter. Apparently that is all. But then is that really all? No. So let us enter the poem and explore the facts.

On the face of it the shape of the poem is very plain and simple. It has three triplets with three lines each evenly arranged. As for sentences, the first triplet has two sentences and second and third have one each. But the moment we enter the poem, it is noticed that the poem has 14 sentences as under:

Triplet 1: I don't seek the stone bowl. Buddha used the stone bowl. Buddha lived here. I seek the rejuvenating sex. People choose sex. People live here. She dwells on moon beams. 3+3+1 (7)

Triplet 2: I can see her smiling in sexless solitude. She is smiling. She has wind-chiselled breast. She is in sexless solitude. (4).

Triplet 3: Her light is not priced. Her light is gifted. Her light enlightens silver linings. (3).

Now when we think of the allocation of these lines and sentences, then it becomes obvious that in the first triplet first three sentences of two lines are allocated to Buddha and his way of life, i.e., the life of austerity, detachment (*Vairgya*), and remaining three underground sentences and one line and the next two complete triplets are reserved for the protagonist and his way of opted life, i.e., the domestic life, the life of involvement with woman as its centre. Evidently domestic life with woman as its nucleus becomes the main focus. And the beauty of this latter part lies in the poet's vision and skill of unfolding the nature and scope of this woman centred domestic life.

A close and careful reading makes one see the act that the third line of the first triplet, viz. "she dwells on moon beams" gets foregrounded as it does not go well with the first two lines. Why does the poet do so? Let us look into the deviation device. The protagonist has firmly refused to go in for the life of detachment and *sanyas*. Naturally the other choice is domestic way of life which cannot be thought of without 'woman'. So the camera moves to 'woman'. Now a woman can be thought of as interested in dreams, whims, creams, etc, a mundane physical sensuous life, or in 'moon beams' and hymns, etc., a higher life of imagination and emotion. And obviously the protagonist opts for the latter. This foregrounded line can be made clearer as follows:

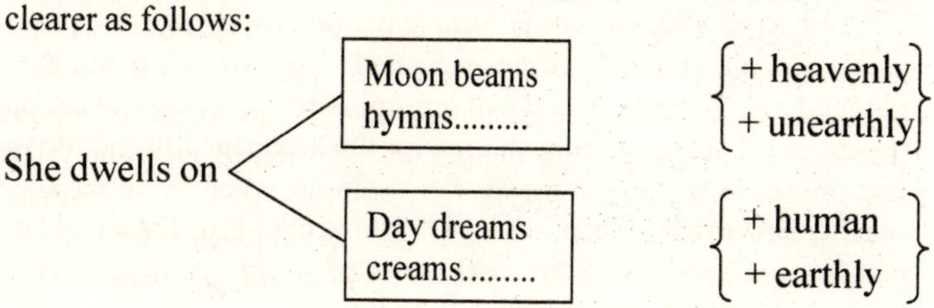

To the protagonist the mundane domestic life is confined to food, sleep, fear and sex, the way it is lived by animals. To him there are higher planes of life. So in the second triplet he talks about the woman and even about himself. Here the third line contains the phrase "In sexless solitude" which is deviant and needs interpretation. The objective 'sexless' takes human and physical noun after it, for instance, Sexless man/woman [+ human/ + concrete] but in the poem it is used as: Sexless Solitude [+abstract/ --human].

Now the fact is that 'Solitude' does not simply mean 'loneliness'. Here it refers to a state which is fully devoid of excitement, agitation, and disturbance. Now such a state cannot be experienced by man as man or woman as woman. The desired tranquil state can be experienced by one who transcends sex. The word 'sexless' mean beyond sex which is the attribute of angels. And therefore the phrase "sexless solitude" would mean 'angelic/divine solitude'. In Sanskrit it is termed as "*Samadhi*" – a state free from dualities and sensual operations. The nature of this 'solitude' can be better understood from the following lines of Wordsworth in his poem 'Daffodils':

> For oft when on my coach I lie
> In vacant or in pensive mood,
> They flash upon that inward eye
> Which is the bliss of solitude.
> And then my heart with pleasure fills,
> And dances with the daffodils.

That is, solitude is blissful state in which one is restored to the third eye, the right vision, the divinity.

Further the phrase "in sexless solitude" has ambiguity regarding its placement. It gets joined to both the protagonist and the woman as follows:

> I can see her smiling ... in sexless solitude.
> She is smiling with wind chiselled breast in sexless solitude.

The two parallel streams present in the first triplet, are also present in the second. Here the first foregrounded feature is the use of the modal 'can'. The structure 'I can see' connotes two things, 'I see' and 'I can see'. That is, the way one sees in the mundane life and the way one can see in unique moments. For example, when Arjun wished to see the 'Brahmadiya Form' of lord Krishna, ten Shri Krishna told him that he won't see that Form with those physical eyes and he needs divine vision (Divya Drishti) to see that Form:

Na tu maam shakyase drashtum a-neineva swachakshusha
Divyam dadaami te chakshuh pashya mei yogamaiswaram

(11/8)

Similarly, here 'smiling' does not mean only a physical act but the divine one denoted by 'moon beams' and 'light'. The 'smiling' or 'shining' or 'brightness' (anand) gets manifested through lips, eyes, breast and skin. And this brightness/anand can be seen as sensuous and also as divine. And it is the physical eyes that see sensuality and the unique vision that sees divinity. And here we see that the protagonist and the woman both have both the gifts. The woman has the potentiality to experience and manifest the divine glow and the protagonist to see it.

Deviation is also noticed in the use of 'wind-chiselled breast' in the second triplet as under:

Wind	blow pollen	Wind	chiselled breast
	{- Human, + Negative}		{+ Human, + Positive}
Wind	scattered grains	Artist	chiselled images

Generally 'wind' scatters, blows, tears things, but here it has carved out the breast. Then the word chiselled 'takes [+ human] [+ animate] subject, e.g., sculptor chiselled the picture: but here it is 'wind' which is [– human] [– animate]. So now the whole interpretation would be as follows: the breast of woman is not simply the lump of flesh and blood but the unique creation of great artist like 'wind' which in Indian context is known as god (Vayu Deva). Again the breast is not only the centre of sensuous attraction but also the eternal source of feeding and fascination. Again it is noticed that here the word 'breast' is used as singular, while it should have been plural 'breasts'. And in singular form it points to be the part of one's body where one's emotions and feelings dwell. Finally, the second triplet can be interpreted to mean that the protagonist has the potentiality to glide into the state of sexless solitude (Samadhi) and see the woman wrapped in divine beauty and light, love and luminescence. The poet talks more about this light and glow in the third triplet.

Surprisingly enough the third triplet itself stands out foregrounded as the first two triplets begin with the first person pronoun 'I', while it begins with the possessive adjective 'her' and noun 'light'. Obviously here the whole focus is on 'her light'. What does this 'light' mean here? A very close reading of the poem helps us see the word 'light' referring to the glow emanating from her lips (smiling), face (moon beams), breast (wind-chiselled) – in brief from the whole body. The light means vitality (Chaitanya), life. This thought becomes clearer from what Othello says in Shakespeare's well known tragedy *Othello* before killing Desdemona:

> "Put out the light, and then put out the light"

It is the light, the *chaitanya* in the person, place or thing that works miracles. No light, no life, nothing. Therefore the poet has very carefully projected the significance of her light as follows:

> her light is not priced
> but gifted to enlighten
> the silver-linings

The poet has three devices, viz., the use of enjambment at the end of every line, the use of juxtaposition in the first two lines and non-finite clause in the third line. These devices beautifully reveal the nature and value of 'her light'.

The first line instead of having a pause at the end moves on to the next line putting up the question: if the light is not priced then how is it? And soon the answer follows 'but gifted'. This results in juxtaposing 'priced' and 'gifted' which are opposite in nature. For instance, the former is concerned with perishable objects like table, chair, cow, horse, etc., while the latter with the eternal like tears, laughter, smile, sadness, etc. Further, 'Price' is man devised act, while 'gift' that of God, Nature. For instance see the following lines from Shakespeare's *Troilus and Cressida*:

> She is a pearl
> Whose price's launched above a thousand ships
> And turned crowned kings to merchants

Here the focus of 'Price' is the 'body' of the woman and not that of 'light' in her which is beyond price. On the other hand, the qualities like joy, smiles, light, and sadness are abstract and spring from within. Let us see the following lines from Tennyson's poem '*Tears Idle Tears*":

Tears idle tears, I know not what they mean
Tears from the depth of some divine despair
Rise in the heart, and gather to the eyes

Similarly, in Taittiria Upnishad it is conclusively said:

'*anando brahmati vyajanat*
anandatev khalu imani bhutani joyante'

That is, joy is god, i.e., joy is the gift of God and joy is at the root of all creativity. Naturally and obviously the poet is talking of that light and luminescence of the woman that comes from within and can be perceived in her eyes, face, lips, breast, skin, etc., as physical as well as divine.

'Her light is not priced but shifted' has one more meaning, viz., in the world there are things available on paying the price e.g., redness on lips by buying lipstick, smoothness and colour on the face by cosmetics, etc., but the light, the joy, etc. comes from Nature alone; the custom of marriage can bring man-woman together, but the feeling of sex can come from Nature; similarly, the protocol of *sanyas* be performed by man, but the real detachment/*vairgaya* could be possible by the grace of Nature/God alone from within.

Again the second line instead of taking a pause at the end glides down to the third line generating the curiosity: 'What does her light enlighten?' and this quest is answered in the third line: 'the silver-linings' which actually means *'jijivisha'* – the strong eternal desire to live and continue living. This desire to live and infinitum is further reinforces by Infinitive clause: 'to enlighten the silver-linings'. In the biblical context also it is seen that initially when Adam was alone, he was sad. But when Eve was created by God and when Adam saw her he was filled with joy, zest and zeal and spoke out – "Flesh of my flesh and bone of my bone". This fact stands verified from Shakespeare's plays as well. For instance one cannot think of Macbeth without Lady Macbeth. Even on the battle field he surrenders to the destiny only after the sad death of Lady Macbeth:

'Out out brief candles.
Life is but a walking shadow, a poor player,
That struts and frets his hour upon the stage
And then is heard no more:'

Thus the poet has tried his best to unfold two streams of life that have flowed from time immemorial. These two parts are as follows:

(i) Buddha way of life, i.e., the life of restraint and discipline *(anushasan)* which helps one see the divinity within and without which is accepted by a few select people and this fact is indicated by allocating only two lines for this sort of life; (ii) Domestic (*grahastha*) life, i.e., the life of worldly pleasure with sex (woman) as its nucleus and which is preferred by the majority of people and this fact is hinted at by allocating seven lines. This two tier pattern of life is pointedly highlighted by: (i) the use of colon (:) at the end of second line n triplet one; (ii) two contractive parallel structures of which one is visible and the other hidden as follows:

I don't seek the stone bowl	I seek stylish belle
Buddha used while here	People choose while here

Further this domestic life equally has two streams, viz., (i) Worldly, life that is confined to sex and sexual joys, (ii) Life that transcends sex and worldly pleasure. This fact gets manifested by two contrastive parallel visible-invisible structures:

Visible	Invisible/ hidden
She dwells on moon beams	She dwells on dreams creams
I can see her smiling	I can see her enticing
With wind chiselled breast	With youth chiselled breast
In sexless solitude	In lustful solitude

However, the protagonist in the poem is inclined to choose the life that transcends routine sex though in the domestic world. And this fact can be seen oozing out from the two parallel opposite symbols:

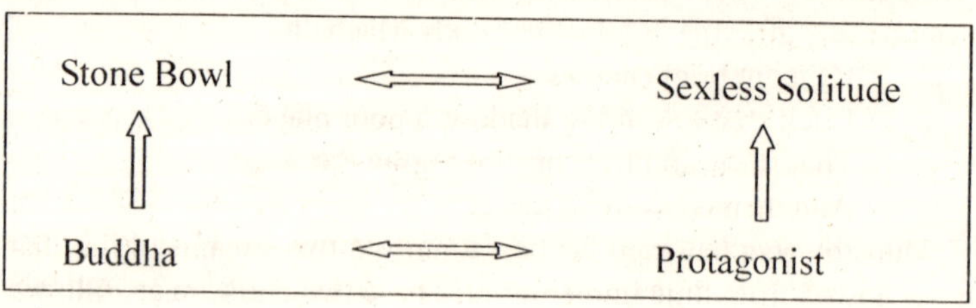

Here 'stone bowl' is a very strong referring to Buddha's mind that had acquired firmness and one pointedness. Obviously 'bowl' signifies human skull in which mind dwells and 'stone' points to passionlessness, firmless of mind. The phrase 'sexless solitude' also refers to the same state of mind which the protagonist acquires in the 'grahasth' life. Here 'solitude' doesn't really mean 'loneliness'. It implies aloneness, 'Zero state'. And 'zero' is a bowl shaped. The 'sexless' doesn't mean without sex. It means the state which transcends 'male' ---- 'female' features. It symbolises an angelic, divine state very much identical to that which is symbolised by 'stone bowl'. Thus these two phrases have unique cohesion.

'Divinity' in 'mundanity' is equally suggested by the lexical nad their cohesion as follows:

moon beams
smiling
wind-chiselled breast
light
silver linings

It is seen above that 'stone bowl' and 'sexless solitude' point to the state of divine joy. The similar joy is communicated by the lexica items above. This joy and light emanates from the key organs of the woman, e.g., moon beams (face), smiling (lips), light (eyes) and bewitching breast. The interesting thing is that all these organs are bowl shaped and have been the eternal source of both, the sensual and ethereal fascinating and gravitation, illuminating silver linings in man. For instance, when Allauddin saw beautiful Padmini, he becomes lascivious, but when Vivekanand saw a beautiful woman, he glided into the divine state.

Generally a man as man thinks of woman and a woman as woman thinks of man. This way of thinking makes one biased, partial, etc. For instance, a man finds a woman fascinating in one moment, and the next moment the same woman become repulsive to him. This is because the sense perception keeps changing from moment to moment for very many reasons. Obviously the protagonist seems aware of this fact of life and so he talks of that what he sees in 'sexless solitude' and as it has already been stated that in this state one transcends his duality and see things beyond sense stratum. In Mandukya Upanishad 'aum', i.e., God is depicted as follows:

'*eishah yoni sarvasya*
Prabhavapyayohi bhutanaam'

Here 'yoni' means sex-male or female and either of this 'yoni' is the abode of God in everything and this God alone is instrumental for all creativity. This fact also makes it obvious that the attraction, the gravitation between male and female is not the attractions of the opposites but that of the likes, i.e., divine and divine or sense and sense.

This prolonged discussion can now be summed up thus: Broadly Life offers two ways of living, viz., of detachment – attachment, of withdrawal-involvement, of *sanyas-grahasth* etc. Very select people go in the former. Mostly people including the protagonist opt for the latter. In the domestic sex centred life, too, one can have exclusively sense centred life as well as that of transcending the senses. And the protagonist in the poem prefers the latter. Either of the ways is not superior or inferior but with different scales and qualities of experience and consequences hinted at by the parallel structures.

WORKS CITED

1. Singh, R. K. *Sexless Solitude and Other Poems*, Bareilly: Prakash Book Depot, 2009.
2. Radhakrishnan, S. ed. *The Principal Upanisads*, New York: HarperCollins Publishers, 1953.

5

R. K. Singh's 'Karmic Credit': A Study in Text

— *D. C. Chambial*

'Karmic Credit' is a short poem of eighteen lines by R. K. Singh published in Poetcrit 23.1 (January 2010). There is hardly any critic and poet who have not read his poems. He is one of the major poets writing today and widely published and highly acclaimed not only for the thematic content of his poems that is innovative and unique but also for his technique. He has evolved a highly condensed technique. The intent of this paper is to explore its text and technique for its complete understanding.

The very title of this poem insinuates readers to look for its interpretation in the Hindu philosophy of karma as propounded in the *Bagvadgita*:

karmanevadhikarste ma phaleshu kadachana,
ma karmaphalheturbhoorma te sangoastvakarmani.

(Gita II: 47)

It embodies the philosophy that a person should do his/her actions without caring for the result of that action(s). The Hindu philosophy identifies two types of actions or deeds (karma): one of which is good or directed towards good with good intentions; and the other is opposed to it, bad, or directed towards bad deeds with bad intentions to bring about harm or sorrow to others. The Hindu dharma teaches that it is sin even to contemplate someone's harm which means that one's actions, deeds or karma should be directed towards others good or welfare. Leaving aside the second type of karma, our concern here is mainly towards the first one when all deed(s) are directed towards the promulgation of universal good. This karma is like an account in a bank: if it is good it is credited in his account and if bad, it is debited from his account. Thus one's karma increases or decreases according to one's good or bad actions done in this human life.

The second word that the poet has used in the title is "credit" which is a noun and qualified by the first word "karmic" which is an adjective of the English version of the word "karma." The two, thus, constitute one whole phrase "karmic credit" that becomes the root of the thought in this poem from which springs the entire poem. Thus, the title embodies the principle of sum total of one's karma towards positive direction. This "karmic credit" becomes the quest of the narrator—"the house"—that tells its tale thus:

Karmic Credit

The cracks, cobwebs, dusts and spots
in the house reveal how neglected
I have been. The roof and base tell of
the wild growth, the expanding peepals
snakes, scorpions, lizards have free time
round the year it's the deserted look

an extension of my existence
without repair or maintenance for
decades their apathy disturbs sleep
I suffer scars and sparks, burn my skin
measure my shadow at different hours
yet I couldn't become the skeleton

I watch the earthworms on the corpses
that swell stomach of headless mummies
or lie dormant to kill the spirit
the elements, ochre moon, sun tongues –
the Buddha's fan fails to renew faith
I can't redeem my karmic credit

(*POETCRIT* 23.1(Jan. 2010): 117.)

The citation of entire poem becomes necessary for its explication. For the study, the poem can be broken/split into several units and then these units/parts taken for exploration one by one.

The first sentence, in two and a half lines, forms the first unit. It tells about its neglected state as-

The cracks, cobwebs, dusts and spots
in the house reveal how neglected
I have been.

These lines very clearly express the sorrow of the protagonist that is because of continuous neglect. It seems that sufficient time has elapsed since this house has been forsaken. There is none to look after it: repair, clean and dust it. This neglect is manifest in "The cracks, cobwebs, dusts and spots" that abound in the house. There is no mason and even no servant to clear it of its cobwebs. It seems the spiders have almost taken charge of the house and are weaving their cobwebs as they like. Dust has also settled unchecked. The cracks and spots remain untended and unrepaired. The omnipresence of "cracks, cobwebs, dusts and spots" gives vent to the agony that the protest suffers: "reveal how neglected / I have been". The present suffering, according to the theory of karma, is the result of past karma. The past karma of the house, in the present context shows that once upon a time when the owner of the house lived here, was very good. Then, because of some unknown reasons, the owner has deserted it and gone somewhere else without assigning it to the care of some person, not even a servant. The suffering also mounts due to the loneliness in which it is now.

The second unit is:

> The roof and base tell of
> the wild growth, the expanding peepals
> snakes, scorpions, lizards have free time
> round the year

Now the protagonist, after telling about its interior, tells about the "roof and the base" of this house. There is "wild growth" that has remained unchecked and uncleared. The peepal tree is ever "expanding" and its branches are growing. Naturally, such a place where no one lives and is abandoned for good, must be the habitat of animals like "snakes, scorpions, lizards" to thrive happily. These insects and reptiles have "free time / round the year". There is none to check them. All this condition of the house and spectacle, "the deserted look," add to the suffering of the protagonist. The roof appears to have become the nursery of wild grass and dust. The snakes, scorpions and lizards have enough space to play unrestrained. Though this deserted look gives unchecked space to wild growth and animals, yet it gives unchecked sorrow to the protagonist.

The third unit has four lines:

> it's the deserted look
> an extension of my existence

without repair or maintenance for
decades

to tell his tale. He avers that "the deserted look" of the house is the "extension of my existence": the interior and exterior state find expansion in its surroundings. Now this "look" of the house and the surroundings has become the very reality of the protagonist which can never be forgotten. The present state of the house is due to the fact that it has remained "without repair" and also without "maintenance" continuously "for / decades" - for a pretty long time. How long can one bear such neglect? It is bound to give rise to an unending angst in the mind of the protagonist or person in question.

The fourth unit is of two lines:

their apathy disturbs sleep
I suffer scars and sparks, burn my skin

It unambiguously discloses the inherent suffering that is augmenting with every word that comes out from the lips of the protagonist and every moment passes. It is not the physical suffering. It has now taken the persona's mind in its grip. He is thinking and thinking about the present state of the house. The psychological suffering is so overwhelming that it has made him insomniac. He is unable to sleep. All this is because of "their apathy". But who are "they"? Here "they" certainly refers to the owners of the house: the animals that have it their habitat cannot be as they are free to come in a deserted place or house when there is none living in it. And what is their "apathy"? It is their indifference towards it. The suffering is so acute that the protagonist admits: "I suffer scars and sparks, burn my skin". These "scars and sparks" are not of any physical burning but mental angst that he suffers due to the disregard. He feels that these "sparks" singe, besides mind, his skin gives him unbearable pain. It also suggests that in his imagination, he experiences physical pain.

The fifth unit brings the time element in the thought process. It also has two lines:

measure my shadow at different hours
yet I couldn't become the skeleton

The subject of the verb "measure" is in the previous unit. It is the protagonist, who, under present state of his mental agony after facing the deserted look of the house, tries to measure his "shadow at different hours", which suggests that shadow changes every moment as it is not static like the time itself, but in flux. This change in the size of shadow also suggests the growing of the persona in age and heading towards evening. His statement, [I] "measure my shadow at different hours," also suggests his consciousness about his growing old age like that of the house about which he feels so much concerned. It is this concern that makes him so sorrowful. This sorrow, in turn, makes him restless. He thinks that his worries, and insomnia too, about the house will take their toll and reduce him to "skeleton" but the truth is quite contrary to it. He avows: "yet I couldn't become the skeleton." On the one hand he thinks about his worry that will have its ill effect on his health, while, on the other, the reality is adverse of it. This situation brings him to a state of *trishanku* : he resonates between two states, one of his imagination and the other of veracity. It is the most painful state of existence.

In the sixth unit, the protagonist's imagination contemplates death in various forms:

> I watch the earthworms on the corpses
> that swell stomach of headless mummies

Now the protagonist watches "earthworms on the corpses." Earthworms convert the bio-mass into soil. Now, these are at work. They are busy with the bodies of those who were laid to rest in the soil. The degradation of these bodies has begun. As they consume the flesh of these bodies, their bellies increase in size – "that swell stomachs of headless mummies" – and these bodies under soil are headless. The word, "headless," adds another dimension to the whole argument. It is just possible that the owners of the house were murdered; their heads were severed from their bodies before giving them a burial. These are addressed as "headless mummies." It is on such dead bodies that these worms thrive and grow in size.

The seventh unit-

> or lie dormant to kill the spirit
> the elements, ochre moon, sun tongues –

hints at another possibility at the existence of "earthworms" with the dead bodies. The persona thinks that the alternative reason of their existence may be "kill the spirit" of the dead. By killing the "spirit" of the dead, they think of destroying even their spiritual existence. And that will be the complete abolition of these dead: bodily, they are already dead and spiritually, these worms will decimate them. Besides the spirit, they will also put an end to "the elements" – perhaps, the five elements: earth, water, air, fire, and void. Here it seems that the persona is contemplating about the annihilation of the universe. When this unit is read together, this meaning becomes apparent. But the paradox remains: how these worms can bring about this catastrophe?

The eighth unit has two lines:

> the Buddha's fan fails to renew faith
> I can't redeem my karmic credit

The persona meditates upon Buddhism that considers this world as the home of suffering. That Buddhism is also unable to give birth "to new faith." Here, the belief that suffering leads to enlightenment by developing an indifferent attitude, an attitude of sameness, *samatva* as propounded by the *Bagvadgita* "*sukhadukhesamekritva labhalahou jyajayou*" (II 38), towards it also seems futile. And the persona concludes; "I can't redeem my karmic credit" — that having suffered so much could not deliver him from the present situation of suffering.

To conclude, the poet has successfully put forth his thesis of suffering and that this suffering has been fruitless and useless in redeeming the "karmic credit" – the fruit of suffering – by mitigating suffering. In this poem the poet has yoked together the concept of Buddhistic suffering and of Hindu karma which earlier remains clouded in the argument of the poem but comes to the fore in the last two concluding lines of the poem.

WORKS CITED

1. *Srimadbhâgvadgîtâ.* Gorakhpur: Gîtâ Press, Samvat 2053.
2. Singh, R. K. 'Karmic Credit'(a poem) pub. in *Poetcrit,* 23.1 (January 2010):117.

6

Philosophy as Figure?: A Study of the Poetry of R. K. Singh

— Mahendra Singh

Poetry is the onto-hermeneutical structurality of self that creates a horizon of noumenal-intentionality for consciousness to electirify the circuit of being connecting from the wave-length of Encompassing. For the poet, the Encompassing is not a horizon within which every determinate mode of Being and truth emerges for him, but rather that within which every particular horizon is enclosed as in something absolutely universal which is no longer visible as a horizon at all. The subjective notion of textual poeticity is like the Encompassing that appears and disappears for us in two parallel perspectives: either as being itself, in and through which we are—or else as the Encompassing which we ourselves are, and in which every mode of Being appears to us. Thus poetry never appears as an object in experience, or as an explicit thematicity of thinking, and therefore it might seem to be empty. But precisely here is where the possibility for the poet's deepest insight into being arises, whereas all other knowledge about Being is simply knowledge of particular, individual being. I must presuppose a poetic attitude whose passion for the truth, in a continuing attempt to assimilate one's own existence, achieves awareness of an unlimited range by continued searching. Poetry and philosophy both are very close to one another expanding the epistemological-ontology of the quest of 'being'. It is philosophy that widens the dimensionality of quest for 'being' in order to solidify the onto-heremeneutical grammatoloy of metaphysics. This paper makes a close analysis of R. K. Singh's poetry in the light of David Hume, Immanuel Kant, W. E. F. Hegel, Friedrich Nietzsche, Soren Kierkegaard, Edmund Husserl, Martin Heidegger, Rene Descartes, Sartre and Merleau Ponty's philosophical theories. The poet seems to be very close to the theory of 'impression' as he sketches the image of 'moon' in an appealing manner. Mark the lines:

She is no moon yet
she drifts like the moon, takes care
of him from the sky-
... she looks too sad to have
any sweet dream: (*The River Returns*, p.3)

The above stanza could be explained in the light of Hume's theory of impressions and ideas. The most basic causal principles of the poet's nature would be generalizations about type of mental states; they would describe the mental process by which we understand his thoughts, imaginations and feelings. The above lines seem to suggest that the varying degrees of liveliness in the perception of the poet are a felt aspect of his experience that he will all immediately recognize to point. Hume identifies liveliness with the capacity of a perception to influence our passions and dreams. This is the idea of the poet about female figure when he says 'she looks too sad to have any sweet dream'. Hume claims that if an idea is a belief, it has same influence on us that our impressions have, and "(t)his effect it can only have by making an idea to approach an impression in force and vivacity."[1](p.119) This sounds as though Hume intends for the varying degrees of liveliness of perceptions to pin point the varying effects of our impressions and ideas. Intuitively, a greater force can produce more changes than a lesser force and here the poet seems to think that there is a natural explanatory link between degrees of liveliness and degrees of influence. The impression of 'moon' on the poet engages him to make a comparison 'she drifts like the moon' rendering the immediate realities of passions and imaginations. The idea of the poet is a link between perceptual judgement and causal belief to concretize the very being of 'liveliness'. Hume believes that dream is neither sensation nor impression but the structured idea of unconscious state. He distinguishes between two kinds of impressions: original impressions, or impressions of sense, and secondary impressions, or impressions of reflection, which include our passions, desires and emotions. Original impressions include the impressions conveyed by our five senses, of course, and they also clearly include bodily pains and pleasures. The 'sad' appearance of female figure is the original impression on the poet through lively perception leading him in the zone of pain. The word 'sweet-dream' derives the 'direct passion' of the poet known as secondary impression that proceeds immediately from pleasures. What the 'direct passions' are "about" or "of" is the pain and pleasure state that causes them; for example, the melancholy state of female is the anxiety of the poet. A notion of generosity that the poet expresses on the painful state of female's 'sad appearance' may cause him pain, but it would cause him pride only if he recognizes it as his own. In the same sequence, further the poet continues:

> Yearning to meet him
> she turns a silk-worm spinning
> love-silk in cold night –
> stands in a shade melting tears
> like a candle, drop by drop (*The River Returns*, p. 4)

As per Hume's view, the content of the poet's idea would not have changed, but at first his idea would have been an idea of imagination, and later, after the flash of recollection, it would have been an idea of memory: "as soon as the circumstance is mentioned, that touches the memory, the very same ideas now appear in a new light, and have, in a manner, a different feeling from that they had before"[2] (p.628) Hume draws from this the conclusion that imagination and memory "are only distinguished by the different *feeling* of the ideas they present"[3].(p.628) and he describes such feeling as 'liveliness', the same feature that distinguishes impressions from ideas. 'Love-silk' is the basic content of the poet's binaries of ideas generating the desirability of impression for meeting, in beloved's heart. Here I find a notion of contiguity that produces association because "the senses, in changing their object, are necessitated to change them regularly, and take them as they lie *contiguous* to each other"; thus "the imagination must by long custom acquire the same method of thinking, and run along the parts of space and time in conceiving its objects."[4](p.11)The phrase 'melting tears' has association with 'cold night' and 'candle' in terms of causal relation that serves as 'constant junction' for the noumenal objectivity of female's love. Hume writes:

> "no objects will admit of comparison, but what have some degree of resemblance", and he notes that only some of these resemblances will produce an association of idea... [W]hen a quality becomes very general, and is common to a great many individuals, it leads not the mind directly to any of them; but by

> presenting at once too great a choice, does thereby prevent the imagination from fixing on any single object".[5] (p.14)

The phenomenal feature of 'candle' produces an association of ideas for the poet comparing with 'melting tears' of female that falls 'drop by drop.' The simple impression of 'candle' is attended with a corresponding idea of beloved's 'melting tears'. Hume's account of simple perceptions may be even more complicated if I take into account his distinctive theory about the poet's ideas of extension, that is, ideas of spatial extension.

> From the sea of days and years
> I gather white sand
> drifted on the beach
> in the shells waves bring.... (*My Silence*, Poem 65)

The following lines give us the panoramic view of Descartes' "intuitionism" that appears in Meditation III, where he begins to set out his own conception of knowledge. The poet's image of 'the sea of days and years' sketches the 'mathematical propositions' of Rene Descartes to know the 'criterion of truth'. The poet like mediator turns to the one basic truth in his possession, namely, *cogito ergo sum*, and extracts from it a standard of truth, clarity, and distinctness of perception, to replace the discredited idea of relying on the senses. Descartes writes:

> I am certain that I am a thinking thing. Do I not therefore also know what is required for my being certain about anything? In this first item of knowledge there is simply a clear and distinct perception of what I am asserting ... So I now seem able to lay it down as general rule that whatever I perceive very clearly and distinctly is true.[6] (p.35)

In this way, then, the self-refutation of the skeptic delivers the very basis of a new, non-empiricist conception of human knowledge. 'White sand' refers the 'karmic deposits' of human life that he accumulates from the 'sea of days and years'. 'Shells' are the precious treasure of the sea referring to notion of certainty for the existence of being. Here again I quote Descartes: "I have freed my mind of all care (*curis*) and have arranged for my-self a solid stretch of free time (*otium*)"[7] (pp.17-18). When time is short and resources limited, when practical concerns are in play and we must act, we cannot afford the luxury of rejecting every belief for we can imagine the slightest ground of doubt. The waves of sea are fickle in nature and they are dependent on the stroke of wind to reach nearby the seashore sketching the mathematical line of doubt for the existence of being sheltering in shells as 'white sand'. Here *derivative beliefs* on waves are the superstructure to solidify the epistemological ground in order to maintain the sustainability of the ontological grammatology of being. Descartes writes:

> ... there is I-know-not –what deceiver, supremely powerful and supremely cunning, who deliberately and constantly deceives me. Then I too undoubtedly exist, if he is deceiving me. And let him deceive me as such as he can, he will never bring it about that I am nothing, so long as I think that I am something.[8]
>
> (p.25)

It is wave that deceives like demon to the very being of the 'I-ness' of the poet who looks to the 'days and years' that disappeared under the vast scanner of past. 'Years and days' have their temporal structurality of time-consciousness that also tries to surface the layer of trans-temporal zone. Further, in another context the poet writes:

> I search my name
> like a timeless thought
> from first to last it remains
> revolving like the earth
> the sun in me rises and sets
> and I dance my silence on the ocean floor
>
> (*My Silence*, Poem 65)

The search of name for the poet is the *cogito* (I-ness) of Descartes claiming 'intuitive certainty' for his existence. Descartes presents the *cogito* as a demonstration of his existence from his thought. The 'timeless thought' derives the existential notion of restless being for the search of self-hood on the seashore of life. In the end, though, Descartes acknowledges that his argument does, in some sense, assume a general connection between 'thought' and 'existence'. He admits this when he presents his philosophy in synthetic form in the *Principles of Philosophy*:

> When I said that the proposition *I think, therefore I*

> *exist* is the first and most certain of all those which occur to any one who philosophizes in an orderly way, I did not thereby deny that one must first know what thought is, what existence is, and what certainty is, and that it cannot happen that what thinks does not exist.[9] (p.8)

Firstly, I must clarify that thought can never be timeless on account of its empirical nature and always comes in consciousness with the temporality of time as phenomenal reality to concretize the 'circuit of being'. The poet, like meditator, infers his existence from his thinking presupposes the general principle implicitly, but does not need to be explicitly conscious of it. In fact, he discovers the general connection between thought and existence when he finds himself unavoidably making the inference from 'his' thinking to 'his' existence. The line: 'the sun in me rises and sets' leads us to the extreme of two different streams that widens the horizon of faith and doubt for the certainty of existence. Sun is the universal phenomenon of Nature that justifies the certainty of existence of Absolute to make collapse the citadel of reason and doubt. We have got birth not life because life is the belonging of Supreme who is free to take it any time. The individual should not bother for the certainty of his existence while stating that the sun is setting and rising in him. The sun (life) is the property of Supreme and one must have a very strong notion of infatuation to devote his life like tree that offers soothing shade to the weary traveler but never claims that shade is its belonging. Here one metaphor of epistemology is appealing in the line 'I dance my silence on the ocean floor', that 'silence' symbolizes wisdom that can be attained through self-contemplation. Silence is the sister of Nature and the poet endeavors to develop healthy companionship with Her. In another context, the poet talks of his being that are very close to Sartre's 'human reality'. The poet writes:

> The expanding rings of the sun
> cobweb my being and things
> all around cluster from dawn to dusk....
>
> (*My Silence*,Poem 58)

Consciousness is central to human reality, according to Sartre, not simply because human beings are necessarily conscious but because a full exploration of consciousness entails explorations of its subjects, its objects and its modalities, and these ultimately yield a fully rounded description of the 'being' of human beings as what Heidegger called 'Being-in-the-world': embodied free subjects embedded in an intersubjective world of meaningful and value-laden objects. The above stanza is purely existential and the poet is enforced to characterize his consciousness as a 'perpetual lack'. The second line: 'cobweb my being and things' deserves interpretation in terms of 'human reality', 'intentionality', 'being-in-itself' and 'being-for-itself'. The claim of Sartre that all consciousness is consciousness of something certifies that all consciousness is intentional. Sartre's assertion that every consciousness is consciousness *of* something provides a further wrinkle to his previous claim that consciousness is nothing: it is not a thing but, rather, a relation. It is a relation between subject (poet's being) and object ('and things'), though a note of caution is required: the subject is neither Husserl's transcdental ego nor Descartes' immaterial mind but a body subject ; the object (things) of poet is neither a representation in consciousness nor an isolated physical object but a meaningful whole within a field of his perception and action. The poet's 'being' derives the notion of Sartre's 'in-self' corresponding that 'Being is' and 'things all around cluster' refer 'for-itself' which is the origin of nothingness that exists in the universe. In terms of phenomenology, the words that occurred in third line 'from dawn to dusk' can be compared with Sartre's 'life-space'. R.K. Singh's characterization of life-space, and of the objects of perception within life-space draw heavily on Gestalt psychology and when he says that 'things all around cluster from dawn to dusk' he gives an opportunity to correlate with the spatial situation of objects. If life-space is hodological, the spatial location of objects within life-space will like wise be given hodologically. According to Sartre, Objects are revealed to us as the heart of a complex of instrumentality in which they occupy a determined place. This place is not defined by purely spatial coordinates but in relation to axes of practical reference.[10](p.321) Here Sartre is identifying the place of an object hodologically : in terms of potential *paths* to the object and in terms of *difficulties* and *obstacles* along those paths. If we look at the things phenomenologically, we find 'a complex of instrumentality' in the locatability of thing. So we find phenomenological error in 'things all around cluster' that destructures the phenomenological locatability of objects existing in universe. At another place where the sketches present the panoramic view of Nature we find that how phenomenality reality takes place at the time of changing season. The poet writes:

The withered leaves
blown away in autumn
come again with the tired rains
the season confers
through the soft grey clouds
the growing freshness on naked trees (*My Silence*, Poem 53)

The above stanza reflects the cyclic view of Nature that is determined to change. Her cloth is blown away in autumn to wear new one in spring. The lines make us aware that the poet is Nature conscious 'that never betray the heart who loved her'. Now we notice not simply the negative differences, but also the positive bonds that hold the two terms together. The meaning of textual being suggests us to concentrate on Hegel's *Philosophy of Nature*. In his Introduction to the *Philosophy of Nature* Hegel asserts that Nature is to be regarded as a system of stages, where one follows another with a kind of necessity. For example, the arrival of autumn is necessary to make the leaves shed for the new one that will come in spring. Following Hegel, the poet advocates some kind of natural evolution. Hegel goes on to say that this not to be understood as if each stage is generated by a *natural* process. It happens rather within the implicit, internal idea that constitutes the ground of Nature. In other words, "metamorphosis does not occur in Nature, but only in that conceptual thinking which grasps the underlying rationality of the universe... The way of evolution, which starts from the imperfect and formless."[11](p.249) The fact that experience does offer something that matches the template offers evidence that Nature is ultimately in reason and mysticism. The negativity involved in words, 'withered leaves', 'autumn', and 'tired rains' does not itself convert into trans-substantial time. Rather, the images of the poem notice this negativity. The process in which negativity or non-union is integrated with union or identity that happen mystically in Nature and within individual living organism is like 'naked tree'. Here 'naked tree' denotes the Absolute Idea of Hegel that can be compared with the sacrifice of Lord Buddha who left his palace for attaining enlightenment. Tree attains the state of *tatthagat* when it detaches from leaves to justify the philosophy of *Gita*. Attachment is the cause of grief. Knowledge, music and art all come through the corridor of suffering. The phrase 'growing freshness' projects the state of *para-nirvan* that tree attains after perennial suffering. The poet sketches the view of the sea that symbolizes knowledge and self-consciousness. The poet is standing nearby the seashore and watching the waves:

Watching the waves
up and down
I stand
like an island (*My Silence*, Poem 48)

It is sea that eliminates our ego, notion of pride, false rhetoric and pseudo-conception and offers dialectical methodology to understand being. The sea that the poet has depicted is not just a consciousness but self-consciousness whose waves go upward and come downward independently and assimilate the self-consciousness of the poet. The rising movement of the wave denotes 'the absolute Notion' of Hegel that enables the poet to transcend the mundane world through negation of his consciousness. The movements of wave in the object of self-consciousness has, for poet or in-itself, returned into itself and become life. The effort of the poet while standing like 'island' to touch the surface of 'absolute knowing , is a wholehearted counterpart to the activity of apperceptive spontaneity as Kant conceives it in the Transcendental Deduction. What I feel that the 'rising wave' develops the forms of a pure determination process in such a way that in it the process—as that which determines or as that in which the dynamic of determination itself is displayed in its pure form—receives complete autonomy from any ontologically fixed substrate. The poet witnesses the 'rising wave' because it offers the 'movement of truth' that can be grasped neither by a determinate concept nor by an intuition. Hegel is inclined to believe that truth is not a concluded, fix object, event or proposition of *which* a concept should be provided; truth is a complex movement of transformation that the poet feels for his sublimation at the seashore standing 'like an island'. The next view comes to us is that of a river where the poet makes an appeal to the boatman for carrying him home:

... O boatman
I must reach my home

before the snakes of the river shroud my bed
and my being is questioned
by the silence of the watery night (*My Silence*, Poem 69)

The poet seems to be well aware about the philosophy of 'being' that reminds us of Heidegger's 'question of being' raising traditional ontology. Heidegger writes: "Man alone of all beings, when addressed by the voice of Being, experiences the marvel of all marvels: that what it *is*. Therefore the being that is called in its very essence to the truth of Being is always attuned in an essential sense."[12](p.261) The being of the poet is Heidegger's Da-sein who exists factically (facticity, thrownness), and that thus factically existing, he is already falling away from himself to the things he meets within his world. Similarly, when we speak of thrownness, we already imply that this thrown Da-sein is in the way of existence, because only in coming back to himself in the possibilities of his being can Da-sein find himself already thrown into a world. Similarly, when we speak of falling or fallenness, we are already implying existence and thrownness, for only a 'being' of the poet who understands his being in a world can lose himself to the things he meets within it. It is 'watery night' that projects the fallen state of the poet (Da-sein) and 'the snakes of the river' derives the notion of 'temporal facticity' enforcing Da-sein to walk in the range of 'thrownness' rather than reaching 'home'. It is the 'voice of Being' that awakens the poet to make an appeal to the 'boatman' for carrying him 'home'. Heidegger always emphasizes that Da-sein has an ontological circle-structure: the 'light' of existence is only possible to a thrown and fallen being. And the individual must remember that the whole being of a possibility lies in its being disclosed as a possibility. With Da-sein, the factical existence of a unique self is required to be its own possibility rather than to have a tendency of dependency on 'boatman' to whom the poet makes an appeal. The essence of De-sein is to understand his being, in place of questioning it, as the possibility that is singly and uniquely his. The poet is not happy of his past and expresses a deep notion of dissatisfaction sketching the line of intentionality in terms of phenomenology:

Couldn't be happy with
my present nor could realize
any dream all these years—

there is nothing to look back
to say I lived my life well(*The River Returns*, p.21)

The above stanza clearly depicts the predicament of the poet who feels himself as thrown being on the sea of life swinging in the waves of past and present to solidify the scriptology of human existentialism. The world of the poet's own existence is the horizon in which his everyday understanding moves, so that it forms it and in reference to it the things he comes across are intelligible as the 'range of past' and 'notion of happiness'. The horizon from which things are to be understood is the substantiality of matter. But in existential term, this horizon gives nothing from which things could even be questioned as to their possible relevance to a purpose; their only possibility now is to show themselves in their material properties as moving bodies in a space time continuum. The horizon which makes it possible for us to understand being as being is itself the meaning of being. What is this horizon? The poet exists such that his being is manifest to him, and it is *manifest* to him as his own. The tendency to interpret the being of the poet from the being of things may be provisionally explained by one of the basic ways in which he can and usually does exist: he loses himself to the things he meets in his world. In this context, Martin Heidegger writes in *Being and Time*:

> The way the present is rooted in the future and in the having been is the existential and temporal condition of the possibility that what is project in circumspect understanding can be brought nearer in a making present in such a way that the present must adapt itself to what is encountered in the horizon of an awaiting retention, that is, it must interpret itself in the schema of the as-structure.[13] (p.360)

Here Heidegger is intended to project the existential-temporal "schema" to cast light on the obscurity of Kant's doctrine of the 'schematism'. The phenomenal temporality of present enforces being to indulge in the root of past to minimize its essence (meaning) and the horizon of universal life widens from the horizon of individual being. The poet's notion of dissatisfaction is constituted by the temporal present in which his consciousness is destructured by the intentionality of phenomenalogical reduction and future is overclouded by the fog of uncertainty.' All these years' are the deconstituted possibility of time's temporality and the poet lost his 'being' in facticity of negation. The growing movement of the fall is made possible by interacting modifiability of the whole temporal structure. The more fleeting the presenting, the more 'flightly' it conceals a definite ability-to-be, the less able is the futural here-being to come back to its thrown self. The 'running away' of the present of the poet misleads him into envisaging it as an ontic happening in which one thing breaks loose from another thing. But the presenting is not anything; it cannot 'stand' in and by itself at all but can only bring itself forth (temporalize itself) in the unity of time. Even the unheld presenting is still in some way 'held' in here-being's coming-to-itself awaitingly. The running-away of the poet modifies the awaiting in such a way that the awaiting 'runs after' the presenting. The awaiting of the poet can no longer fulfill its proper function of 'running ahead' and holding out possibilities before and toward the presenting it gives itself up, it abdicates its role of leading and guiding the thrown self in its choice of 'present' opportunities. By taking over the lead, the presenting modifies the inauthentic future into an awaiting that runs after. It is this ecstatic modification that makes possible the 'dispersion' or 'scatteredness' which is a constitutive character of falling. The self-grounding character of the poet is in turn, 'grounded' in the temporality of care, which holds the present in an ecstatic unity with the future and past.

The poet is well aware about the existential suffering of man that we come to know through the lines:

> While I lie alone
> shapeless fears rest on my eyes
> heavier than time
>
> searching salvation... (*The River Returns*, pp. 74-75)

Fear is the sickness of consciousness that offers deranged view of anxiety for being that rests in state of solitude. The poet again shows his existential concern for the despairing state of being that is blackened in the totality of negativity. Fear makes home in the 'house of being' when being maintains distance from faith to widen the black horizon of trembling and despair. In the Hegelian state of consciousness, the poet has supposedly gone further than faith, and in doing so, faith has been placed in its proper place in the fundamentally rational scheme of things. One sees oneself merely as a product of the Creator and totally indebted to this Creator, so one renounces the temporal world of form in order to find 'salvation', but in doing this, one remains a permanent outsider to the world of forms, and little or no pleasure is derived from worldly existence, which is now considered unimportant and meaningless. The poet's perception of reality, however, unlike those living in the ethical state of consciousness, is no longer exclusively constructed by the rational mind, for he sees and believes, primarily through the eyes of faith. According to Kierkegaard, a man of genuine faith is questioned, he will always be prepared to admit the impossibility of his beliefs and will nevertheless still have utter faith in them clarifying that *infinite resignation* is a prerequisite to faith. Kierkagaard writes in *Fear and Trembling*:

> "Infinite resignation is the last stage before faith, so that anyone who has not made this movement does not have faith; for only then does my eternal validity become transparent to me, and only then can there be talk of grasping existence on the strength of faith"[14].(p.75)

This is how in infinite resignation one becomes aware of an infinite relation to reality which in turn opens the caves to the possibility of receiving the grace of faith. The poet says that his 'shapeless fear' is 'heavier than time' because fear has designed a 'circuit of despair' to shatter his faith. Disowned existence, as a movement manifests a threat from which Da-sein flees. This threat, according to Heidegger, is revealed by dread, on the ground of which Da-sein flees from himself into his occupations with things within the world.

The possibility of the poet's 'lie alone' leads to the flight of disowned existence that is not an occasional, isolated act, but a basic way in which Da-sein is-in-the-world. This implies that threat also cannot be occasional, isolated experience, but must constantly tune Da-sein and reveal to him a threat to his existence. Heidegger believes that dread is the basic mood that lies at the ground of Da-sein's being, although it rarely rises to the surface and few of us might recognize it as fully and explicitly experienced by us. The next stanza tells us the time-consciousness of poet who tries to locate his being in the 'empty cell of time':

...empty cell of time
is me weaving heat
in unholy solitude... (*My Silence*, Poem 61)

The above philosophical stanza is very close to Kant's theory of time and space and both are considered as object of cognition rather than mere forms of sense experience—as 'formal intuitions' rather than 'form of intuition'. Kant believes that time is an *apriori* intuition that contradicts our natural conception of sense experience as an entirely a *posteriori* affair. Kant views on time in section II of *Critique of Pure Reason*:

> Time is not an empirical conception. ....Time is a necessary representation, laying at the foundation of all our intuitions. With regard to phenomena in general, we cannot think away time from them, and represent them to ourselves as out of and unconnected with time, but we can quite well represent to ourselves time void of phenomena. Time is therefore given *apriori*. In it alone is all reality of phenomena possible.[15] (p.28)

According to the stanza, it is contradictory that time cannot be outwardly intuited without being inwardly intuited: if our mental states are not in time, we cannot experience outer phenomena as being in time. And here, the poet is being a witness to 'unholy solitude' in the conscious range of time as the negation of his instrumental essence that leads him to 'absolute negation'. The poet faces the hammer like stroke of 'weaving heat' that is the result of 'time void of phenomena' representing his mental state. Time is an unmanifest phenomenon of Hegel's 'life-world' that refers 'empty cell' and deeply rooted in the representation of given *apriori*. Whereas Hegel believes that time is a being that exists in being and is "intuited becoming". Time signifies a transition from being of the poet to his 'unholy solitude'. The image of 'weaving heat' is a thought which grasped in the poet's being; only if the negations do not simply subsist in their indifference, but are superseded, i.e., themselves negated. In the negation of negation, the temporality of time posits itself for the poet's being and thus emerges from the indifference of subsistence. In positing itself for itself, it posits the succession in which it stands, the sphere of his being-out-side-of-itself, that is, the 'negated negation. Lastly, while concluding

I assert that as the immediate intuition, time is "empty", and must be so if it is to be capable of taking up into itself: all things appear in time, that is, project themselves, and become themselves "viewable" in time. At another place the poet feels that he has failed to see the image of objects in the 'mirror of time' and his inner environment is overclouded by 'foggy blackness'. The poet writes:

> Seeing no image
> in the mirror of time—
> foggy blankness (*The River Returns*, p. 76)

Here the poet is not in a condition to witness the 'image' of things (objects) justifying the subjective conditionality of object that he endeavors to locate in the 'mirror of time'. Kant was so much concerned with the subjective conditions of objective knowledge that he came to assert that we can never know things as they are in themselves, but only as they appear to us conditioned as we are by certain subjective cognitive structures. In the above stanza, 'time' appears as inner intentionality of consciousness that the poet experiences the world in the fractured possibility of his perception blocking the door of cognitive faculty. It was Edmund Husserl who rejects the "objective" view of time as a punctilinear row of "nows" that stretches both back and forward to infinity and constitutes a one –dimensional line, the objective time line. In this term, Husserl offers us a three-dimensional view. The present, for him, is not the nondimensional point of the instantaneous now. Rather, we might say that the present is 'thick' to the extent that, 'within the present, we find both the past and the future; that is, we find all three dimensions of time. Perceptual consciousness of the poet seems to get marginalized in the past dimension of point of time to cease the present one. There is a vital gap between the 'time past' and 'time present' and this gap sweeps away the recalling dimension of the circuit of memory from his consciousness creating a horizon of blank panoramic view. Merleau Ponty writes in *Phenomenology of Perception*:

> Thing and instants can link up with each other to form a world only through the medium of that ambiguous being known as a subjectivity, and can become present to each other only from a certain point of view and in intention. Objective time which flows and exists part by part would not be even suspected,

> were it not enveloped in a historical time which is projected from the living present towards a future. The alleged plenitude of the object and of the instant springs forth only in face of the imperfection of the intentional being. A present without a future, or an eternal present, is precisely the definition of death; the living present is torn between a past which it takes up and a future which it projects.[16] (p.388)

The cognitive faculty of the poet is searching the point of perceptual consciousness where his present could touch the surface of subjective conditionality for the perception of object in order to minimize the circle of intentionality. It is inner time- consciousness that generates a wave length of reflexive uniformity and reflective materiality for creating space in the faculty of perceptual circuit through which one can mediate on the 'eternal present ' of Merleau Ponty.

> I see boats sinking and life
> bewitched by suffering... (*My Silence*, Poem 44)

The lines project the paradigmatic perspective of despair, that is, the sickness of spirit. The poet's life seems to be filled with constant and intense suffering. Existentialism denies the priority of objective truth. What is important is what we do about ourselves, how we live within the light we have, the decisions we make. The poet seems to "thrown" into existence, afloat over several fathoms of ocean water, and he must somehow keep afloat. A key question comes up , why not drown? However, the urgency of finding a purpose to life radically transforms the relationship between objective truth and subjective apprehension. Passion is the way to truth, and the way may be more valuable than the end. The father of Christian existentialism Kierkegaard writes in *The Sickness unto Death*:

> We have here a great consciousness of what despair is, since despair is indeed loss of the eternal and of oneself.... For when the earthly is taken away from the self and one despairs, it is as if the despair came from outside, even though it always comes from the self; but when the self despairs over this very despair, then this new despair comes from the self...For just because it is more intense, this despair is in a certain sense closer to salvation. A

> despair of this kind is hard to forget—it goes too deep; but any moment the despair is held open, there is also a possibility of salvation.[17] (p.93)

The despair of Kierkegaard is very close to Buddha's *dukkha* that originates from the self to see the misery of world. Thus the despair that comes from within leads to perennial contemplation so as to transcend the world through self-consciousness. The suffering of the poet that comes from despair and angst may lead to salvation, but for this, individual has to transcend himself from mundane affairs.

> I wanted to touch a sun
> vanished before my hands
> became titan to reach
> the horizon (*My Silence*, Poem 43)

The following lines offer us a wide range of philosophical dimension for interpretation in the light of Jaspers' 'Encompassing'. The concept of horizon encourages Jaspers to elucidate form of "the Encompassing". The modes of the Encompassing distinguished by him are Being in itself. Like the poet, every individual is the eventual phenomenality of "the Encompassing" to create space inside and outside for manifolding the situationality of consciousness on the surface of 'determinate mode 'of transcendent being. Jaspers writes:

> ... everything that is an object for us, even though it be the greatest, is still always within another, is not yet all. Wherever we arrive, the horizon, which includes the attained itself, goes further and forces us to give up any final rest. We can secure no stand point from which a closed whole of Being would be surveyable, nor any sequence of standpoints through whose totality Being would be given even in directly. We always live and think within a horizon. But the very fact that it is a horizon indicates something further which again surrounds the given horizon. From this situation arises the question about the Encompassing.[18] (p.211)

The way objects represent themselves in the world create phenomenal range of perceptual manifold in the structured narrativity of consciousness for widening the horizon of cognitive realm. The term 'Encompassing' refers to the vibrating subjectivity of phenomenal world where objects are 'intended' to project themselves as per their different configurational nature and situationality to fabricate the noumenal line of horizon, for being in the conditioned possibility of time and space. In fact, horizon gives rest to the meaning of being where being tries to detotalize the contextuality of reflexive materiality. The poet is searching a definite 'standpoing' for the expansion of his conscious reality in order to give a magnitudnal sublime to his intuition. The appearance of 'sun' is the magnitudnal reflectivity of Nature that offers a temporal constitution of horizon. The objective purport of intuitions is to be understood, then, in terms of their exemplifying logical unities that are characteristic of judging. That intuitions are of objects, Kant's urging, is to be understood in terms of their possessing the kind of unity that results when, in judging, one brings cognitions to the unity of apperception. So Kant places spontaneous apperceptive activity at the centre of his picture of the objective purport of sensory consciousness. The sensory consciousness of the poet is awakened by the absolute notion of object as 'sun' to form spatiotemporal horizon. The free activity of bringing cognitions to the unity of apperception is a precursor, in Kant, to what figures in Hegel as the free self-development of "notion"—a setting within which the idea of "the Encompassing's" directedness at objects no longer includes anything that could appear as a gulf between subject (poet) and object (horizon). The further stanza of the poet creates a havoc of contradiction leading to express my view on 'celebrity' and 'tree'. Friedrich Nietzsche's view on 'will to truth ' and 'will to value' is also very relevant that can be projected well in the light of tree's life and service.

I am no celebrity
but they don't want me
to grow like a tree… (*My Silence*, Poem 76)

The word 'celebrity' refers false and fraud rhetoric created by so called postmodern people having pseudo conception, formation and mentality. The moral and truthful value of life and world never get sustainability by the person having power, post and position known as celebrity. The value of world maintains its long durability with the favour of unsung one who suffers a lot at the cost of his life justifying the aesthetic phenomenon of existence for the beautification of world. 'Celebrity' is a very cheap and mean word for the isolated and forgotten one like Sartre who refused to take 'Nobel Prize' on *Being and Nothingness* and certified the authenticity of statement that work can never be truly evaluated in the light of Prize. Work is bigger than Prize. One who suffers in his life for the noble piece of work is very lucky than the person who has a notion of pride for Prize and calls him as celebrity. Like tree, individual has to pay heavy amount for service in the form of suffering. Tagore says that if one leads his life truthfully and calls for companionship, the world does not listen to him. Despite this crucial condition, he has to walk alone. This encouraging view appeared in his famous song 'Aikla Chalo Re'. The growth of tree appears to the world as easy going phenomenon but the same world fails to see the amount of perennial suffering that the tree faces for its growth and maturity to serve the world while offering fruit and shade to the tired ones. The top of the tree faces the extreme heat of the sun silently without making any complain and man nurtures false pride while stating that he is at the top. And moreover, the tree faces the heavy stroke of tempest, harsh weather and the beat of rain patiently for attaining the state of perfection to serve the world. Now it is right to assert that the service of tree is bigger than the success of celebrity. And suffering is necessary for the individual through which he gives value to the world in order to enhance its sustainability.

Now I concentrate on Nietzsche who holds that pleasure and pain are 'mere epiphenomena' of our physical and unconscious natures devoid of metaphysical relevance. Nietzsche writes in *Beyond Good and Evil*: "Life is the sole locus of value, and its preservation, flourishing, and enhancement are ultimately decisive in the determination of value".[19](p.4) Whether we believe in life or not, life is an invitation for living and creation to offer value for the world. According to Nietzsche, our being is like a tree that derives its roots into the depths and at the same time embraces the heaven even more lovingly and broadly. Thus these two aspects of the tree stand for the 'will to truth' and the 'will to value'. The 'will to truth' leads us to "the earth," to what is known through the senses. And it leads us to acknowledge and pursue the "rootedness" in the "the earth"—in our affective, and decidedly "earthly" nature- of those things that seem to tower above it, the values that appear as if in "the heavens," to which we are driven by our 'will to value'. The relationship between these wills leads to those aspects of his thought that make him incomprehensible.

> Like tree we grow - it's hard to understand, like all life—not in one place, but everywhere; not in one direction, but upwards and outwards and downwards equally; our energy drives trunk, branches, and roots all at once; we are no longer free to do anything singly, to "be" something single.[20](p.371)

My line of argument is what makes Nietzsche incomprehensible is not simply his growth, but the manner of that growth, like all life, he grows in more than one direction at once. And the poet could not find "will to truth" that tree represents in its rootedness of the earth in order to take stand firmly against the challenges of life. If a tree were not rooted, it would not surge into the heavens; if didn't grow toward the heavens, its roots would perish. This suggests that Nietzsche is like a tree in that the growth of his 'will to truth' depends on the growth of his 'will to value', and the growth of his 'will to value' depends on that of the 'will to truth'. For a creative writer it is moral obligation to show spiritual awareness for the solidity of universal paradigms—"will to truth" and "will to value".

It is poetry that brings sublimation for the world, but before this, the world assimilates it in its within, while indulging in the process of self-contemplation and meditation. Scriptural consciousness, grammatological notion of ontology, metaphysics, mysticism, spiritualism and configurational projection of epistemology all are the 'will to truth' and 'will to value' for the poetry, through which, it creates space to take everlasting stand on the sand dunes of time. The poet feels subjective truth of ages in his nerves and arteries through his transtemporal connectivity of consciousness to incarnate time, so that, the seed of atemporal vibration could germinate in the soil of sublime narrative of time to heal the wounded humanity. The ontological notion of epistemology lies in the textuality of mysticism and scriptural awakening through which the real poetry springs out like fountain from the realm of metaphysics.

Have I been off the mark? Perhaps yes? Perhaps no! That is what judging and interpreting poetry is all about.

WORKS CITED

1. Hume, David. *A Treatise of Human Nature*, eds. David Fate and Mary Norton. Oxford: Oxford University Press, 2000.
2. *Ibid.*
3. *Ibid.*
4. *Ibid.*
5. *Ibid.*
6. Descartes, Rene. *Oeuvres de Descartes*, eds. Charles Adam and Paul Tannery, Vol. vii, Paris: Vreny, 1957.
7. *Ibid.*
8. *Ibid.*
9. *Ibid.*
10. Sartre, Jean Paul. *Being and Nothingness*, tr. H. E. Barnes. London : Routledge, 1986.
11. Hegel, Georg Wilhelm Friedrich. *Philosophy of Nature*, trsns. A. V. Miller. Oxford : Clarendon Press,1970.
12. Kaufman, Walter. *Existentialism: From Dostoevsky to Sartre*, ed. "The Quest for Being", Martin Heidegger. New York: A Plume Book, 1956.
13. Heidegger, Martin. *Being and Time*, trans. John Macquarrie and Edward Robinson. New York: Harper and Collins,1962.
14. Kierkegaard, Soren. *Fear and Trembling* , trans.H. V. and E. H. Hong. Princeton : Princeton University Press, 1983.
15. Kant, Immanuel. *Critique of Pure Reason* ,trans. J. M. D. Meiklejohn. New York: Dover Publication, 2003.
16. Ponty, Merleau. *Phenomenology of Perception*, trans. Colin Smith. New York: Routledge, 2003.
17. Kierkegaard, Soren. *The Sickness unto Death*, trasn. Alastair Hannay. London : Penguine Books, 1989.
18. Kaufman, Walter. *Existentialism: From Dostoevsky to Sartre.* ed. Jaspers's Existent Philosophie.

19. Nietzsche, Friedrich. *Beyond Good and Evil.* Trans. Marion Faber. Oxford: Oxford University Press, 1999.

20. Nietzsche, Friedrich. *Gay Science*. trans. Josefive Nauckhoff, 2nd edn. Bernard William. Cambridge: Cambridge University Press, 2001.

21. Singh, R. K. *My Silence*, Madras: Poets Press India, 1985.

22. __________.*The River Returns*, Bareilly: Prakash Book Depot, 2006.

7

"Sanjaya" and "Dhrutrashtra" Reconstructed in the Capsule Poems of R. K. Singh

— *G.D.Barche*

After going through R. K. Singh's poetry volume *Sexless Solitude and Other Poems* Gwilym Williams says: "What's really behind R.K. Singh's unceasing output of verse is a question I have asked myself more than once. Why does he strive so long and hard? Is there here an eternal search for some universal truth? Or is it simply anger at the way the world, and India, is?"(*Sexless Solitude and Other Poems*, 'Some Opinions', p.83)

Now the questions that arise are: Does a poet carry something at the back of his mind while writing poetry? Does he deliberately strive so long and hard, while writing? Does he try to give vent to his hidden anger, hatred, etc., through his poetry? And surely the answer to any of these and similar questions won't be straight this or that.

As a matter of fact 'to think this way' is misreading a poet and his poetry. The fact is that broadly a poet, like all others, lives a two tier life, viz., private and personal, and social and scriptural. Now the common people simply live and keep living, but a poet being gifted with more lively sensibility, wider knowledge and esemplastic imagination, he sees and feels more and even reconstruct what he sees and feels. So when a creative artist writes, may be a novel, a drama or a poem, he creates a mini world with very many characters representing different facts of life. Therefore, it is not just to associate protagonist or characters of a poem with the poet. As a matter of fact a genuine creative artist transmutes his personal and private agonies into something impersonal and universal. When we go through the poetry of R.K. Singh, we see this very executed.

While going through the capsule poems, i.e., short poems with cognitive content in Sexless Solitude and Other Poems, it is noticed that he has tried to project two categories of people in two sets of poems, viz., (i) Sanjaya type people in set-I, i.e., those who remained detached and can see things as they are. Sanjaya is a well known character in *The Mahabharata*. He was blessed with special vision by Lord Krishna. As a result, he coud see what was what was on the Kurukshetra, the battle field, the place of the great Mahabharat war; (ii) Dhrutrashartra type people in the set-11, i.e., those who get attached to the things and fail to see their real nature. Consequently they suffer. Dhrutrashtra, in the epic, suffers and makes people also suffer simply because he fails to see truth as truth. Here the protagonists of two sets of poems can be looked upon as two different persons of the same person with twin facets.

Now first we take up those poems which have Sanjaya type characters: the first poem to be taken up in this context is "Awareness Matters". The poem runs as follows:

> Each death has a passage
> to surprise the dead
> awareness matters
>
> no solace the cow's tail
> in the river's midst
>
> heaven, far, too far (p.10)

Here the pointed eye of the protagonist in the poem is quite evident. He sees two types of persons, viz., one dying and the other dead who receives the news of the former's death. That is, a man dies. The news of this man's death fills another man, living dead, with surprise. The point is that here everybody is dead in the sense that every moment he is in the fear of death. Therefore, Shakespeare has already said, "Cowards die many a time before their death..." (*Julius Caesar*). The very idea of death fills dread and depression in every body. He is surprised and shocked by the deaths like 'untimely death', 'unnatural death', 'unkind death' and so on. But then the protagonist can see the cause of this dread and surprised to be 'the ignorance' or 'the absence of knowledge' about death. The cycle of death is eternal as it is said in *The Bhagwat Geeta* "*Jatasya hidhruvo mritu, druvam janma mrityascha*", i.e., if birth is there, then death definitely follows it. So according to him instead of surprise and fear one should develop 'awareness', 'awakening' regarding the incident of death. He also refers to the orthodox religious faith according to which after death one goes go to hell, then there he comes across a river which he has to cross to go to heaven. And for crossing this river cow's tail can help that person. But then protagonist pooh-poohs this idea. He is sure about the idea of heaven and hence 'far', 'too far' and that 'awakening' alone matters.

In another poem '*Death*' the protagonist traces out another tendency rampant among people in our country or rather everywhere, viz., 'Without living/life lost in existing'. That is, people do not know 'how to live life'. They simply continue existing by 'evading the fact/ of living in fear/and manipulations'(p.35). Their all endeavours 'for thoughtless peace' are directed 'to fight off death'. Again instead of 'living life' properly, they waste their time and energy in rationalising their follies and failures and resting faith in're information or resurrection' of some noble soul to right the wrongs. On the contrary the truth is that man is the architect of his faith which is rooted in 'living life' properly with well planned things and rightly directed actions. The main idea of the poem 'Without living life' can be explained thus: when our country got freedom, its population was roughly thirty six crores. Then in succeeding years, many efforts were made in promoting hospitals and doctors to fight off death, but nothing was done to check the growth of the population. Then the growth of the population was allowed, but the relevant resources and moral values were not taken care of. And now people are resting their hope in the faith of 're-incarnation or resurrection' of someone to face and find out solution for the present explosive situation pertaining to peace and population.

The way T. S. Eliot has projected modern man's life in a long poem like '*The Waste Land*', the protagonist of 'Is This All?' has done that here is a short space of two triplets. In the first triplet he unveils the lifestyle of modern man which is characterised by three acts, viz., (i) propitiating gods through the cocktail prayers; (ii) living animal life, i.e., confined to food, sleep, fear and sex; (iii) boasting and advertising the worldly achievements. And hence he raises the question whether this tier life is all. Then he very vividly highlights the mind of modern man in the second triplet. That is, his mind is dominated by negative and narrow thinking, 'fungus of illusions' and 'toad-stools of damned tracts'. The answer to the yes/no question – 'Is this all?' seems to be that such a negative and narrow thought-based life is not worth. Perhaps he wants to point Vivekanand's message that each soul is potentially divine and the goal of life should be to manifest that divine as against simply 'live animal existence'.

The protagonist in the poem 'Journey' is equally very minute and mature observer of the usual phenomenon of 'journey' very often undertaken by the people. He is of the view that a meaningful journey should have proper direction, definite destination and duly discerned destiny. But then the fact is that most of the people do not bother about any of these corporate considerations. And that whosoever sets out on journey, they have either flickers or flashed, i.e., ever changing scales of brightness on their faces. And the protagonist finally states that he does not give any credit to such shifting shades of joys. To him the joy that oozes from proper understanding of the goal is steady and non-shifting. He also observes the fact that the journeying people inside the train and distantly drifting hills, houses, trees, etc., outside 'bear the same indifference'. That is, he sees no life, no sense of sharing, relating or love among the people inside and natural phenomenon outside the train.

Then, a very common but crucial observation is noticed in the poem 'Arriving Early'. The scene is of 'a waiting hall'(p.29), may be at the Railway Station or Cinema Theatre. It is full of men and women. The protagonist here observes that men are happily engrossed in chatting and commenting on the topics ranging from love affairs to '*Shariat*' (Marriage contract) without any fear or care, while women and particularly wives find themselves uneasy and chained as their range in all respect is bound and binding. And hence a man's wife 'murmurs about arriving early', while the hubby of that wife 'looks for some poetically active faces' in the waiting hall. This, in a very poignant way, points to the position of women in our society. All taboos and defined tracks are for women and none for men. This inequality and partiality have vitiated men-women relationships and created distances and distaste in social life.

The protagonist's subtle eye also notices the newly growing tendency of arrogance and shamelessness of the new generation in the 'Barbed Wire Fence'. Here he has tried to show how the garage guards make the water in the open and even show 'their dick'(p.2) to the maid in the adjoining house. Similarly, boys and girls 'make love in the bush' unmindful of the children's park, on one side, and the residential house, on the other. The protagonist is concerned about this fast growing phenomenon of young boys and girls chatting for hours together and even at times resorting to the forbidden acts least bothering about the time, the place and the public opinion.

The protagonist who is so perceptive like Sanjaya about the word around is blind Dhrutrshtra with regard to his personal inner world. For instance, just see his pain and suffering in the poem 'Overload'. Here we see that he does not get a normal sleep. So he drinks to have sleep. In that drugged state 'the electrical circuit in the brain' (p.2) goes awry and he starts muttering unwanted things in unparliamentarily language unmindful of the concerned victims. His mind is so much overloaded with deep discontent that its unloading alone seems the way out. He finds himself helpless regarding this process of loading-unloading that has sent in and continued unchecked. Now the point is that the protagonist considers this problem to be chronic and incurable, but the fact is quite the opposite. There are ways out, one only needs the eye and the will which he does not have. For instance, here is a way suggested by Maharshi Vashistha to calm down the mind: "*Manah Prashamanopayah Yogah*", i.e., the yogic practices calm down the mind.

The protagonist's pitiable condition is seen in the poem 'Again And Again'. He cannot relax, meditate or even dream on his so called sacred bed. Further, now he fails to have the unusual 'naked company'(p.7)of his beloved 'with tingling laugh' and 'slurred with passion'. Above all he fails to have successful love making. Now here we easily see his ignorance about the basic facts, e.g., one cannot have the same experience again and again and infinitum; change is the law of nature, and that one can have meditation, relaxation, happy company of any one and successful sex, only if 'mind is in proper order. Milton has rightly said "The mind is its own place and in itself can make/ A heaven of hell and A hell of heaven" (*Paradise Lost*, 254-55). So what is needed is to explore the right way to set the mind right.

We see the protagonist in a slough of despair in the poem 'The Dead Too Are Restless'. The protagonist is of the opinion that his onetime 'misplaced dreams'(p.12) has now 'turned nightmares' causing havoc on him. Those 'nightmares' have become highly chronic and gone beyond cure. To him even the path of meditation, gods, yoga or any other 'psychic mumbo-jumbo' does not seem to be of any help. They are like 'beats', the outcome of years' nourishment, and can now die only with his own death. But then he does not see peace and panacea even in death as 'the dead too are restless'. This fact has to be understood in two ways: (i) there are dead bodies which do not burn easily on the funeral pyre, in the sense that either their tongues came out or certain organs fall apart, etc., while getting burnt. And this fact can be seen as their restlessness; (ii) there are people who leave their houses and retire into the forest as Sanyasis. Now such people are as good as dead for the society. And the fact remains that even these so called Sanyasis no longer remain at ease within and without. But again the truth is that the protagonist is wrong. He does not have the 'Vision Proper'. The channels like meditation, prayers, yogic practices, etc., are competent enough to restore any chaotic person to his sole self, to his blissful self provided he practices them under proper care and training.

Intense miserable condition of the protagonist is evident in 'I Want to Sleep'. Now the sleep is the nature's gift to the human as well as non-human creatures. The sleep comes to anyone in the same way as light enters the house the moment the windows and doors are opened. But here we see the protagonist complaining for not getting sleep. His argument for not getting the sleep is 'the sick and the sickening'(p.6) people around him from whom he has carried 'germs and allergens' which keep him 'tossing and turning' the whole night. He also believes that right from the time of his birth he has 'never slept well'. He now wishes to sleep without the help of 'pills, drinks, magazines or sex'. And the type of sleep, that he wishes to have, should be 'thoughtless prayerless in peace'. This whole account simply shows the protagonist's blindness to the natural phenomenon of sleep. The sleep snatching factors highlighted by him are groundless. I have seen people sleeping in the hospitals beside the serious patients and even beside the dead. When the body and mind are free from all sorts of traffic jams, then the sleep comes to the person the same way as the beloved goes to the lover of her choice. Huxley has rightly said "rolling in the mud is not the way of getting clean". Instead of lamenting over the loss of the sleep, one should explore and expel the sleep breaking basic factors.

The protagonist is seen in the inferno in the poem 'Passion'. He suffers from worldly worries and anxieties, on the one hand, and from the strong sexual urges, on the other. Then the growing age comes in the way of the sexual gratification. So he turns to the drugs which 'hardly help reach climax anymore' and his quest for 'ecstasy' remains 'a far cry'. During the day he keeps working the whole day without any rest and respite as he says:

I smell hell all day
suffer shrinking passions
in the hollow of my mind (p.74)

Here again we see his blindness to the fact that senses can never be gratified. Maharshi Vedvyas has very firmly put it as "*na jatu Kaam Kaamanam upbhoge na samyate*" that is, the sensual desires can never be satisfied. Even Bhagvan Buddha has said "*trushna doospur hai*" i.e., desires can never be gratified.

The short sightedness or even the blindness of the protagonist is quite visible in the poem 'Conclusion'. Here he wishes to 'clean the cobwebs of legends'(p.22) because they 'veil the vision' and offer moral lessons for the future generation 'with doubtful glories' and they, instead of pushing people forward, make them 'move backward'. Now the fact is that everything of the past or present cannot be held out for 'forward' or 'backward' movement. The stream of life goes on flowing with its own built-in mechanism. Further he sees the whole country and particularly the mega cities like Delhi and Bombay in the jaws of 'empty slogans', cheating and lust. Particularly he is more concerned there about the ceremony of 'midnight lust' concluding like 'a tragic poem'. In brief, the hero of the poem feels hurt to see the present tragic state of things. He wishes to do something, but being weak and confused, he simply gets excited and poetic like Bahadur Shah Jaffar, the last emperor of our country.

The protagonist is seen devoid of any hope of salvation in 'Nirvana-I'. The word 'nirvana' is made of two units: nir-vana' of which 'nir' means without, and 'vana' means burning, i.e. without burning or suffering. Unfortunately he has no chances of 'nirvana' in the present setup of life. Generally 'lightning' and 'rain' are life givers but to him 'lightning' 'frightens'(p.77) and raises no fire, and 'rain' does not quench 'the earth'. He sees no creativity in his daily work and no joy in 'a kiss' of a parting partner. Finally, at night he is 'sulking with a glass' in the dark and the idea of 'nirvana' seems 'stupid' to him. Now this can be called a defective, flawed or mono-directional thinking of the person. There is solution, salvation, nirvana; the only needed requirement is the proper training and growth of the mind.

Thus, here over a dozen poems have been discussed concerning two opposite aspects of human mind. The attempt is here made to show as to how the poet has very pointedly projected two visions, viz., that of Sanjay and Dhrutrashtra through very short but well knit poems. Very novel and creative use of language which is the poet's forte has not been ever touched upon. The present article helps us mark the eagle eye that the poet has regarding sweet-sour aspects of human behaviour, human life as a whole. Before closing this talk, a humble suggestion is that the poet should show a ray of light, a way out, even while projecting the darker or negative aspects of life through the protagonist of his capsule poems. For instance, instead of saying 'I smell hell all day', cannot the protagonist say, 'Hell I smell' though heaven is not far to seek?

WORK CITED

1. Singh, R. K. *Sexless Solitude and Other Poems*, Bareilly: Prakash Book Depot, 2009.

8

"Living in uncertainties/ it's life in death": Death Motif in R.K. Singh's Poetry

— *Rajni Singh*

Death is built into the very structure of existence and is particularly and peculiarly ones own. It signifies itself and treats itself through its own happening and realization. This enigmatic nature of death has generated a good amount of philosophical and literary discourse. Philosophers and poets, since ages, have found it as a latent truth and have assiduously investigated it. In literature Death has been a thematic field extensively explored and more than preferred. Some authors give personal accounts of their impending death on their sense of bereavement; some use literature to structure and order our thoughts about death; and some treat death as a literary device, using it, for example, as a symbolic representation of the decay of society.

R. K. Singh's taste for Death is the outcome of the poet's realization of 'Being'. He is no graveyard poet to reflect on the dead or to lament on the lack of *an Other (*In Heidegger's perception presence is an act of 'co-being' and the lack of an Other is something caused by that Other's death, or when one is trapped in a state of solitude). There is neither any resonance of personal loss within the context of family and friends nor a direct reference to death through images of tomb, graveyard and epithet. Despite the fact, Singh's poetry is endowed with the motif of death which stems from the awareness of 'self', of 'Being' and of 'Being- there' i.e. *Dasein.* Singh's *Sexless Solitude and Other Poems* showcases the existential angst of the persona, who poem after poem puts on the mask of a solitary figure, agonized and restless, voyaging through trails of chaos and trying to seek solace amidst it. Interestingly, everywhere the persona is aware of his 'Being', of ' Being –there', *Dasein* that necessitates the elaboration of the idea of mortality from the point of view of the prominent 19th century philosophers who made a detailed study on the concept of mortality and linked it with the idea of Being . Martin Heidegger, Jean- Paul Sartre, Albert Camus and other existentialists stressed that 'Being' is the characteristic aspect of human being (in Heidegger). The individual is aware of its existence and that this existence is its own. In Heideggerian sense "*Dasein* always understands itself in terms of its existence- in terms of a possibility of itself; to be itself or not itself." (*Being and Time*., p.13) This 'Being- there' is more than a mere spatial relation. It is, in fact, encountering, having being absorbed- in- the- world, and it is this state that stirs in one the awareness of his temporality and makes him anxious and concerned about whether this life has any significance. This search for meaning in life is due to the knowledge of one's life being abbreviated due to Death. It is from this existential view point that I propose to analyze the motif of death in Singh's *Sexless Solitude and Other Poems*.

R. K. Singh's interest in the theme of 'being' is an indication of his consciousness of one's restricted time on the earth which, though indirectly, spills out in most of the poems of this volume. Possibly, the speakers of the poems seem to have been born out of the poet's self- exposition to the perilous superficiality of social equilibrium and mimicry. On the surface level the speakers might appear as multiple, however, these multiple souls sing in one strain that echoes the crisis of 'being'. Thus, there emanates one single self caught in the consciousness of his existence, and tide like rises and subsumes within his monotonous routine:

> Each day ends in fear
> of one or the other kind:
> living in uncertainties
> it's life in death (p.71)

Heidegger's contention is that the true being of the individual is hidden in everyday experience- though revealed by clues. Likewise, in the above lines the agitated soul in a confessional mode muses over the uncertainties that he lives in and also recounts his unknown fears. He, like Prufrock, feels crippled, cabined and confined in the inferno of his monotonous existence. He experiences death every day; rather his very existence is death- like. Prufrock, too, lived in self-doubts and was inflicted with indecisiveness but he did not dare to examine the crisis of his living nor had the courage to resolve the complexities of this life. The helplessness of our persona is no less than that of Prufrock but unlike him, he possesses the courage to comment on his situation. He might be 'pinned' by his own fears and anxieties but doesn't 'wriggle on the wall' and in a way succeeds in escaping death. His self- cognition and the capacity to endure the crisis assert his existence. However, his admittance of his condition 'it's life in death' brings forth the horror of his experiences, 'death-in-life', a cursed living. Thus the persona experiences his death in his Being.

The knowledge that death looms over life and can occur at any moment gives significance to the present. One realizes that one is superficial, is wasting, is dissipating life. Death produces anxiety and anxiety exposes superficiality of everyday life. A similar kind of situation is experienced by the speaker of 'Leeches':

At the end of the day
when I look back and see
my knowledge and insight
rusting with ageing colleagues
I pity my age and wish
to give up; I can't change
the means and the ends frustrate
the will to work anymore.... (p.69)

The speaker muses and broods over his past, present and future. He has the capacity to comment on his everyday lived experiences and to expose the authentic which lives hidden in experience. He is aware of his being trapped in Time and his failure to foresee the validity of his existence. He finds nothing for him, except stupefaction, confusion, horror and death. The wish to 'give up', to quit, is an indication of his weariness, discontentment and restlessness. The place where he had been for years has offered him no solace. The languishing soul finds itself damned forever in such a place. He possesses no courage to 'change' and thus desires to surrender, to escape from the illusions of the world. There is a profound awareness of his inability, rather his failure of handling things or rectifying the situations. The realization of his belittled existence breeds in despondency in his attitude towards life and perhaps the escape from reality, the desire to release himself in inaction:

I want to rest now burying

ambitions and achievements
that ache the soul.... (p.69)

The fleeing away from the world of action to inaction is totally owing to his disenchantment with the present, his acute loneliness and feeling of being alienated from his co-beings. This state of living, the termination of the self from the world, is in itself an assertion of one's 'death', even if this death may not occur at the physical level. Further, another interesting fact comes to the fore when one ponders over the declaration of the persona in the first line of the concluding stanza: "I want to rest now burying/ ambitions and achievements." "Burying" is a metaphor for death and the choice made by the self 'to rest' carries undertones of suicide. The individual knowing the inevitability of death experiences anxiety. This anxiety is the "acceptance of the potential non-being of ones Being (*Being and Time*, p.25). Any attempt to assuage this anxiety is but an attempt to alienate oneself from life. Thus Heidegger says that anxiety reveals to *Dasein* the possibility of fulfilling itself in a "freedom towards death". This acceptance makes temporality a concrete fact. Being towards death is the absolute condition of human freedom. Death "is the possibility of the impossibility of any existence at all." (*Being and Time*, p.307).

In, yet, another poem we encounter a prototype of the two speakers discussed above, who confesses at the very outset " I can't hide fears" and further admits "...the terrors of death are real."

Again, in the poem "Stripped and Naked" we come across an introspecting soul "crushed between the heart and head" and confesses his failure of getting along with his actions. Standing at the cross roads 'stripped and naked' he experiences the nothingness of his existence:

now stripped and alone
with hands over my chest
I stand in the street (p.39)

The act of probing into the 'I' and exploring the 'self' breed in the realization of one's state. According to Heidegger, the self, truth and freedom should not be approached by abstract concepts. The true starting point is everyday existence, Being-in-the-world. Man finds himself thrown into existence and it is there that the quest must begin. ("At any street corner the feeling of absurdity can strike any man in the face"- Albert Camus). The rendezvous of the 'I' with the 'self', the fear of being exposed to, results in shame ('hands over my chest'). This is the purgatory state which is followed by void, vastness, immensity and the ultimate realization of life's journey: thus the ongoing quest for the very nature of existence finds value and meaning in its ultimate abode:

> await the coffin
> to reconcile the truths
> I could not conceive (p.39)

The poem, 'Death' objectively comments on the validity of existence and retrospects those claims that offer meaning in existence and thus exposes the hidden fears of man related to death. Man is always conscious of his existence which is due to his anticipation of death. Till he is alive he is aware of his end and constantly engages himself in evading the fact. The dismissal or the non- acceptability of death is just a means to rationalize one's existence, i.e., one's temporality which itself is metaphorically transient in nature:

> Without living
> life lost in existing
>
> no use rationalizing
> re-incarnation
> or resurrection
> is an escape
>
> evading the fact
> of living in fear
> and manipulations
>
> we close all doors
> for thoughtless peace
> to fight off death (p. 35)

The speaker of the poem " Don't Condemn Me" suffers from the anxiety of his Being and the loss/ death of his potency: "I am too much with me and worry/ about her dying libido and my / own shrinking sex amidst salsa chill…/ ringing emptiness day and night shake / the age- wrapped youth…."(p. 1) He laments the loss of passion in his life and is a fit symbol of inner decay. The 'ringing emptiness' symbolizes the persona's lost sexual vitality and his brooding on this loss. "Love and sex are the only aspects of life which make life worthwhile to live." (Emmanuel Levinas: Beyond Levinas)

Thus the persona's declaration of the death of sex is symbolic of his own death. The awareness of his debilitating sexual powers shows his sense of helplessness which is reaffirmed in the title of the poem, 'Don't Condemn Me' that carries an overly self- defensive tone.

The same kind of decay is experienced by the speaker of the poem 'Winter'. He experiences 'the dark', i.e., loss/ the death of activity in bed:

The day is shorter
the night longer
and yet sleepless

suffer the dark
in the air in bed (p.5)

The way the speaker measures his day and night showcases his obsession with his existence.

A similar sort of restlessness is witnessed in the poem "I want to Sleep". Here the persona, too, measures his life: "from 10 p.m. to 4 a.m." and "perhaps from the day one". The obsession with time reveals one's anxiety and makes one confront the Nothingness, existing in each and every moment of one's life. Heidegger claims that the individual knows time because the individual knows it is going to die. The past, the present, and the future penetrate one's existence and one's existence, through and through, is temporal. "Living among the sick" the persona also feels sick of his "tossing and turning" and fears his meaningless, valueless existence and finally expresses his desire for a sound "...sleep without pills/ drinks 'zines or sex/ thoughtless prayer less in peace."(p.19)

The hopelessness of the persona's situation is well expressed in 'Psalm':

Where shall I find my rest?
at the doors of Sheol?
in dust? or in the light
of living? standing still

among the ungodly? (p. 21)

This awareness of one's absurdity of life and of mortality may serve as an awakening experience, a profoundly useful catalyst for major life changes:

...bless the spirit in
time and me that I feel

your healing touch in thought

and bear without regret
the burdens of the world
loss of love, or even hope
to live like a lotus leaf (p.21)

Despite being trapped in spiders' network gleaming with 'corpses' and 'funeral' or living amidst all complexities, loss and decay, the 'self' can see the eyes:

Shrieking in the sea
my knotted self
the lines on the palms

spiders' network
gleaming with corpses
that have no face

yet their funeral
mirrors the eyes
waving with dying light. (p. 36)

'Eyes' stand for hope. In spite of all gloominess and redundancy there lies a hope, the individual's subjectivist urge to own life exclusively through self- cognition, self- appraisal, through introspection. The realization that life may end at any moment frees the individual to interpret personal experiences and act on them as he/she sees fit and this is why the persona of 'I'M Different' asserts:

I'm different; I live in my poems

I enjoy the self,...

I live in me and am happy with
my little images that lift up
the sight and soul and please for a while. (p. 53)

These 'little images' could be the 'body' even, for it is the essence of one's existence. Therefore in one of the poems the speaker avers "I love Him through the bodies He made." (p. 1)

Thus the images of emptiness and death in life pervade *Sexless Solitude and Other Poems*. The several speakers of this volume appear identical and emerge as a single lonely figure, 'a knotted self' trapped in the 'spiders' network' that gleams with corpses that are faceless. He moves from the void of thought to the fear of the void of action- the need to fill life with something. In fact, the poet makes the persona his mouthpiece to assert his own self- definition and self- evolution that appears to be ongoing, endless till the finality.

In its last analysis, the poet's metaphor of death is search for life, meaning in existence. It is not a negative presence but a positive response to what is negative in general and in his life, in particular. If one tries to look at in a 'usual' way then it is likely to create confusion rather than clarify something substantial. To my mind there are more fearful aspects of life to encounter than the so called fearful aspects of death, normally seen in poets everywhere.

WORKS CITED

1. Singh, R. K. *Sexless Solitude and Other Poems*, Bareilly: Prakash Book Depot, 2009.
2. Philipse, Herman. *Heidegger's Philosophy of Being: A Critical Interpretation*, Delhi: Motilal Banarsidas, 1999.
3. Grimes, John. *Sankara and Heidegger: Being, Truth, Freedom,* Varanasi: Indica Books, 2007.
4. Clive, Geoffrey. *The Philosophy of Nietzsche*, USA: Meridian, 1996.
5. Barnes, Hazel E. *Jean-Paul Sartre Being and Nothingness*, New York: Washington Square Press, 1984.
6. Heidegger, Martin. *Being and Time,* trans. John Macquarrie and Edward Robinson. New York : Harper and Collins, 1962.

9

Contemporary Social Issues/Anxieties in the Poetry of R. K. Singh

— *P. C. K Prem*

In order to understand the poetry of R. K. Singh, one has to comprehend that nature and woman occupy a pivotal position in his philosophic wanderings. If Singh gives an uninhibited expression to thoughts about love, woman, beauty and nature, or talks about the exploitation and poverty, he in reality also shows genuine concern about the modern social predicaments of life. He exposes man to prevalent corruption, hypocrisy and questions of morality without malice or prejudice.

Like any other creative man R. K. Singh is deeply concerned about man's existence and identity: the existential crisis in a multilingual, multicultural, multi-religious, and plural society vis-à-vis the ethos of Indian society and inheritance. Here, the poet's thoughts and reiteration of emotions and ideas reinforce his argument in varying contexts, creating a pervasive interest which one would like to redefine and interpret in the light of contemporary social scenario. He discovers new meanings via imageries of woman and nature; he explores life and its purpose, and relationship between the body and the soul through unmitigated passions; from silence to noise unheard, Singh searches for identity. In this context, he does not forget the sufferings of man in the present socio-political frame that is callous and unreasonable at times where a poor man suffers unmitigated hardships. Most of such poems, relate to the influences politics and present day's netas and babus have on the lives of the poor, the underprivileged and the subjugated.

As we read Singh's poems from *My Silence* (1985) to *The Face in All Seasons* (2002), we discover the poet's many dimensions: his social awareness in terms of contemporary life and values exposing man's innate instincts, pretense and nakedness; his understanding of myths, legends, history, politics, culture and religion; philosophy of humanity, and interpretation of art and tradition.

One of the disturbing trends in the contemporary world is its misuse of religions for petty gains. It is applicable to individuals' whims as well countries around the world with a shade different. For purely personal gains, a man can go to any length to fulfill his vicious desires and manipulate religious teachings the way these suit his reprehensible designs for self promotion. Religion is being adopted as a ruthless method to settle social issues to prove a point.

While painfully conscious of the contemporary violence, he is not very happy with men in power who behead women and children for personal gains to achieve power and this is done in the name of God. Thought it is not a new idea yet the poet relates it to the mindset of modern men who want to dominate the world using religion as a conduit. This takes the poet to the nerve-racking violence that plays havoc in Algeria, Zaire and such other countries where religious men want to rule. In another context, he also points out the amount of horrifying destruction on earth the Taliban brought to their country. Singh is terse and reproachful when he observes:

> ...who must spread
> their values and shun truce for power
> in the name of God turn the clock backward
> imposing ordeals of all sorts
> next door political fanatics
> in the name of social justice
> close eyes to sadhus killing housewives
> teachers raping girls in classroom
> and hoodlums burning women in slums
>
> (*The Face in All Seasons*, Poem 8)

Politics is corrupting social and economic life while the poor man perspires to make others' lives happy and yet there appears little hope of redemption. He observes:

> Pseudos, shams, crooks and
> politicians pervert:
> empowered by their
> own corruption swing
> ... ...

their head moves ahead
unreal their rhetoric
pull up if you can (*Above the Earth's Green*, Poem 47)

In a few sharp words, the poet delineates the awful modern attitude of powerful men. He surveys the entire scene around the world and speaks eloquently of the deplorable plight of helpless men and women. Obviously, it is not religious fervour or love of ethics enshrined in all the religions of the world which worry men in authority; it is in truth a consistent attempt to pattern religious teachings to benefit hunger for more and the spirit of aggrandizement of a few ambitious men. In the process, the real growth suffers.

Strange logic works in the minds of politicians who are more fanatics than religious with a personal agenda where administering of social justice is just a slogan and thus reducing the noble thought of bringing equality in social, economic and political areas to a bitter farce. Society is ailing; he appears to tell fervidly when he reminds us of teachers who rape girls in the classroom and rogues burning women. Unfortunately, a sinister thinking is being translated into violent realities of life when men forget to behave, and demonstrate beastly prowess towards women. This anxiety is quite recent and probably it is an offshoot of virus of materialism and misplaced concept about free life and living. In another short verse 7, the poet is pained to recall the terrible advent of 'sand storm' where Taj is just a symbol of working bleeding hands when miseries of poor men are hidden in the dome of betrayal whether old or new:

Looking for Taj in grains
through sand-storm find history
trapped between the toes

bleeding fingers draw
new domes of betrayal in
windy matrices (*The Face in All Seasons*, Poem 7)

The world is not very convenient now and man is to be blamed for the contamination and pollution that is spreading around without any visible solution. Socially it can be easily termed as a step towards collective suicide and this shocking awareness reveals poet's painful anxiety. One is coarsely amazed at the revelation of naked realities.

The poet is dangerously cute and correct when he talks of Banaras and Lucknow. These two cities become symbols of ills, sins and foul play. Words like law and liberty lose meaning:

> They repeat blunders
> out of ignorance
> or kindness

It is a society where bureaucrats:

> ...politicians and journalists
> who appear
> in mating season
>
> like dogs in
> October and November
> and perpetuate the blur
>
> ...of decaying ancestors (*My Silence*, Poem 38)

Look at the following lines:

> The morning in Banaras
> along the Ganges
> is no longer fresh:
>
> smell of urine
> dried and fresh excrement
> merge with smoke, sweat and
> stench of the rotting river
> ... .
> and the river awaits new birth
> dream brokers promise
> in convulsion of lust (*The Face in All Seasons*, Poem 14)

The awful pollution of Ganges –a symbolic warning- pursues man everywhere and if he fails to make amends soon, a total annihilation will engulf this earth. The thought gets fortified as he observes:

> The bamboo garden
> we picnicked and made love in
> is now a concrete
> managing environment
> and pollution control (*The Face in All Seasons*, Poem 21)

An oblique hint at the spread of Hinduism does not hearten or enthuse but depressing scenario emerges as neta-log – the politicians in the modern age, indeed an universal worry - use even religion to further self-seeking motives. On the other hand, the conduct of priests does not provide hope and here secular thoughts invariably get the beating:

> Preaching Hinduism
> they've lost God for politics:
> pull down churches
> shed crocodile tears
> killing the priest they kill truth:
> pseudo seculars (*The Face in All Seasons*, Poem 18)

In a world of market-economy, shares do erode to a large extent the credibility of honest business and this makes life difficult for a simple man of modest means:

> We must wait
> till the share scam
> is smoked out
> and resources
> restored. (*Some Recent Poems,* 'Share Scam')

Thus contemporary issues disturb and the poet finds that politics plays an extremely destructive role in life. He fails to understand 'why dogs defecate' around on the one hand and on the other 'mental miseries increase'. In a slightly changed scenario, the poet says:

> Politics is based
> neither on knowledge
> nor principles but scams
> irresponsible
> power for free money
> hawala, gawala and
> loots to strip democracy
> voters' faith for five years
> connive with criminals
> raring to patronize
> rival systems from within...
> (*Above the Earth's Green*, Poem 29)

Without directly putting in straight words, the poet has the inkling that bad politics leads to corruption and miscellaneous ailments in the society for which a vulnerable man has to pay dearly. Now politics is too much with the people and this not only brings condescension and miseries but violence and terrorism also. Says he:

> Each day ends in fear
> of one or the other kind:
> living in uncertainties
> it's life in death
>
> and here they are
> setting dreams
> and winning votes
>
> their 'proactive politics'
> adds to the list of
> dead and dying
>
> they may or may not sleep
> in high security houses
> but it will be too late
> by the next election

(*Sexless Solitude and Other Poems,* 'Terrorism')

In the above verses, Singh's scathing criticism of politics, principles, scams, patrons, system of government, God and god men, religions and corruption with horde of social evils attracts attention. It is realistic description of society and man's outlook on life devoid of scruples.

Everything is done in the name of a poor man without actually doing anything. A similar strain of present gruesome scene instills distrust when he says 'encroach on public land/without murmur politics/plays its own logic:/ who can protest when/wolves mate bitches to create/a democratic rate' (*Above the Earth's Green*, Poem 30)

> In the name of faith
> and god
> politics fuels bigotry
> strips the prophets
> corrupts clarity
>
> reasoning ceases
> when mind purveys prejudice:
> age shuts the door
>
> everybody paves

his own way to the grave
(*Above the Earth's Green*, Poem 27)

The poet is sad over the present state of affairs. The freedom has not brought hopes but only pessimism fills the lives of people who want a better life. The country is still feeling the heat of violence, insensitivity and corrupt practices and the so called democratic life is meaningless where faith of the people stands tainted. Democratic rules do not provide honest and fair government and an irritating debate continues over the rich and the poor, reaching nowhere.

...the new rulers are blind
to common man asking
a fair share and honest rule
everywhere obscenities stare
I worry my country is dying
with too little democracy
too much Hindu and Muslim
too much rich and poor
(*The Face in All Seasons*, Poem 25)

Immense and manifold scientific and technological progress and expansion in no way has helped man to remain happy in the contemporary world as too much materialistic outlook creates scarcities unbelievable. Still man is suffering acute lack of basic amenities of life including food; and the horrible thought of water shortage scares. In the name of free economy, man is stifled which makes contemporary life quite choking.

honest bread and peace
the hungry billions seek
no hi-tech slavery

the global cheats promote
liberal economy
stealthily purvey

rights and environment
with politics of control
doom the future (*The Face in All Seasons*, Poem 75)

It is a tragic irony that realities of life agitate and injure the soul of the poet when he finds all pervasive tensions, fanaticism, loss of ideals, political corruption, degeneration of values, evils of drugs, orgies, chaos, life in dark voids and doubts are suffocating life of man. Sufferings mount as he does not find an easy escape from these ailments eating into the vitals of society and man. He says:

> the anger over fanaticism and loss of ideals, politics and corruption
> the degeneration all-round and struggle for survival amidst lying and conniving
> and these burdens, death of desires, drugs, orgies, promiscuities
> ... ...
> I can't suffer the crises I haven't authored even in thought
> I can't endure aches of incompletion, dark void that sounds aloud
>
> (*Above the Earth's Green*, Poem 34)

Conscious of the modern sufferings, a bitter lamentation stays in the heart. In extreme worry, he talks of education, knowledge, repression and dependence. Failure is driving him to a new century without redemption. He takes up social issues confronting man but fails to find a definite solution in all enveloping pollution, squalor and degradation. He observes:

> Pseudos, shams, crooks and
> politicians pervert....

and thus man, alas poet, lives through pains and:

> alone I suffer sins
> I didn't commit
> now unembraced she turns
> her back pressing
> pillow between the thighs
> curls no apology
>
> (*Above the Earth's Green*, Poem 49)

A definite and weird current continues to flow in all the untitled poems but these demonstrate tangible unity in various fragments and one gets a feeling that it is one long poem. Singh is unsympathetic and partially negative towards life but down deep an impression sustains that he is realistic in defining purpose. Loss of human values and morality disturb the poet. He is aware of the socio-political situation and fully knows the rotten conditions to which society is moving ahead, suffocating man. The sufferings on the surface seem multidimensional.

Modern life persistently asphyxiates man but he is wide awake. The modern metros don't provide solace and contentment but kill man with deafening noise and contamination. Many insidious and unholy deeds keep man occupied and he cares little for the excellent and pleasant things of life. The poet does not want to complicate life which is already unwieldy and intricate. It is a tragedy of times that in materialistic surfeit man is unhappy and in the intensity of activity he is thoughtlessly in need of releasing tensions and bodily exhaustion. Life of speed and rashness also spells dangers to physical pleasures:

> Trucks on G.T. Road:
> invasion of the body
> for a quick release

A terrible thought shatters all goodness that man nurses:

> He survives in bones
> brittle like hers in forties
> it's winter again (*Above the Earth's Green*, Poems 98, 102)

Singh is seriously worried about the sufferings of a common man. There is wide spread corruption and so are the vociferous words against the corrupt. Its eradication not only puzzles the leaders pledging to eliminate it from private and public life but it also has assumed a colossal destructive postures to pollute public life though out the world. Even world bodies like the UN fail to make any difference. The poet is rather ironical when he observes:

> He is amazed to see
> so much corruption
> in the system
> of world peace:
>
> his colleagues envious
> of his foreign jaunt
> with the UN
> and earnings
> ... ...
> while I worry about
> freedom in Congo
> untamed humans
> safe sojourn
> (*Sexless Solitude and Other Poems,* 'Peace Mission')

Unfortunately, for men who matter, individual material prosperity is important. It is a depressing commentary on people in authority from whom the general masses expect relief so that public money is not eaten up by the men who govern. Corruption is a wide spread disease and the schemes meant to help poor men in the rural and urban areas are also jeopardized for want of honest and upright people engaged in the implementation of such projects. Nothing tangible appears to have been done if one looks around and finds that little has been achieved in the areas of manual scavenging, latrines, toilets and such like little things that make poor men a little comfortable. The poet observes:

Human Rights activists
discuss eradication
of manual scavenging
and construction of
wet latrines in villages
in the conference room
complain about poor flushing
in NHRC toilet
and routinely censure
the junior staff
before seeking provisions
for rehabilitating
liberated scavengers

(*Sexless Solitude and Other Poems*, 'Human Rights')

Not for a moment, poet is at peace when he observes around that those who must devote attention to better the pitiable conditions of poor people, are not sincere. Even faith is in danger:

I don't endorse their pact
to squeeze adulation and
control faith of the masses
to shed blood and spread darkness:
... ...
the temple doesn't attract me
I want to forget the myth

after the fascist owned him
Ram had ceased to be my god

(*Sexless Solitude and Other Poems*, 'Hey Ram')

Thus personal convenience takes precedence over the general cause and this reflects on the wisdom of those who are supposed to care for the downtrodden.

Singh's poetry candidly depicts the crude realities of life, contemporary anguish, social iniquity, inequality and injustice that man is trapped in. disturb him. As a teacher of linguistics, one finds terrific economy in the use of words. There is a curious use of words with various shades of meanings and while reading poems one has to cautiously take care of each word used with multiple layers and meanings. Amidst enormous human sufferings, he is truthful and candid in expressing distress and agony he undergoes in the contemporary world and that is precisely his poetic strength.

WORKS CITED

1. Singh, R. K. *My Silence*, Madras: Poets Press India, 1985.
2. __________. *Memories Unmemoried*, Berhampur: Poetry Time Publications, 1988.
3. ______________. *Flight of Phoenix*, Berhampur: Poetry Time Publications, 1990.
4. __________. *Music Must Sound*, Dhanbad: Author, 1990.
5. __________. *I Do Not Question* (Two Poets), New Delhi: Bahri Publications, 1994.
6. ______________. *Above the Earth's Green*, Calcutta: Writers Workshop, 1997.
7. ______________.*Every Stone Drop Pebble*, New Delhi: Bahri Publications, 1999.
8. _________.*Cover to Cover, A Collection of Poems* (jointly with Ujjal Singh Bahri). New Delhi: Bahri Publication, 2002.
9. ___________.*Pacem in Terris* (a trilogy collection with Myriam Pierri and Giovanni Campisi, 2003.
10. ___________.*The River Returns*, Bareilly: Prakash Book Depot, 2006.
11. _________.*Sexless Solitude and Other Poems*, Bareilly: Prakash Book Depot, 2009.

10

Profession and Performance: R. K. Singh's *Sexless Solitude and Other Poems* - A Study

— *V. V. B. Rama Rao*

With steel flow
the rolling water
pierces the rocks
and shapes them into song
the sun and the moon fail
to march (sic) its sharpness
the wailing of the rocks
turns into song

R.K.Singh, with considerable reputation even abroad, is well-known to readers of poetry in India. His poetry volume, *Sexless Solitude and Other Poems* appeared in 2009. The present article intends to study some poems from this volume with a view to assessing them in the light of some statements the poet made in an interview with Arbind Kumar Choudhary on December 2006:

> I write to seek a release from myself as much as from others; to feel free by unburdening myself in verses; to experience an inner balance, feeling, probing, sensing, recalling, or whatever.
>
> A good poem generates some physical, emotional or psychosexual sensation,stimulates some sensuous, spiritual or exalted pleasure, or provokes some ideas.
>
> I have no taste for didacticism in poetry. I love brevity, rhythm, and

> "colouring of human passion"; personal, lyrical, honest and free expression, with seriousness in reflection and interpretation. Poetry lies in creating the image (like the painter who celebrates sensuality), and in capturing momentness of a moment, which stirs the mind.
>
> ...But here (in the body of the poet's total work till 2006) one may discover my formal taste, personal vision, and sexual orientation rooted in Purush-Prakriti union. It is significant for open eroticism, seriousness, candor, and exaltation of Rati.
>
> I believe in unity of mankind and equality of sexes, and am secular and non-moral in my attitude and values.

The title poem, usually, is the one the poet considers his best to illustrate his point of view, his world vision and his own individual stamp, his signature-tune, if you will. The endeavour is to tune in into the reader's mind to make sure that the complex web of feeling is put across.

The poems culled into this slender volume have something suggestive, something that has a quality of homogeneity with the poet's perception. A lot of deliberation must have gone into the choice and decision of the title. The title, in many cases, may have already been chosen before the poet picks up the individual poems to fit into the scheme in the imaginative artist's mind. Very easily this volume could have been titled God, Sex and the World too with equal gusto since these are the principal themes. The titles can be seen as falling into two clearly differentiated stances – call them postures, if you will. 'Nirvana -1', 'Nirvana -2', 'Shiva's Third Eye', 'Hey Ram', 'God, Awareness Matters', 'Eyeless Jagannath' have a thematic proximity while 'Stripped and Naked', 'Sodomy', 'Body Bliss', 'Barbed Wire Fence' have a basic unity of their own. 'I'm different' is a matter of the understanding by turning the searchlight inward. The whole thing is a Song of the River, ever flowing, ever serene and ever life-giving.

Sexless Solitude is a coinage to signify a state of mind when solitude takes the main stage with sex driven into a no-longer-significant-part to play. This, paradoxically, makes existence significant. There are moments when the reader feels that the poet in Singh is tossed on the tightrope of spirituality and the sexy but surely this volume bids goodbye to the tossing. The scabrous and the scatological, normally vulgar or loathsome cease to be so with a widening of the intellectual horizon. Sin becomes behovely, as that great Saint Juliana of Norwich convincingly declared: "Sin is behovely, all shall be well and all manner of things". There is no more tight-rope-walking, and hence the pronouncement in the title composition:

> I don't seek the stone bowl
> Buddha used while here: (p. 23)

The poet's vision has come to full maturation of the kind of ripening attained by mystics after a strenuous effort at understanding the ultimate reality. All the poems display this maturation as seen below in the sampler from the slim collection of poems included in this volume.

The poem 'Barbed Wire Fence' records the experience of an illumination at the end which comes like a revealing flash, not a blinding one:

> My window opens
> to the back of a garage
> where guards make water
>
> at times show their dick
> to the maid in my kitchen:
> they care for none
>
> how can I complain
> if boys and girls make love
> in the bush between
>
> the children's park and
> my backyard? They are distanced
> by a barbed wire fence (p. 2)

The scabrous and the scatological are part of the actuality around. The thinking person feels that the crudeness cannot be helped. The fence does exist and what happens on the far side needs to be included to make the vision complete. This is essential to stay sane and cultivate a state of equanimity – cultivating a saint's understanding and inclusive vision.

The poem 'Eyeless Jagannath' is a frank admission of man's helplessness to comprehend the mystical thrills and depths of existence. Headpiece filled with straw, standing on the precipice of physicality, man is Prometheus bound. The title could be construed differently, (I'm) Eyeless! Jagannath! Or, one may prosaically attribute 'eyelessness' to Him. The Supreme Lord of the Universe promenades in effulgence. The poet feels eyeless: this could be an explanation for the earthy actuality. There is a sense of bewilderment that, in spite of His Lordship, there should be so much gloom and emptiness both within and without. Singh is rightly attracted by breathtaking splendour of the promenade – the *rath yatra* – the Lord seated in a fabulous chariot drawn by innumerable devotees. Man's existence between physicality and the 'eylessness' are poignantly communicated. Like the pithy grand declarations in the Upanishads, the *mahavakyas*, Singh's admissions of frailty, bewilderment and cerebration. He impresses the reader with the genuineness of his feeling:

> I stand on the edge
> of earth's physicality
> waiting on the brink (p. 9)

On the brink of what, if it is not on the edge of sanity and saintly insight!

'Awareness Matters', again, is a realization: Birth, Copulation, and Death – this is the way the world goes, goes and goes on. A cow's tail does not help anyone cross *bhava sagara*. This point is driven home:

> Each death has a passage
> to surprise the dead
> awareness matters (p. 10)

The brevity and the pithiness of the expression and the insightfulness of the reflection are striking.. Salvation is matter of sharp awareness, which comes from living in the faith and conviction *aham brahmasmi*!

'Body: A Bliss' is a feeling of complacent physicality. Lorca rises up from the physical to the metaphysical in a sudden flash in the line quoted 'To see you naked is to recall the earth'. Body shines momentarily and passion does not last long. This is a truism no doubt but the understanding is valuable. It does us good to remember that 'parts arouse dead flesh'. Three things are signified in the brief flash: movement, journey and evolution. Man must play seasons first Spring:

...the thirst is ever new
and blissful too

to recreate
the body, a temple
and a prayer (p. 30)

The supreme realization is the function of the body. *shareeramaadyam khalu dharma sadhanam.* The body is the primary requisite for *dharmasadhanam*, achievement and fulfillment of *dharma* – in one word, prayer.

'God' is a composition very incisive – a realization by intuition. Sermon on the Mount is a creation of mind. 'The word is not God/ but the mind creates/ it after its own image'. One's attainment and accomplishment come only by growing outside the known, without thought, without drawing – just by intuition, illuminating intuition. Nirvana it is

when seeking nothing
experiencing nothing—
stillness become (s) divine (p. 33)

This nothingness is not a negative or uncomplimentary thing. Paradoxically, it is a positive concept, not substantially different from either *nirvana* or *mukti* - the metaphysical visualization of the ancient Aryan scheme of things. Singh is obviously concerned with the consummation devoutly to be wished – the ultimate of existence.

'Stripped and Naked' is in the mode of a confession. The head-heart dichotomy is part of the poet's metaphysical vision and this in this poem this gets a poignant portrayal. The speaker is 'crushed between the head and the heart'. He realizes that he cannot produce a mate for his creation's peace and bliss. 'She raises her eyebrows/ and isolates herself as if/ I authored all her grief'. He regrets the lot that has befallen him – all his own doing:

now stripped and alone
with hands over my chest
I stand in the street

await the coffin
to reconcile the truths
I could not conceive (p. 39)

'Sodomy', another electrifying title, deliberately thought up to shock prude minds, is at one level an acerbic criticism of mine mafias. 'Burning stones to ashes/ and feeling good politicians/ idolize criminals and cartoon'. The mafia usurped not merely the mounts of money but also the pinnacles of power as in a part of this country in the South. The speaker of the poem is befuddled:

...with chameleon hues

(they) ritually smuggle power
to perpetuate wanton rut
of intellectual sodomy
crying foul after checkmate (p. 45)

'I'm Different' opens a window on the psychological condition of the speaker of the poem which is in line with the Nirvana duo. 'I secrete (not ejaculate) poetry like semen/ in consummation leave smuts at times/ to reveal the horse they try to hide ... I'm different: I live in my poem/ dressing or undressing like sex act/ long or short, in bed or kitchen'(p.53). All poets are unique persons and this is Singh's assertion. 'I live in me and happy with/my little images that lift up/ the sight and soul and please (himself as well!) for a while'. The most significant fact is that the speaker explains here the origin of the springs of his creativity. We may consider his *apologia pro vita sua*, his prolegomena of poetic fancy. (Parentheses mine) The secret of the springs of his creativity are spelt out in the little gem of a poem 'River's Song'. The rolling river pierces the wailing rocks and sculpts them into song. The Sun and the Moon cannot match its sharpness.

'Hey Ram', the title is the dying utterance of the Mahatma, the great martyr. It is a condemnation of violence and Fascism. Singh believes in peace and staying human. Pacts to squeeze adulation are detestable for any thinking person. Faith is something not to be manipulated by the rich or those in power. There is a thinly veiled reference to Ayodhya carnage when the poet says: 'idols may draw crowds to kill/ and the spell may not last long'. Singh goes above the denominations of religions. He avers:

the temple doesn't attract me
I want to forget the myth

after the fascists owned him
Ram has ceased to be my god (p. 58)

'God, Sex and the World' deals with the prime preoccupations of almost great poets and so it is with Singh:

learning and unlearning
each moment synthesizing
god, sex and the world (p. 64)

Great truths are always simple clothed in a language which goes straight to the head like Newton's Laws of Motion or to the heart like Upanishad *mahavakyas*. Part of the prayer it is to have the *lingam* (Shiva's form) kissed or kiss it to feel. The body is to be thanked too to feel God. We are told assuring: *shareeramaadyam khalu dharma saadhanam.* God-consciousness is essential for those who are blessed with Faith. The body houses the divine spark and the theist seeks and finds relief first (from human misery) and salvation ultimately. The diurnal change is meeting and separating – day for meeting, day being consciousness and night for slumber in separation. There are spaces leavened by awareness. Unfortunately the lucid intervals are few and far between. Wisdom entails the synthesizing the existence of God, Sex and the World. It is an act of playing the trapeze.

False faith stems from ignorance and arrogance. Miscellaneous gods sin against God. They break the covenant in betraying creation. Shiva's third eye, opened, fire is burnt out by the resultant Fire. 'Agni defiled sexact/ outraged love in action/ sacrileged union'. The ignorant fear fire, question freedom and dictate codes of love. This makes the poet deliver the dictum: 'worship lingam/ forget Shiva'. The metaphor, the symbol is the thing: the name is just not all. In other words the wise one knows the relevance of symbol and its essence ignoring the mere stone.

'Nirvana – I' and 'Nirvana –II' can be considered companion pieces. Nirvana in Buddhist terminology refers to a state where individuality becomes extinct by being absorbed into the Supreme Spirit. Here Singh uses the term suggesting the lover and the ladylove coalescing into one another or the male losing himself in and into the female. In pedestrian expression it is physical union – copulation. Nature is benign in the sense that lightning and rain do not cause fire or submerging. The poet looks back at his own sense of frustration, and disappointment. Ritual kissing does not lead to creation: when bliss is missed talking about *nirvana* – extinction, losing one's self into the sex-partner, never happens: 'it's stupid to talk about nirvana'. Here, Nirvana is spoken of merely as the bliss of union. Nightfall, the beloved gone with a parting kiss, sulking, - Nirvana is unthinkable. The latter composition is an unavoidable continuation. Abandoning desire does not put an end to yearning – yearning for coalescing. Growing sense of disappointment (from past, passions and delusions) dims the light. Hope of consummation too rises with dawn. Once again the poem is about passion and at a sublimated level it is just a manifestation of the yearning of the bliss of nirvana, the bliss that passeth understanding.

Each of the professions cited above at the beginning of the study has been performed and the promise is solemnly fulfilled in the poems penned by this illustrious, unpretentious thinker. His exercises are attempts at some kind of purgation, securing release by unburdening himself. All these poems without exception stimulate us and provoke thought as to what existence is both in actuality and ideal in the poet's imaginative perception. As he has professed, Singh has not tried to moralize, preach or reform. Moralizing and lecturing are modes which are pitfalls that good poets carefully avoid. Didacticism unless very subtly veiled would degenerate into boredom. Singh has always sought to look deep within and intuit conditions and situations powerfully and convincingly. He tells the readers about himself: takes them into the recesses of his thought processes with conviction and genuine feeling. There is seriousness, authenticity and scope for interpretation. A good poem should lend itself to interpretation at various levels, revealing depths of understanding the human reality, the human condition. For example the symbol of Buddha's Bowl is very rich. The stone bowl has a significance that is very appropriate to the Wise One's throwing it away in a gesture of abandoning his last human possession. A lot remains to be written if we go by what the Internet provides on Buddha's Bowl. Every one of the poems I chose to be the base of my brief study illustrates the fulfillment of the essence in Singh's profession.

WORKS CITED

1. Singh, R. K., *Sexless Solitude and Other Poems*. Bareilly: Prakash Book Depot, 2009.
2. Sharma, I.K. ed. *New Indian English Poetry: An Alternative Voice*. Jaipur: Book Enclave, 2004.
3. "Prof. R.K. Singh Interviewed by A.K. Choudhary". http://www.lit.org/view.php?viewed=36990

11

Erotic Consciousness in R.K. Singh's Poetry: Depiction of Feminine Enamouredness

— *Jindagi Kumari*

Erotic consciousness means the awareness of experiences and ideas that are evocative of sexual desires; pleasures and sensations as "erotic" is concerned with the arousal and satisfaction of sexual desire and its study involves the varied aspects of sexual or amatory love.[1]

R. K. Singh's poetry reflects an unmistakable awareness of erotic as it abounds in portrayal of woman and her beauty as a means of attraction and arousal. Besides eroticism appears considerably in his delineation of carnal communion between man and woman, sexual life of married couples, nature of physical urges. One also finds radical reflections over the aspects of sex and sexuality such as loss of vigour, prostitution, masturbation, and sexual perversion in general. The paper, however, limits to focus on the reflection of eroticism in the poet so far as it shows in his depiction of feminine charm; her body and beauty.

The speaker in R. K. Singh turns to woman as he fails to find a source of inspiration in the world marked by pollution, corruption, and deceptiveness. Woman and her company remains the single possible arena where solace, peace and pleasure (through sex) can be found. The poet's depiction of woman as divine being seems to be an outcome of similar implication. The poet talks about woman, her nudity, and her beauty in a number of verses such as 'Love Moods', 'Fount of Poetry' (*Some Recent Poems, MSAOSP* 33)[2], 'Poem 5', 'Poem 49', 'Poem50', 'Poem 56' (*Flight of Phoenix, MSAOSP*), 'Poem 6', 'Poem 13', 'Poem 36', (*Memories Unmemoried MSAOSP*), 'Poem 3' ,'Poem 4', 'Poem 13', 'Poem 19' 'Poem 21' (*Music Must Sound, MSAOSP*), 'Poem 1' , 'Poem 2' , 'Poem 3' , 'Poem 5' , 'Poem 7', 'Poem 18', Poem 23' 'Poem 24' (*My Silence, MSAOSP*), 'Poem 17', Poem18', 'Poem 57' (*Above the Earth's Green*).[2]

The persona in R. K. Singh seems to be on an eternal quest for woman as she signifies beauty, pleasure, and creativity:

I seek new strides
in each of your moves
new dreams in your eyes and thighs

nude lyrics in lips
shape the night's sway
set my heart afire

I seek the lingering fragrance
the rhythm that frenzies the soul
the timeless joy you conceal

('Fount of Poetry', *MSAOSP* , 33)

The persona attains new heights in company of woman "each of her" "moves" seem to aid to his ecstasy; her lips seem to be encompassing "nude lyrics", evoke the speaker's desire for communion and his heart start to burn with the urge. The speaker finds all the excellences of nature such as musicality, colour, rhythm, and aroma arising from the source of timeless joy that is woman. It is notable that the excellences attributed to women don't exist in ideal form only, rather they are part of her concrete and personified form; her beauty is not exclusive of nudity but integrated to the same. The speaker finds his dreams personified not only in his beloved's "eyes" but also in her "thighs". The aesthetic and spiritual values of woman are, thus, combined in her concrete and personal form:

I seek hues that blaze being
and shade the nest I rest in:
your chains renew my freedom
each time I look at you
I see natural woman
the fount of poetry. ('Fount of Poetry', *MSAOSP,* 33)

The beloved woman encompasses "hues" that colour the speaker's life and enlivens his bleak self. The woman protects and nurtures the spirit as a "nest". Her nude, natural form is as soothing as 'Fount of Poetry'. The speaker extracts elements of pleasure implied in the sensuous charm of the nudity of a woman:

In the fragrance of her breath
blooms the bud of joy
I gather the fruits.

Flickers of peace hide
god in heart like running brook
love in nudity.

She gives me of herself
each day and night fulfills in me
God smiles in her eyes. ('Love Moods', *MSAOSP,* 32)

The lines also show the sensuousness leading toward tranquility and spirituality. The realization of self sacrifice of beloved in lovemaking makes the persona aware of her superiority to him and he finds "God" smiling "in her eyes." Here one finds the close association of erotic to spiritual.

Nudity of woman, a symbol of sensuous pleasure, becomes a mean to experience "peace", and "God". The same idea recurs in Poem 5 (*FOP*) where the speaker finds himself hidden in the eyes of his lady who signifies "hope", "love" and "mercy":

... he whom I seek is
hidden in her eyes

shedding hope and love
all around her mercy (*MSAOSP,* 54)

The speaker's search for self ends in finding woman who conceals within her higher virtues of hope, love, and mercy. Further, woman in R. K. Singh is also considered analogous to poetry. She has been recurrently depicted as "flesh and spirit of poetry" signifying "eternal love thirst." However, one also comes across derogatory comments about woman in a number of his poems,

...a woman's mind
resides between her thighs joy
and satisfaction (Poem 56, *FOP*, *MSAOSP,* 72)

Here, the speaker seems to highlight woman as a mere physical being. The phrase "between her thighs" used in the context of her intellectual capacities is derogatory and exhibits the cynical mentality of the speaker. Nevertheless, one turns back to the previous positive vision of the role of women where the speaker finds "...all calm/ in her presence." (Poem 13, *MU, MSAOSP* 85*)*. Woman's "face" becomes a means to "light up" the "dark chamber" and is like "the moon" reclining on his "bosom"; her charm is so pervading that even nature ; "evening" tries to steal the "fragrance" of the woman. (Poem.3, *MMS, MSAOSP,* 103)

The speak^r goes on to outline the body of woman and present it in association with various qualities such as comfort, pleasure, novelty, freshness and protection as in the lines:

> I want to rest in your lap
> and drink from your golden breasts
> hide me in the curtain of your hair
> shield me in the grove of your flesh
>
> (Poem 4, *MMS, MSAOSP,* 101)

Here, images such as "lap", "golden breasts", "curtain of your hair" and "grove of your flesh" are highly evocative and seems to be symbolizing erotic and spiritual in combination with each other as the woman in the verse represents an image which is at once indicative of a beloved and a mother. The same idea recurs as the speaker in Singh perceives in woman a "tree", "green" and "wide", " abundantly dresses", "overflowing" and as one who "blesses all" in her "cool shade"(Poem1 *MS, MSAOSP* 137). Woman as a tree is symbolic of life; the image also evokes the physical excellences of woman; the effect is not only tantalizing but also gratifying. Such a charm is a conveyance of "breezy songs" even when one is in "solitude" and that is why in the company of woman the poet feels "nearer god".

Again a tree in "autumn" seems to be representing "a young woman", "naked". This nakedness of woman is shown as "exciting birds" to "come /kiss and play". However, the instinct which is evoked by the exposed beauty, however, the lines "when spring will return/ she will be too lovely/ to touch" imply that beauty of physique in exposure is evocative but beauty concealed is even more appealing. The speaker in intimacy with woman feels his senses leading him to self realization:

> ...love...
> (from) her breath runs through my veins:
> this vassal of the flesh blushes
> as I drink the infinite in her (Poem 3, *MS, MSAOSP,* 138)

The speaker feels dwarfed before his beloved whose love seems to be endless whereas the speaker's love is limited to sheer physicality represented through the image "vassal of flesh". In another poem the poet draws the contours of a woman's body and evinces how the captivating charm encompassed in each part of her body incites one to helplessness:

Is it the perfume
or your body
that makes the night drunken?

your lush lips
ripple fire (Poem 5, *MS*, *MSAOSP,* 138)

The lines celebrate the intoxicating and bewildering impact of the sensuous charm of woman; the speaker is swayed by the aroma of her body and feels as if the night itself is drunk. The lush lips of beloved is arousing as it "ripple(s) fire" even in beautiful silence. The speaker fails to control his urges and pleads for a communion:

can I seek
my voice
in your breasts? (p. 138)

The lines explicitly express the erotic desires of the persona. Physical communion with woman is always associated to the feeling of assurance, inspiration and spiritual bliss and repeatedly the speaker expresses his wish to sit under the "tree of love". Also the poet establishes woman on a higher pedestal than man:

...just one pace
if I could take
I enter
the pavilion of eternity (Poem 6, *MS*, *MSAOSP,* 139)

Woman as a source of love is emblematic of creativity and leisure; the qualities leading to eternity. The poet also represents woman's body in terms of natural images quite frequently as in the verse: "In the forest of her body/ and steeps of her breasts..." (*MSAOSP,* 144)

In R. K. Singh, physical urges as evoked by intimacy or sensuousness with a woman is mostly leading to the higher realms and is uplifting and elevating. The speakers in his verses find: "... repose/ in the wrinkles / of her face and:

...feel her crimson
glow in my eyes

her holy scent
grows inside
a sea of peace
multiplies
in the mind (*AEG*, 29)

The lines imply the psychological aspect of physical union as closely linked to harmony at the level of thought. The same idea is stressed in the following verse where the persona finds his ultimate repose and resting place in the body of woman:

When I have no home
I seek refuge in the cage
of your heart and close
my eyes to see with your nipples
the tree that cared to save from sun
(*AEG*, 30)

To conclude, erotic charm of woman is pleasurable, refreshing, and uplifting. It not only intoxicates and bewilders but also transcends; providing one refuge from darker forces it becomes a motivation to survive.

WORKS CITED

1. (http://www.chacha.com/questions/what_does_erotic_mean) July 24th 2010.
2. Singh, R. K. *My Silence and Other Selected Poems*. Bareilly: Prakash Book Depot, 1994.

12

Mirroring the Contemporary Society and Culture: The Poetry of R.K. Singh and P. Raja

— Jayshree Goswami & Md. Mojibur Rahman

The paper aims to make a comparative study of the depiction of culture, both personal and societal by R.K Singh and P. Raja, one belonging to eastern India and the other to southern. It focuses on personal/ individual identity; depiction of Indian culture; Indian rituals and myths, family, man/ woman relationship, treatment of love and sex; and reflection of modern societal system— political, academic, cultural, economic, and social.

Poetry is both personal and social criticism. The contemporary poets are dissatisfied with the present state of unrest, corruption, ignorance, misery, and identity. For them poetry serves as a medium through which while denouncing the societal blemishes they reveal their ideology, attitude, prejudices and vision. Apart from this, a writer also confronts the problem and challenges to one's identity in a multicultural nation; where one feels alienated, rejected and rootless. Sometimes they even suffer the politics of rejection at the national level. R.K Singh depicts and probes into the question of isolation and rootlessness, which is caused not due to transmigration, but due to rejection in one's own land. The persona in these lines confronts the treatment of an outsider in spite of being an insider. The expression of disgust is noticed in the following lines:

> I do not question the sun
> adding wings to wounded giants
> or depressing them to crouch down
> the memory's lanes or erect
> new walls with odours of hate
> and love cagily crumpling
> the shades between earth and sky.[1](*SRP*, 2)

In these lines, the persona through the "sun" image expresses his grudge against the superior authority, for they with the aid of their motivation either privilege the fragile and the marginalized men, or deprive them off their rights and individuality. He considers himself and he likes to be the "wounded giants", denoting their inherent potential, and at the same time their adverse treatment. The protagonist in order to attest his indifference at this discrimination restates the opening statement "I do not question", but actually reveals his excruciation at being alienated and distanced. Therefore, he is forced to "crouch down the memory's lanes". Consequently, he becomes lonely creating "new walls with odours of hate". Though being worthy of identity, he shrinks into himself unnoticed and unrecognized.

A similar poetic agony arising out of rejection is sensed in the poem 'The Writer at Home' by P. Raja. The persona, a writer expresses-

> Hailed by fans from all corners
> the writer is
> a non- entity at home. [2] (*TLGH*, 19)

Against the background of "home", the writer connotes to his homeland, India. He uses the image of "unsympathetic eyes/ of a practical housewife" [3] (*TLGH*, 19) for the unsympathetic readers and critics, who are professional enough in disapproving and ignoring his "cerebral excitement" [4] (19), or the creative composition. The writer presents the anguish, and psychic trauma of a native writer who despite receiving acclamation from abroad is subject to rejection in his own country. The noun "fans" expresses the complacency of the persona resulting out of his plaudits. However, at the same time the agony of exclusion is exhibited through his becoming a "non- entity"

We find an affinity between the characters of Singh and Raja, as they have similar concerns. The sense of rejection in their own homeland agonize them. In Singh, the rootlessness is because of the character's failure to assimilate in a multicultural nation like India. Besides, we find Singh's images to be more complex and ambiguous than Raja's. Raja is more direct in his expressions.

Singh also depicts rootlessness, existential crisis and alienation in poems like Seek the Roots' (SRP,), 'Wordless Plaints' (SRP, 16), and 'Aloof' (SS, 3). The poet expresses his crises of identity in the lines

The colour of night is the same everywhere
what if my identity is not known
let's fuck the moment and forget the place (*FOP*, Poem 26)

The directness in tone generated through the expression "what if" clearly states the grudge of the narrator. The trauma and anxiety for being unrecognized, unknown is implicitly expressed through the image "night". A similar darkness, like that of the night, prevails in the heart of the poet. The slang used "let's fuck" bespeaks the prevailing grievance and hostility towards the authority. Failing completely to denounce the society, the persona alienates himself from the society. He seeks recluse in solitude. The character experiences: "I feel alone/ like a wandering bird/ without a nest:"(*FOP*, Poem 17)[6] Singh carefully chooses the images of a "wandering bird" and "an island" to convey the present state of rootlessness, seclusion, and isolation. The persona seems to undergo diasporic alienation due to multiculturalism and regional dislocation.

Nonetheless, we do not find instances of alienation and rootlessness in Raja's poems, since the writer is rooted to his native place unlike Singh. Though Raja's characters too, are in search of establishing their identity, they try to do so through the medium of poetry. The poet persona projects the commercialization of prose writing and the marginalization of poetry in 'Why I Write Poems'

Poems don't bring money.
Sometimes they fail even to fetch
a complimentary copy.
...Perhaps that's why wife
-the inspirer of my works-
advises me not to write poems,
but concentrate on remunerative prose-pieces.(*TLGH*,59)

Identity created through poetry is at stake. It is because in modern times poetry has been marginalized for lack of readership, as a consequence, it has become so unpopular that "sometimes they fail even to fetch/ a complimentary copy". On the contrary, the word "remunerative" for prose pieces indicates the commercialization of prose and its widening readership. Yet the poet considers that for a poet poetry serves to provide aesthetic pleasure rather than means for a livelihood.

While in Singh we find the characters to be reflective with the issues of identity, in Raja one glimpses pathos with a slight humorous touch.

Depiction and Negation of Religious Rituals and Myths

Apart from articulating their individuality, both the poets project the Indian social culture. Rituals and myths are central to all cultures. They reflect the cultural orientation, and are strictly adhered to even though they do not possess any scientific basis or justification of the phenomenal world. In their poetic microcosm one can find the criticism of those rituals which retard progress, and recommendation of those which are iconic.

> Is it the love for ritual
> or the ritual waste:
> every year they steal light
> to illumine *puja pandals* (*SRP*,41)

In this instance, the social critic projects the religious corruption. He unveils the cultural dualism through his reflective question "is it love for ritual/ or the ritual waste".The stealthy act of the practitioners, who steal light for illuminating puja pandals, attests the diminished sanctity of these rituals and its substitution with flamboyancy. This is an illustration of a cultural degeneracy in a country that boasts about its classic culture. The "stealing of light" and "blaring of non- stop nasty songs" enhances the ironic situation when "but the goddess keeps mum/ perhaps self-loathingly/ sleeps for demons to write histories"(*SRP*, 41). "mum", "self-loathing", and "sleeps" hints at the helplessness of the goddess. Further, she "sleeps for demons to write history". Here "demons" evokes the hegemony of corrupt and shrewd men in creating history since time immemorial. These men influence the social ideology through their existing power by justifying their deeds. The critic attacks the religious practitioners and holds no opinion about the rituals themselves. He considers that it' the people, who by abasing these rituals, are denuding them off their religiosity.

Likewise, in P. Raja too, one observes the critique of certain superstitious and religious practices. However, unlike Singh, Raja's comment solely reflects the religious hypocrisy and not the political one. The persona, a socio- cultural- economic critic depicts the pathetic condition of Hindu gods and their believers :

> India speaks through its temples.
> Its hindu pantheon boasts humbly
> of just two million gods.(*TLGH*, 34)

The persona ironically depicts the Hindu religious tolerance through the phrase “hindu pantheon”. He mocks at this pantheism by confirming it to have ‘just two million gods”. Further, the ironic contrast of non- Indian and Indian religious ideology is humorously depicted in

> All other countries are paupers.
> They can’t afford to spend on their god.
> For them charity begins at home. (*TLGH*,34)

There is an essential religious cultural difference between India and other nations. While a majority of Indians still practice pantheism or idol worshipping for their sustenance in the phenomenal world, all other countries believe in humanitarian. For them “charity begins at home”. The persona further highlights the anti- humanistic attitude and irrationality of those Indian rituals that causes economic waste. He comments:

> While babes whimper for a cup of milk
> cauldrons are poured on sacred stones.
>
> Tones of pure ghee drench our gods
> to their very stones.
> But hotels here display the broad:
> “The sweetmeats sold here
> are not made of pure ghee”.(*TLGH*,34)

The irrational belief of the religious rites is depicted here. “while”, and “but” depicts the contrast between the real needs like “a cup of milk” for the hungry babes and “sweetmeats of pure ghee” and the superfluous practices like pouring of “cauldrons of milk” on sacred stones and drenching the gods with “tones of pure ghee”.

Apart from religious ignorance instances of traditional extinction is viewed in the poems of P. Raja. In ‘My Grandpa’s Desk’ an old father beholds the contempt for the traditional assets, which probably is due to the emerging materialistic choices of the present generation. The father reflects on the issue of a “desk” that is considered to be an inheritance of loss by the son. The persona expresses his concern and agony in-

My son, I do not know, what he would
do with the desk! Keep it as a momento!
Or simply reduce it to splinters
to feed his empty oven! (*TLGH*,67)

However, Raja is not critical of all the rituals, superstitions, beliefs, traditions, and cultural practices, he in certain cases even highlights typical south Indian cultures that are revered and adopted. For instance, the drawing of kolam, a traditional art form practiced in south India. He also presents the mindset of a Hindu wife as shaped by the religious texts: she believes that "...God sleep/ in that lump of sod?"(*TLGH*, 21) But, it is to be noticed that Raja exhibits a common Indian male ideology in considering woman to be irrational, emotional, and gullible. This is evident from the following lines :

Believing is feeling.
She believes.
...Isn't God omnipresent?
Oh, yours may not be.
But hers is. (*TLGH*, 21)

The title 'The Hindu Wife' suggests the poet's perception as guided by the psycho- social opinion of a female psyche.

On the other hand, R.K Singh is critical of most of the cultural practices and customs. In poems like 'Orgasm' (SS, 37), 'Fresh Future' (SS, 52), 'God' (SS, 33), 'They Call God Loudly' (SS, 38), the persona believes that these rituals have undergone severe modification in both their purpose and meaning. The persona visualizes the retarding nature of these mythsprobably his visualising is subjective in tone. He believes that these myths by constraining the thought framework and the human action limit the vision and freedom of an individual. Therefore, he wishes to "...recoup/ the elements' balance/ and create new suns/ and moons that could light the cave"(*SS*, 52)

Family

Another socio- cultural dimension that one discovers in the poets is family. Though Indian family system is known for its togetherness and unity, both Singh and Raja trace urban family life, where the household is segregated after marriage. Singh deals with the discordance and distancing of couples in his poems. In the poem 'Bulli' the wife lives with her husband in spite of strife, disregard, hate and dissatisfaction. The husband reveals:

She sees
many faults in me
points out all I shouldn't do
...yet life
rolls on mocking
compromise of living
to keep home she conceals within
our angst. (*SRP*,26)

The Indian wife adheres to the cultural values and chooses to compromise. The husband in order "to keep home" circumstantially forces the wife to "conceal within" her "angst", failing to which she is destined to lead a helpless and agonized life. Further, in the poem "sleepless night", one can notice the bitterness of an otherwise cordial relationship. The husband detects, "The anxiety/ on her face tells of/ the gap in relationship"(*SS*, 28). Singh tries to present the bitter relationship of a husband and wife, hence, reflecting only one aspect of the relationship.

P. Raja, on the other hand, highlights that aspect of family where a daughter-in–law is seen to be the cause of distancing and enfeebling of familial ties. In poems like 'Fool and God' and 'Curtain Lecture', he exhibits the relationship between a daughter and her in-laws. The persona in the latter poem speaks: "My brother is now an acquaintance. / My parents are only occasional guests."(*FZTI*, 32). The notion of "an acquaintance" and "only occasional guests" highlight the inherent love of the husband for his family members, which the wife is believed to have disrupted. And at the same time, the husband is shown to be helpless as he silently witnesses to whatever is being done to his parents. In this instance one notices the projection of a chauvinist ideology in considering women to be solely responsible for misfortunes and discordance. In contrary, the husband is seen to be a dummy character that has no role to play. Similarly, the persona in these lines demeans woman as:

Forget, you stars!
to twinkle.
O, moon! Drive the nights.
Worry no more,

O, Sun! about the day.
Stop, O Stop,
till the dead God
resurrects
and creates a new Adam
who never in his life
will ask for an Eve. (*FZTI*, 38)

The persona's exhibits a biased perception in denoting apathy for the pathetic condition of Indian woman. The character seems to be unhappy with the lady as he considers her to be the sole cause of his agony. And hence, he wishes to live without "eve" or woman in the world.

It is detected that Raja projects an opposing ideology to that of Singh. This may be due to the cultural and situational differences of South and North. Moreover, in Raja's poem we find an omission of those circumstances where woman is deprived off of the power to think, feel and act. The true picture is a majority of women are still harassed by men. They still have the status of subalterns. Though it cannot be denied that this biased attitude is noticed only in the treatment of husband and wife, for in case of man-woman relationship, a different set of ideology, attitude and treatment is noticed in Raja's works.

Indian Philosophy

In Singh's poems one comes across the philosophy of androgenity of soul. Woman is supposed to be the feminine principle, the initiator, or shakti in the Indian context. "her shiva and/ shakti a dual-single/ me and she, one".(*FOP*, Poem 6) Shiva is the male power and Shakti the female. He believes that both of them are incomplete without each other just as Purush cannot exist without the assistance of Prakrati. Creation is possible only when "lingam and/yoni harmonise"(*FOP*, Poem 52). Here, the union is divine, generating harmony. In this instance, we find Singh to present a contrary code to that of the Indian society; where male and female are binary oppositions and the relation, status and positions are hierarchical. Similarly, P. Raja too, addresses woman as Shakti. The character of 'An Opportunity Missed' speaks:

In vain did I wander

in the temple of Shiva
while my Shakti prayed for me (*TLGH,* 23)

The character considers himself to be Shiva, the male principle and woman to be the embodiment of Shakti. He realizes that love and peace resides in the presence of Shakti and not in the temple of Shiva. The persona considers his quest for himself, Shiva, to be "vain" because union and harmony is possible only when man and woman become one. This concept of the poet is devoid of all the societal values and prejudices. It is the poet's perception of man-woman relationship.

The Opinion of Love and Sex

Apart from the man- woman relationship the concept of love and physical union, too highlights the culture of a nation. In Singh's poetry we find the concept of sex to have many connotations, most of them adhere to the Indian philosophies that have permeated into its culture

It's part of prayer
to have the lingam kissed
or kiss it to feel
the creator's pulse (*SS*, 64)

Sex is a ritual, "the climax of creation"(*MS*, Poem 63) just as the lingam of Shiva is divine and one can feel the divine pulse of Shiva by its sacred touch. Similarly, through the union of bodies, one can realize God. The poet writes: "thank the body too/ that houses the spirit"(*SS*, 64) The poet considers the body to be a temple; bliss, for the spirit too, requires the body to realize the divine. He wishes "to recreate / the body, a temple/ and a prayer" (*SS*,33)

Influence of Sangam Literature

P. Raja also presents his concept of freedom of love. Moreover, Raja's love poems exhibit traces of influence of ancient Tamil poetics, as embodied in Sangam poetry and expounded in 'Porul Athikaram' (The Book of Meaning). Tolkappiyam part III is unique in its combination of ecology and aesthetics, for it codifies literary themes and forms based on categories of space and time. The basis of Sangam poetics is the division of life and literature into 'akam' and 'puram'. 'Akam', as Thaninayakam puts it, is supposed to be "the most internal, personal, and directly incommunicable human experience, and that is love and all its emotional phases." In addition, puram is "all that does not come under this internal and interior experience" while, love poetry is akam, all the other poetry, elegiac, panegyric and heroic, is puram. The aspect of love is called 'uripporul', or the subject matter of the 'tinai', the region, the season and the hour are called the 'mutalporum' or the material, the objects of environment are denoted as 'karupporul'.

However, Tolkappiyam clarifies the relative importance of the three components of tinai. According to him "karupporul' is more important than the other 'mutalporul', and 'uripporul' is more important than the other two". That is, the aspect of love is the most important part, the objects of environment come next and the region, the season and the hour are less important.

Considering this notion, we find in Raja an adherence to 'uripporul' only, as also found in some of the poems of akam poetry. In akam poetry, the poems on the theme of love are all in the form of dramatic monologue and name of the hero and the heroine is never mentioned. Similarly, in Raja's collection *To Live in love* we find his characters expressing their feelings and thought, without reference to any particular person/ name. His characters are intended to be universal and common to all times. However, he deviates from the strict pattern of form and writes in free verse. The persona speaks to his ladylove:

> You are an oasis
> my dear!
> In my life's vast desert.
> … When we came face to face,
> thank Heavens,
> we had no attack of lock- jaw.
> Warm embracing
> crazy, fervent kisses,
> '-our very existence now.(*TLL*, 2)

The image "desert", indicates aridness due to desolation and separation. And the image "oasis" suggests hope or love, which would quench his desires. The excitement of the lovers union and the consummation of love is depicted through the expressions "warm embracing", "crazy", and "fervent kisses". Here, the poet presents that aspect of love when a lover separates, and then re-unites with the beloved. This eternal moment is subsequently followed by the exchange of their feelings and thoughts. Next, in the poem 'Burden of love', the poet presents the trauma of a lover who earlier shared a loving relationship, but now is separated.

Depiction of Modern Society

Both the poets portray, discuss and criticize all the proponents of contemporary Indian society— the political, academic, cultural, economic, and social. Singh in his poetry raises basic issues like corruption, poverty, perversion, prejudices and pollution.

Singh's social consciousness is reflected through the issues raised and the scenario presented by him. He criticizes the political system and their leaders. He considers politics to be a profession of convenience where the leaders:

> blinded by politics
> of convenience
> ...as leaders create
> a new elitism
> a new tyranny
> of mid-term poll (*SRP*, 42)

The poet presents an Indian picture where there is no democracy. The expressions "a new elitism", "a new tyranny", "mid term poll" intimate the fascist regime that is tyrannous and favourable to only one class, the leaders. The expression "mid term poll" also indicates the dystopian system. The words "create" and "new" have a negative implication, these hint at the concept of a society to be inhabited only by dictatorial and tyrannous rulers. The poet uses animal images to describe their shrewdness, treachery, and deceit in *My Silence* poem - 36 and *Music Must Sound* poem– 75. He also unveils political perversions by referring to the different scams and scandals in poem 29 and 47 of *Above the Earth's Green.*

On the other hand, P.Raja does not explicitly communicate political depravity. However, he borrows the image of mosquito for the political leaders and in a humorous way criticizes their misdeeds thus:

> How well with your charming song
> you mesmerize mankind!
> Oh! Scrounger of man's fuel.

We toil and sweat.
We pray and eat.
Yet our bread is not a full loaf.(*FZTI*, 48)

This is an apt comment and image which describes the situation of an Indian as well as the political leaders. The "charming song" suggests the gullible promises of the leaders before elections. The condition of an Indian citizen is accurately portrayed through the statement "Yet our bread is not a full loaf". Additionally, being in academics, Raja authentically presents academic corruption in poems like 'After the Interview' and 'Ragging'. In poems like 'Refresher Course' and 'Seminar' he humorously narrates the causes of falling academic standards. R. K Singh, on the other hand, depicts the administrative loopholes and politics in higher academic system in the poem 'Why Should I Suffer'. Apart from this, the poet exposes, discusses and criticizes the contemporary problems of terrorism, population, communal conflicts, and poverty that the nation is encountering. Corruption is a major theme in his poetry, and he exposes corruption of all kinds: Sexual, religious, social, academic, and political.

Both the poets seem to be dissatisfied and unhappy with the present societal condition, as is reflected through their attitude, and perception of the society. It is to be noted that both R.K Singh, and P. Raja do not provide any resolution, whether implicitly, or explicitly, to the problems they discuss. They do not seek to direct men, to judge events, to reform morals, or to present a philosophy. Poetry is their only object, an art that exists for itself.

WORKS CITED

1. Singh, R. K. *My Silence and Other Selected Poems*; *Some Recent Poems*: 1990-1994. Bareilly: Prakash Book Depot, 1994. Print. Abbreviated in the text as *SRP*.
2. Raja, P. *To The Lonely Grey Hair*. Pondicherry: Busy Bee Books, 1997. Print. Abbreviated in the text as *TLGH*.
3. Singh, R. K. *My Silence and Other Selected Poems*; *Flight of Phoenix: 1987-1989*. Bareilly: Prakash Book Depot, 1994. Print. Abbreviated in the text as *FOP*.

4. Raja, P. *From Zero to Infinity*. Pondicherry: All India Books, 1987. Print. Abbreviated in the text as *FZTI*.
5. Singh, R. K. *Sexless Solitude and Other Poems*. Bareilly: Prakash Book Depot, 2009. Print. Abbreviated in the text as *SS*.
6. Raja, P. *To Live in Love*. Pondicherry: Busy Bee Books, 2003. Print. Abbreviated in the text as *TLL*.
7. *http://www.tamilnation.org/literature/ancientliterature.htm*
8. *http://www.tamilnation.org/literature/anthologies.htm*

13

The Asexuality of Sex: A Study of Sex Expressions in R.K. Singh's Poetry

— ***Raghuvanshmani Tripathi***

In one of his early poems, collected under the title *My Silence*, R. K. Singh writes about his involvement with sex when he looks at a woman. The act of looking is meaningful for the poet as it leads to the poetic process and the expression of his feelings. The poetic lines that underline his reaction to the beauty of a woman tell us that it makes him 'blind', 'deaf', 'ignorant', 'poor' and 'indrawn', various states connected to his being overpowered by a mystic sense inspired by her beauty, but the darkness of 'dust' veils his being so opaquely that he is not able to follow the hidden words.[2.6] The hidden words are related to the spiritual and the mystic and, thus, by not following the hidden words, he is bereft of the entry of the 'pavilion of eternity'. The eternity is related [contrasted too] and signified in terms of the uneternal that surrounds him in spite of his reaching the condition of getting 'blind', 'deaf', 'ignorant', 'poor' and 'indrawn', the psychic states that may lead him to the desired realm. As a reader continues his journey through the poetry of the poet, he comes to know that the notion of eternity as expressed in his poetry does not exclude sexual acts like copulation, climax, and bodily fulfillment. Unlike the sonnets of Shakespeare, love is a part of sex, and lust is never denied or taken as a hindrance to achieve the spiritual state, and the 'eternity' is one of that. Thus, the 'eternity' is to be explained as a state of bliss, the extension of sexuality in the realm of poetry. In his journey of love even the savage is not unacceptable as it flows in 'the arteries in the tulip silence'. [2.4]

The darkness and blindness of 'dust' is not the blindness of 'lust'. The poet forgets the decree of the coal dust when she enters with her warmth in the wheezing and sleepless winter discomfort [26.3]. The poem underlines the importance of passion in life. Sexual exploration is mystic and it is done in her 'privates' with 'handgun'. [6.19]The metaphors used by the poet, here, are not confined to eroticism. They cross the realm of erotic to enter the realm of obvious sexuality. The primal image of snake from Bible does carry a different sort of connotation, devoid of sin and suffering. [7.23&24] He describes himself as a snake without Eden. [29.19]The problem lies only when age is countered with passion, a question that reminds the poet of time rather than sin. These two aspects of sex, time and sin, are well delineated by the poet. [7.22] Instead of acknowledging the presence of sin in his sexual acts, he finds that the presence of her 'presence' makes him feel nearer to god.[1.1] The Indian god Shiva, associated with enjoyments of life, is planted deep and the serpent is eternal. [17.59] The poet, without mincing words, records that he exults as he drinks the infinite in her [2.3] and her body or its perfume makes the night drunken, [2.5] another state associated in literature associated with the bodily pleasures. [One may remember the Rubiayats of Omar Khayyam and its long prevalence over a literary tradition that discarded the orthodox religion in the favour of the joys of life.] For the poet, a woman is the best poetry, the best theme of his writing [3.7] and the spring music is hidden between her thighs. This music is beyond birth and aims at the sheer pleasure of sex [27.9]. In one of his poems, the poet states clearly that he wants non creative sex after the birth of two children.[28.17] As the poet appreciates her, and states that her eyes are the source of love and beauty,[3.8] it is not the traditional boundary of taste that he draws around his idea of beauty. The poet feels the presence of sex even in nature, and for him an autumn tree is like a woman naked. [1.2] Thus, R.K. Singh's involvement with woman and beauty is never devoid of sex and it stands as an obvious challenge to the traditional and orthodox in the form of his resisting poetry in the Indian surroundings where sex has remained a taboo for a long time. Even today among the conservative societies of India, it is something to be kept secret in the locker of repression. This is an enough argument to underline the symbolic nature of resistance available in his poetic presentation of sex.

Another interesting aspect of the poems of R.K. Singh is that he depicts the mysterious nature of woman with her Ritikaleen gestures. [6.7] The playful gestures of a woman attracts him in various ways.[6.20] The mystery of such gestures of a woman is, in fact, the creation of the male psyche that likes to see woman in the framework of the notion of classical poetry. This notion is, in fact, not confined to poetry alone but it is an attitude prevalent in the society, enforced by the romantic poems, novels and films. But the difference lies when he presents the sexual act as a metaphor [of the exploration of body?][6.19].In the perspectives of his poems, it is not the question of male domination or patriarchy but the question of the presentation of sex in poetry. How it is presented and what is its significance?

The idea of sex in his poems is highly deceptive as it is the least related to sex. It is needless for the poet to underline the joys that he receives in the sexual acts and exploits. Because it is a thing that is [already] well known to most of the readers and as a form of poetic knowledge it adds nothing to our stock. In recent decades, the underground pornographic literature of the past has emerged 'over'ground and has engulfed the sky in the form of internet explosion of sexual knowledge [?], that is in the form of cyber pornography and erotic literature, once considered to be an offence equivalent to sin. *Therefore, the presentation of the sexual acts in his poetry is, in no way, the significance of his poems. In reality, it stands simply as a celebration of the carnal never fully accepted in our society, a society laden with hypocrisy in the name of social values, culture and religion.* The suppression of sex in the society has led to so many abnormal results, at times, unknown to the society itself. It is in our time, that these suppressed elements have surfaced and spread around disturbing so many from the nightmare of their cultural sleep. The example of the killings ordered by the Khap Adalats is to count one of the numerous abnormal reactions to the unleashed sexuality in our time. It is always shocking to see how such abnormal age-long repressions surface in our society in the forms of new repression. In this context, the rebellious celebration of sex in the poems of R.K. Singh needs more serious and cultural explanation and interpretation rather than a casual passing remark.

Remarkably, in the poems of R.K. Singh sex is not always present as something spiritual and pleasure giving. On certain occasions it is sordid too, and the poet depicts the stark realities of life in the way of his description of the presence of sex in the society. For example, we can take the poem beginning with the line 'she is declared a mental case' [3.9] or the poem written on the widow.[4] In the first, the nakedness of the woman does not inspire any feeling of sex as it underlines her deplorable state as an abnormal woman. In the second poem, the rose which could have become a symbol of beauty and might have led the poet to sexual desires, leads him to the feeling of pity. Rose might, in other sense, have been suggestive to woman's secret parts with the wetness of desire. For the poet the dance of love is dark and unfathomable. The poet wants to seek shelter in the grove of her flesh, [26.6] but this shelter is not always a sure one. The mystery of a woman's flesh is a road to the subjects of poetry existing outside the realm of sex.

This shelter of the grove of flesh is unsure because of the world outside that keeps lurking in his early poetry and occupies a big space in his later poems. As a poem depicts, the outside world is disturbing to the poet's prayer of sex. The disturbing vultures force him to make a show of his person in the sulphurous pond. It is very difficult to live with ones own God while the world around tries to disturb him due to its conservative approach. The society enters our personal life whether we like or dislike the needless social poking. If we don't accept the ways of the world, we are always conscious of our own lifestyle. His poem depicts this aspect of a nonconformist in a humourous but serious manner. This conservatism forces the poet to pretend to hide the semen spots on his pants as tea spots. [30.21] So the question is ever whether it is sex or the suppression of sex that the poet presents in his poem. The question is always double pronged as the expression is presented twofold and forces the reader to look beyond sex. The readings of his poetry is always marred by the conservative approach of glaring at sexual presence with hungry watching or a sort of literary voyeurism which is verily cultural in its essence in the Indian context. This literary voyeurism turns into critical one when inflated with the question of taste. There is usually the brushing of the surface in the appreciation of his poems and it makes the sex shine, but does not look beyond the skin-deep in his poetry.

How asexual is the question of sex when the poet engages himself with the question of religion. The poet questions faith when it is turned into rituals by myths. It is not meaningful for the poet to search faith against oneself. [27.10] The personal convictions based on experiences are discarded by people when they come to the realm of faith and religion. For the poet, a faith or belief without conviction is of little value. His religious experience emanates from his sexual experiences and he develops a moral sense that stands beyond the orthodox notions of religion and spirituality. Sex plays asexual role in his criticism of religion and its real presence in the society. The vedantic discourse of the bearded swami is meaningless as it is unheard in the spiritual blankness. The speakers as well as the listeners are spiritually dead [32.29]. A sexual tinge is given to the asexual theme when the reference is made to Kartik, the month of the mating of dogs, with reference to the denuded women bathing in the Ganges while the gods leer at their wet bare backs. The poet concludes that 'aum' is suitable mantra for Vasanas [lust] [32.30]. The poet criticizes the jugglery through which the religious leaders hide their fractured faith from their followers. [32.32]

Likewise the eyes of goddess Durga can not see the sexual violence which prevails in the society and takes place even before her eyes. One wonders if she can see or do anything in reality. The questioning is about the sight of Durga whether she can see things like that happening during her public worship. Thus, sex is a method of questioning the so called religious in the society. [4] His idea of religion and spiritualism is different from the conservative religion followed by his fellowmen. His love for God is expressed by his love for the people He has created in this world.[154.1] This humanistic notion of religion is not understood by others. But sex is again a way of worship for the poet. His house is glorified by sex and it declares the mysteries of God. This idea of sex as worship is a contrast to the general idea of sex as something impious in the society.

The poet has written many poems on Benaras and the holy rivers. He questions the holiness of the city variously. The river Ganga and Yamuna are not sacrosanct for him. The religious sangam of Ganga and Yamuna is a sterile homosexual affair and these holy rivers don't lead to heaven. [18.64] Thus, the city of religion is the city of sex and copulation of the two great rivers. The sterility of the intercourse makes the city devoid of any religious significance for the poet and his friend who seeks the way to heaven. Heaven is somewhere else. The river Ganga is also a symbol of how culture has been polluted by the modern life style. For him Ganga was once a river now it is lost in a drain. [12.41]

The same is true about repression of abnormal feelings for women in the society [5.13] and the business of sex in our society [5.14]. The state of a woman as pictured by him is certainly grim as she is pictured cleansing her womb [5.16] People show their dicks to women at the pretext of making water, but they object at the young people making love between the bushes and his backyard. This poem clearly shows that the celebration of sex is to be read as a reaction against the sexually hypocritical in the society.

In one of his poems, when the poet tells us not to fall in the trap of life as it is a mere show, [7.21] he is in fact making his reaction against the middle class life. It is the life that the poet is living and he knows the reality of this conservative living very well. The essence of this life is presented in the form of the kick of the prostitute in one of his poems. The prostitute is the symbol of middle class traps that keep us vainly engaged in our lives to make us face its disillusioning reality at last. But it is the stage from where there is no comeback for anyone. One may read it as the notion of Maya [attachment] in Indian philosophy that is the result of our ignorance of the spiritual reality [Agyan]. But, here, the Kick image is too original to be compared to Maya philosophy, and it brings the triviality of the middle class world to our eyes. In the darkness, when the light is switched off, every woman is a Cleopatra. It is the morning light that tells the truth. But in the middle class life the illusions are so many that the light is rarely switched on.

Sex is a shelter in such a life full of boredom. In one of his poems the images of sexual organs and nature do mix up. The poet tired and bored collapses on the open thighed creek and feels the whole city in the glen. [12-13.42] The static middle class life is without any pleasure and there is no release for the poet. [8.26] To use the phrase of the famous English poet S.T. Coleridge, the middle class life is not less than the *death in life*. Thanatos gets the upper hand at times in his poetry which is the result of the middleclass boredom not released even during some travel. [8. 27] Here, again the pleasure of sex is a reaction against the life of ennui and isolation. It is to forget the demeaning aloneness that he involves in sex and not for the thing itself. [92.30] Thus, sex remains a medium rather than an end in his poetry. This is clearer in another poem showing his naughty interest in activities like weeing at a lamp post, peeking at someone's privates, or doodling vulgar graffiti etc. It is the dullness of life that inspires the wish of such acts in his poems [35.44].

The personal of the poet reacts acutely against this middle class life that is full of silence or chaos, two contradictory but similar aspects in his poetry. Inside the poet it is silence, in the society it is chaos. In the society, he stands like an island shielding chaos and live his joy hearing the serenade.[14.4] He considers himself rightful to react against the chill of the silence [icy wind] as he was born in the month of December. [13.47]. It is important to note that the fight against the chill is made by the lower class people in the streets where a huge log is giving them warmth. The petty bourgeoisie is always inside the quilt. But as the poet reacts against the deadness of his surroundings, inside the poet lies the tragedy of man and nature. The broken images reside in him and his poetry. [14.50] Likewise the loneliness inside the poet is increased by the passing of time, poem by poem. [15.52] People love moth eaten reality that floats to emptiness. This realization of his own position in the world is tormenting to the poet's self.

The Image of winter is present in many of his poems which is suggestive of peculiar state of poet's mind when he feels himself isolated from the middle class conservative life devoid of meaning and significance. The hurried happiness means very little for the poet. [15.54] As far as he is concerned, he weaves heat in the unholy solitude in the empty cell of time. [17.61]. He dances his silence on the ocean floor of time where sun rises and sets. The nature images, here, do speak the psychology of the poet. The inside of the poet is highly disturbed while the outside world remains undisturbed. It is compromising and laggard world that has faith in not reacting to the new values emerging in our lives. Thus, the rock stands undisturbed and the shores don't move. It is the sea that returns after striking the seashore. [22.75] He feels the barrenness around himself as there is no tree on the mountain and he sits under the shadow of a wandering cloud.[38.55] Inside him there is a river which is rippled by the ripples of darkness. This river is in fact his consciousness. He hears the shrieks of shadows amid savage hails.[38.56]

To go against the conservative values the poet criticizes the double standards in the society. In one of his poems he talks about free dogs and unfree men. [10. 14] The poet does not feel the comfort in his surroundings which is full of the sounds of Frogs and Owls, and he sings the ritual of flesh and hides himself inside the mosquito net. [27.12] The dust ridden city observes the falling leaves as time passes and the poet finds vultures all around and his corner is not very cozy for sex. It is reduced to the distasteful show of his naked person in the sulphurous pond. [29.18]

The cosmetic values of the middleclass are washed by the rain. It is a phenomenon of nature that discloses all that is hidden behind the mask of culture. [12.39] The same rain like night unwraps their faces and the poet is not able to make distinction between man and beast [33.37]. The Images of night and morning do hold significance in the case of his poetry. After getting tired he collapses on the open thighed creek and feels the whole city in a glen peel off the illusory flesh warmth until/ the rosy fingers of the dawn messes around. [12-13.42]

The criticism of the political system by the poet is at places too obvious to hide behind the images or the language of his poetry. The poet criticizes the police and, in this way, the whole system that has gone corrupt. The police arrests the innocent people accusing them as pick pockets and the real criminals do survive in their white clothes [9.10]. These people in Khadi are described as jackal, fox [45.82] and rats.[46.85] The poet detests the politicians and feels disturbed when he finds bureaucrats and journalists shaking hands with them. They are like dogs mating in the month of October or November, a seasonal image related to sex. [11. 38] His natural appreciation of sex goes against any sort of hypocrisy prevailing in the society. Rain, the time of epiphanic creation of poetry, continues to shake the mortal shell and blasts the hypocrisy. [12.39] In some ways this is his poetic process which involves demystification symbolized by rain.

The poetry of R.K. Singh is the creation of a poet who is a restless soul. To read his poems in a sensitive way involves the experience of the feeling of angst generated by the moral degradation in our time. This shows his rejection of the conservative life lived by the people around him. The life of conservative acceptance of the powerful dominance is not congenial to the poet. The poet has no difficult language to outwit people but people don't like him and even his shadow is disturbing and uncomfortable due to his rebelling attitude. [22.76] In other words he is a nonconformist who is against the status quoits in the society, those who live a passive life and indirectly support the system unacceptable to him.

The presentation of the theme of sex is a medium to explore the society in an untraditional way. The themes planted in his early poems have grown with the passage of time in his later poems but the themes related to sex are always similar in their function. The observations of the poet seem at times objective but in fact they are very personal reactions to the society he is facing. But the personal itself does not remain personal in the poetic process, but involves the social and the political. The calm and fury of the poet shows his inability to change the world and this brings a deep feeling of restlessness getting space in his poetry. He is against the system that tames a man to give him survival in its structure of power. [721. 72]

But, ironically, he is himself a part of the middleclass that he hates and as a result, his reactions turn to himself in his poems. The counter result is more of unrest and crisis getting expression in his later poems. In his drugged sleep he utters expletives and he cannot help his sensory overload. [153.3] He suffers sleepless nights full of nightmares.[154.7] The crisis is represented in the form of themes related to sex and a-sex. *As Freud used to say, the symbols visualized in our dreams look unrelated to sex but in reality they are sexual in nature. In the poetry of R.K. Singh, the process is just opposite. Poems look to be sexual and personal, but they involve asexual and apersonal elements*. Thus, it is from the space of sex that the poems make a journey to the social, cultural and political.

WORK CITED

1. Singh, R. K. *Sense and Silence: Collected Poems: 1974-2009.* Jaipur: Y King Books, 2010. [All the references are from this book. Numbers in the brackets refer to page numbers and poem numbers.]

14

Treatment of Myths in the Poetry of Shiv K. Kumar and R. K. Singh: A Comparative Study

— Jindagi Kumari & Rajni Singh

Myth is an important tool and resource material which is been exploited by all creative minds since time immemorial. Both Shiv K. Kumar and R. K. Singh, the two current Indian English poets, too, take interest in myths to build up their poetic capacities.

In Shiv K. Kumar and R. K. Singh myths are used variously. First is the allusive treatment to myths where the poets deploy mythical allusions as symbols in their poems; the poets allude to various myths ranging from western to indigenous, and harness their qualities as metaphors. The tendency is so frequent that allusion to myths seems very much a part of their poetic style. The second aspect of mythic consciousness in the two poets is reflected in their delineation with rituals or the practices and behaviour originated from myths. Besides, one also notices a third approach to the treatment of myths that can be termed as reinterpretation of myth where the artist freely treats his knowledge of myth; he experiments with it at various levels in course of its presentation and evokes various humorous, ironic, or satiric appeal. However, this kind of approach to myth is available only in Shiv.K. Kumar. Singh doesn't show any inclination towards reinterpretation of myths.

Kumar exploits the device of reinterpretation. In a number of poems in the collection *Trapfalls in the* Sky[1] he presents reinterpretation of the Biblical myth of creation in the section 'Genesis'. Nevertheless, the most noted aspect of the mythic consciousness in his poetry seems to be the employment of mythic allusions.

Study of Mythical Allusions in Shiv K. Kumar and R. K.Singh:

Shiv K. Kumar harnesses the symbolic quality of mythical allusions in construction of his images. He often seems to describe certain traits of an image by alluding to a particular myth. This way he mashes up his images with various associations.

Mythical allusions often present an instance of image within an image. An illustration of this approach is the allusion to "Medusa's hair" in the poem 'Thus Spake the Buddha'. Here, the poet in his attempt to define desire uses the image of "unbridled stallion": "Desire—an unbridled stallion, / mane incensed like Medusa's hair," (*Thus Spake the Buddha*. p.5)[2] The image of "unbridled stallion" in the lines is indicative of waywardness of desire. But the comparison of "mane" of the stallion to "Medusa's hair" seems intriguing. The poet uses the allusion to "Medusa's hair" to suggest the intensity of desire. However, the reference may be puzzling for a reader who is not aware of the myth of Medusa.

The reference to the Greek mythical figure Medusa, who had snakes for her hair and who could turn anybody looking straight in her eyes into stone , is made to denote the destructiveness and intensity of desire which, if left unrestrained, turns cataclysmic as it has deep impact on an individual and it remains the guiding principle of our lives. Here one finds that mythical allusions are not merely decorative but also help the poet to capture and present an idea with all its diminutiveness. The allusions, therefore, are explanatory of the images to which they are associated.

The allusions appear very much a part of the literary mind and thought process and seem naturally woven to the stylistic structure of the poems. By alluding to the myths the poet also highlights a particular event of present time which otherwise tends to skip one's notice. An instance of such treatment is available in the poem 'Rickshaw-wallah' where the poet alludes to the mythical episode of The Last Supper. The Biblical Last Supper refers to the supper of the Christ where he prophesied rebellion of one of his disciples leading to his end. Indeed, shortly after the event, Christ was crucified due to the betrayal of Judas Iscariot, one of the twelve apostles.

In contrast to the mythical episode the poem presents the realistic picture of a rickshaw-wallah's agony. He is shown as "pulling his cross". Cross as the biblical symbol signifies the agonizingly painful death of Jesus. It symbolizes slow and tormenting death. The reference to it in the poem 'Ricksaw-wallah' is representative of excruciating life of poor who, in spite of toiling hard, are not sure of a meal of a day. Their homes present heart- rendering view of desperation and hunger as is shown in the poem; the wife and hungry children of rickshaw-wallah anxiously wait for him at home. The wife fails to console the 'full throated cries of children" for "few grains". It is in this context that the poet alludes to the "last supper":

> the mother-hen is gagging
> her chicks' full-throated cries
> for a few grains of rice —
> their last supper.
>
> (*Articulate Silences*.p.22)[3]

Here, the term last supper gains a new meaning. Since none of the members of the family is sure where or when he/she will be getting his/her next meal, the poet anticipates their next supper as the last supper. Also the last supper seems to be a comment by the observer who anticipated the death of the poor rickshaw-wallah's children due to starvation.

Shiv K. Kumar's strategy in alluding to the myths seems to attract the attention of the audience to the real issues. Myths appear more enchanting to readers than reality. The poet deceives his reader by promising a mythical flavour and in turn bring him face to face with a sour real life situation. It is suggestive of the subtlety of the poet who, by adopting this particular approach, reveals the irony of the situation. In such poems one develops an understanding of the meaning even without having the knowledge of the myth. The way the poet tries to build up a contact between two images, the one which is related to present time and the other related to the past, hardly have any point of commonality on the surface level. But when one intrudes deeper one definitely finds some linkage between the two. The link however is a forced one and is build up with an effort carrying its own limitations. The poet basically designs his style in this manner to define, to elaborate, to illustrate, to highlight, and to intensify the images of present with the help of the mythical allusions.

Moreover, by treating allusions with literal meaning, Kumar reduces their mythical value in the face of reality. He adds to the magnitude of a particular event by presenting it in the light of mythical allusions as in the poem 'Dew Drops on Lotus Leaves, Nagina Lake, Srinagar.' The speaker in the poem seems to be silently observing the beauty and delicacy of the velvety lotus leaves. Dew drops that lay on the surface of the leaves appear like pearls. The speaker is so captivated by the beauty of the lotus leaves that he fails to suppress his desire to possess it. In a fit of impulse he "nipped a leaf off its stem-base". Further, he wants to present the beautiful leaves to his love (his wife) who is still "dreaming away in bed". This act of violating the innocent charm of nature is vividly presented by the analogy between lotus leaves and the mythical platter carrying the head of "John the Baptist":

> And I heard the gods shedding tears
> into my green platter that now seemed to carry
> the head of John the Baptist.
>
> (*Woolgathering*.p.7)[4]

The speaker finds nipping off of the lotus leaf by him as heinous an act as the mythical event of beheading John the Baptist. Also, in both the cases the cut object was conceived to be a gift. Head of the John the Baptist was desired by Salome, Herod Antipas's step daughter because John the Baptist criticizes the illegal marriage of the king Herod, the father of Salome.[5]

Kumar, like Eliot and other modern poets, uses mythical allusions to fill a common situation with religious, historic, artistic, and linguistic tension.[6] However, in each instance he seems to be resolved to reduce mythical in the face of real.

For a common reader who is not acquainted with the myth of a particular culture, reading his poems is like landing in scores of complexities as the poet does not supply any clue or footnote to the dropped in mythical images. Probably the poet has an intention behind doing it .Following Eliotesque track he goes a step further than Eliot in building up the nature of obscurity of his poems.

This approach of treating mythical allusions as metaphor is also available in R. K. Singh's verses. He also exploits mythical allusions as symbolic expressions of an emotion or an idea and as "imaginative vehicle of (his) experiences."[7] However, the poet does not use myth in association to the image in his poems. Unlike Kumar, one finds one to one relation between the idea the poet wants to present and the image and metaphor that is created out of mythical allusions. The poet puts mythical allusions parallel to a particular emotion, idea, situation in the context of his poems and exploits them as vehicle to highlight the significance of that emotion, idea or situation. An illustration of this treatment can be seen in the poem no. 20 (*Music Must Sound*) where the speaker alludes to the mythical event of the "Judgment of Paris". The poem presents the persona who is in dilemma for he has to make a tough choice between his loyalty to his wife and his sexual impulse for a lady other than his wife. The lady, though ugly and old, influences the speaker for her sex appeal: The speaker falls victim of his impulses:

> ...the crone ready to cast
> a new Judgment of Paris
>
> on the mount of Venus
> is an apple
> I wonder if my wife
> too has sensed it (*MSAOSP*.p107)[8]

"Mount of Venus", in the lines, refers to the part of palm between the two middle fingers of a person which, according to palmistry, if prominent, indicates excessive sexual bent of a person. "Apple" here refers to the "apple of discord" in the mythical tale of the Judgment of Paris. The lines imply that the persona's erotic urges for the "crone" may cause discordance in his marital relationship. This idea is reinforced by the speaker's speculation whether his wife has "sensed it" all.

The allusion to Judgment of Paris in the context highlights the persona's situation and his mental condition that is similar to Paris in judging the best beauty among three deities Hera, Aphrodite and Athena. One finds that mythical allusion highlights and explains the context of the poem and is directly linked to the idea the poet wants to present.

So far as the range of mythical allusions is concerned Kumar is seen alluding to mythical figures ranging from Greek mythology such as Medusa, Endymion, Diana, Cynthia, Helen, and others, to Biblical mythical figures such as Adam, Eve, Serpent, God, Delilah, John the Baptist etc. In the reinterpretation of mythical situation he particularly focuses on the various episodes from the Genesis, Bible. However, one also finds him occasionally reinterpreting episodes from

Mahabharata and life of Buddha .Besides, the poet also refers to mythical objects and places e.g. "Hades"(*Subterfuges*,p.38)[9], "Garden"(*Losing My Way*)[10], "manna" (*Trapfalls in the Sky*.p.18), "Noah's Arc"(*Woolgathering*. p.8)etc.

Singh alludes to the Hindu deities "Shiva", "Shakti" (*MSAOSP*.p.100), "Durga"(*Ibid*.p141), "Ganesh""Laxmi"(*Ibid*.p.164), "Kali", (*Ibid*.p.165).The poet also refers to legendary yogis "Aswapathy" (*Ibid*..p.110) and Agastya(*Ibid*.124). Among western myth only one instance of allusion to Greek Mythical Story "Judgment of Paris" (*Ibid*.p.107) and Roman mythical episode related to Rex Nemorensis (*Ibid*.p.149) are found.

R. K. Singh seems more interested in the use of terms and expressions from Indian scriptures. These terms and expressions from Scriptures forward mythical concepts. The poet alludes to the Upanisadic concept of "Shiva-Shakti", "Purush –Prakriti" (*MSAOSP*.p.71), "Abhiviktam –Vibhakteshu" (*Ibid*.p.100). He also deploys Biblical words and expressions in a number of poems and uses them as personal imagery moulding the image by associating it with personal ideas and experiences; instances of this are "Messianic dream" and "mount Sinai" (*Ibid*.p.128).Also, the poet alludes to the religious/mythical figures such as "Moses", "Mohammad"(*Ibid*.p.133) "Christ", (*Ibid*.p.165) as metaphors. Some stray references to "dragon" (*Ibid*.p.159), a mythical creature in Chinese/Tibetan myth, a metaphor is also found in both the poets. Overall, the sources seem to be mixed, this shows the poets' global consciousness as they do not seem to emphasise on any particular culture, religion, or society in choice of the mythical references.

Study of Rituals in Shiv K. Kumar and R. K. Singh:

Another aspect of the treatment of myth available in the two poets is the cross examination or study of rituals which are related to myths and are called offshoots of myths.[11] Both the poets share akinness in their treatment to rituals and their strong disapproval of the same. Also both conceive them as testimony of the degrading values implied in myths.

Rituals in Kumar and Singh have been presented as despicable set of actions which signify nothing more than vacuity and emptiness. They don't appear showing any religious obligation or ideas and scarcely seem to be providing any satisfaction of spiritual or emotional kind. Neither do they appear strengthening social bonds. Rituals in the poetry of both the poets is presented as devoid of all its purpose such as demonstration of respect, submission, statement of one's affiliation, attainment of social acceptance, or approval for some event.[12]

Kumar reflects a severely critical attitude to the ritual of animal sacrifice in the poem 'Kali' .The poet expresses his anger against beastly behaviour of the priest who resumes his 'monotone' in spite of an innocent lamb's bleating as it is exposed to the 'Knife-edge". The persona turns bitter even against the deity who occasions the sacrifice. In the fierce and vituperative mood the persona goes to the extent of analogising goddess Kali with hyena and decries the ideal of creation through destruction:

> If the way to create
> is the way to kill,
> I have hoarded enough blood
> in my throat
> for all the hyenas to suck from.
>
> (*Subterfuges*.p.34)

R.K Singh also seems to refer to the ritual of sacrifice as "crudities in hills" performed by "pervert godheads" in the lines:

> ...I can forget
> gaudy icons, pervert godheads
> crudities in hills
>
> (*Above the Earth's Green*.p.57)[13]

The poet perhaps has in his mind the cult of sacrifice vogue among the tribal living in hill areas. The use of the term "crudities" indicates the poet's conception of the ritual as signifying primitiveness and barbarism of human race.

Kumar finds the position of rituals as essentially ironic since they seem to undermine the very values that they are meant to signify. The poet, therefore, invariably presents rituals as inconsequential. The idea, that rituals can discipline human mind and behaviour seems a fallacy to the poet who seems determined to bring forth the self deceptive conception of rituals. The duality of rituals finds an interesting presentation in the poem "Baptism of Fire" where a youth is shown undergoing his sacred thread ceremony. While he performs various rites related to the ceremony he remains engaged in the erotic thoughts which act as defiance to the essential purpose of the ritual aimed to "control all the tigers" in the persona's "blood stream" and "steer" it toward "cosmic sea". Indeed, the ritual is valued among Hindus as signifier of their spiritual birth. The person who undergoes this ritual is considered as "twice born". Conventionally, the ritual is associated to a youth's vow to celibacy and devotion to studies as he entered gurukula. Even the members of loyal family were trained to live simply without luxury or sense gratification.[14]It is this idea that is ridiculed by the poet who presents the occasion of assumed spiritual awakening making the persona suddenly supremely conscious of his physical urges. This idea is presented in the following verse where fire meant for *havan* reminds the speaker of:

> ...the fire
> that crackles when I touch Sheila's
> nascent breasts under the mango tree.

(*Trapfalls in the Sky*. p.21)

The lines quite overtly indicate the persona's awakening to his sexual desire and urges as he finds the heat of the sacred fire superimposed by the heat of his sexual urges symbolised as "mango tree". The analogy of the spiritual fire to sexual fire is aimed to bring out the conflict of spiritual with physical

By intermingling rituals signifying spirituality with erotic the poet reveals the underlying contradiction of human thought and behaviour. This way he also reduces the relevance of rituals. The idea is reinforced in the speaker's expression of disgust with rituals in the lines:

> A tremor ripples through my hand
> as I hold a spoonful of ghee above
> the fire. I shrivel like a sun-
> flower that droops its crest at dusk
> in shame over the day's obliquities.

(*Ibid*.pp.21-22)

The speaker reflects deep reluctance and feels sick of doing something which he does not want to do. Also, he feels greatly relieved when the ritual ends and resolves to "undo all the knots" of the same.

Further, the poet is particularly critical of pundits, prophets, and soothsayers. This outlook of the poet develops as the result of his deep awareness of the corruption, hypocrisy, and selfishness of the priests whose sole concern in prescribing worship or ritual remains self interest. The poet finds such people responsible for the degeneration of values and decadence of religion. This critical attitude of the poet towards priests shows itself in a number of poems. An instance is the poem discussed above where Kumar presents the priest as "ram-necked". In the same vein, in a number of poems he presents priests through animal imagery. In 'At the Ghats of Banaras' (*Woodpeckers*.p.24) Kumar depicts a priest as a "glassy-eyed crocodile", in the poem 'Crematorium in Adikmet, Hyderabad' priest is ironically presented as chanting "lauder/for a generous tip" while the speaker is mourning his father's demise. The poet highlights the grotesqueness and irony implied in the behaviour of the priests as in the poem VII 'Broken Column':

> ...the high-priest communes with brahma.
> Wrapped in saffron loin-cloth
> he lets his long, grey hair
> cascade down to life's quiddity.
> ...beckons me into the dark chamber
> ...out of earth's orbit
> into blank space
>
> (*Woodpeckers*.p.7)

The lines spotlight the artifice of the priest in his adoption of the appearance. The images of "dark chamber" and "blank space" subtly suggest the void to which these pretending spiritual guides can lead. Again the poet makes humourous comment on the appearance of priest in the poem 'Vandana Weds Ramesh' (*Losing My Way*.p.10):

> ..., four priests....
> ... Tails hanging from
> the middle of their close-shaven heads
> are divine strings that link this world
> to the life beyond.

One finds the poet ridiculing the priests. The image of "Tails hanging" from their "close shaven heads" makes their image extremely humorous. Further, the assumption that the "tails" would link this world to the other world is also highly ludicrous.

R. K. Singh expresses analogous contempt against such religious pretenders. He, nevertheless, targets yogis and sages, who show themselves up as the protectors of India's sage culture. The hypocritical attitude is disparaged as the poet exposes them how they "hung up" the practices of yoga to leer at "bare backs" of denuded beauties taking bath in the Ganges:

at the Ganges in Kartik
...old gods leer at
... wet bare backs
... 'aum' is convenient
to soothe *Vasanas* (*MSAOSP*.p110)

Ironically, "aum" the sound of great spiritual significance proves to these yogis a convenient utterance through which they release their "vasanas". The speaker seems to be fed up with such "Aswapathys" and says desperately: "no more Aswapathys please/...." Indeed one can feel sick of such modern aswapathys who discard their austerity in pursuance of physical pleasures.

R.K. Singh's approach to the treatment of rituals is identical to Kumar. However, Kumar seem to be keener to suggest the need of "secularization"[15] of myth and rituals in view of the fact that "...myths and rituals are all subject to change in the course of time."(*Ibid.*) Also, Kumar achieves an edge over Singh so far as the effect is concerned. He creates vivid humor, brilliant irony and pungent satire while dealing with rituals. This effect is achieved due to keen eye on details and the ability to create fresh images.

To sum up, Shiv K. Kumar and R. K. Singh, in their treatment of myths, emerge as realists and rationalists. They do not reflect any nostalgia to the past values and tradition. They merely highlight the present degeneration by exposing hypocrisy and corruption involved in the use of myths and rituals. The two poets hardly seem to imagine the way out of present rootlessness in mythical past in the manner of Eliot. Instead, they seem to seek a release of the society from the fetters of deadly rituals which distances one from reality by provide an "ideal kind of fulfilment"[16] .The poets emphasise the need of development of a new awareness among people adequate to the situations of life at present time. They are not against myths or rituals; they are against their misinterpretation and misrepresentation. So far as the use of mythical allusions is concerned both Kumar and Singh use mythical allusions as a source of artistic embellishment. They stud their poems with mythical allusions to increase artistic appeal of their verses.

WORKS CITED

1. Kumar, Shiv K .*Trapfalls in the Sky*. Madras: Macmillan India, 1986.
2. ____________.*Thus Spake the Buddha*. New Delhi: UBSPD, 2002.
3. ____________.*Articulate Silences*. Calcutta: Writer's Workshop, 1970.
4. ____________.*Woolgathering*. Mumbai: Orient Longman Limited, 1998.
5. http://www.answers.com/topic/john_the_baptist Jan the 24th 2010.
6. Singh, Rajni. *Tennyson and T.S. Eliot: A Comparative Study*. New Delhi: Sarup & Sons.2005.53
7. http://query.nytimes.com/mim/archieve_free/pdf?_r=1&res Nov the 5th, 2009.
8. Singh, R.K. *My Silence and Other Selected Poems*. Bareilly:Prakash Book Depot ,1994.
9. Kumar, Shiv K. *Subterfuges*. Delhi: Oxford University Press, 1976.
10. ____________. *Losing My Way.* New Delhi: Peacock books, 2008.
11. Abrams, M. H. *A Glossary of Literary Terms*. Delhi: Thomson, 2007.
12. http://en.wikipedia.org/wiki/Ritual Jan the 2nd 2010.
13. Singh R. K. *Above the Earth's Green* .Calcutta: Writers Workshop, 1997.
14. http://hinduism.iskcon.com/practie/602.htm Jan the 2nd 2010.
15. *The Encyclopedia Britannica.* Vol.12. (Printed in) USA, University Press. p.93.

15

Major Themes in R. K. Singh's *Sexless Solitude and Other Poems*

— Ram Sharma

R .K. Singh is an established name in Indian English Poetry with thirteen poetry collections to his account. Among the many collections of poems by the present day Indian English Poets, the poems of R. K. Singh attract us by its content and style and we get a rare pleasure by reading them. In the foreword to poetry collection I. K. Sharma opines about the poet:

> 'A poet of modern sensibility, Dr. Singh has drawn inspiration from diverse literatures of the world , from the English-speaking to the non-English , such as Japan, France, Chile, Yugoslavia etc.'(p-1)

There are 99 pearls in the form of poems in this volume. In the first poem of the volume entitled 'Don`t Condemn Me', the poet requests not to condemn him for the conversation of sex.

> sins of races flowing in my blood;
> I love Him through the bodies He made
> but don't understand redemption
> in churning and parting of the sea (p. 1)[1]

Again, it is worth mentioning I.K.Sharma's view on Singh's poetry:

> 'Singh manages to tell his experience, bitter or sweet, mostly bitter, in minimum possible words. He would eliminate all the non –essentials from the composition. He would chiefly exploit, like Hemingway, the vigour of verb in his poems, and avoid the pomp and vanity of adjective altogether. This way of writing makes his poems far different from the poems we often come across in Indian English poetry magazines.'

In the next poem entitled 'Barbed Wire Fence' the persona discusses the love making of boys and girls in the bush.

how can I complain,
if boys and girls make love
in the bush between .... (p-2)[2]

The persona ponders over sex when he is alone and in wintry nights but his verses is not obscene. His sweaty desires compel him to scribble verses when he is alone. Again and again he thinks about naked company with laughs. Such poems like 'Overload', 'Hazy Sun', 'Aloof', 'Winter', 'Again and Again' expresses the above thoughts.

...now fail to have
what I always had,
her naked company
with tingling laugh,
slurred with passion ('Again And Again', p-7)[3]

Singh doesn't consider it bad to talk about sex in solitude He is against those persons who take law in their hands to stop lovers for the celebration of Valentine's day. Poems such as 'Group Dance', 'Liberation', 'I Hang Nobody's Picture', 'Portraits We Fear To See' convey this idea:

Culture is not repression
but sublimation through expression

why do they police
art for lesbianism
homosexuality
naked sex or blasphemy? ('Portraits We Fear to See', p-25)[4]

The poet Stresses on open love and he does not care of psalms to sing or going to churches. For him this is not devotion to supreme authority but this is open business.

I see no saviour come
to rescue me when mired
I seek freedom from myself: ('Valley of Self', p-26)[5]

The poet creates his own world of sexless solitude and he enjoys this world without any barrier. These poems entitled ' The Other Poetry, 'Sleeping Light', 'Arriving Early', 'Total Image', 'Body: A Bliss', 'Creation Orgasm', 'Stripped And Naked' carry this idea:

To create is to die:
die to love, to time

to memory, to god
to everything we know
do or experience ('Creation', p-32)[6]

Singh revives the old tale of Adam, Eve and snake through poems such as 'Snake', 'God', 'Sex And The World', 'Erotics of Bygones':

Hiding or waiting
it raises its head when least
expected, a snake ('Snake', p-61)[7]

The poet also diverts our attention towards present day problems of peace, human rights and terrorism in poems like 'Peace Mission', 'Politics Defies Silence', 'Human Rights', 'Terrrorism':

Each day ends in fear
of one or the other kind:
living in uncertainties
it's life in death ('Terrorism', p-71)[8]

Further, the poet boosts our morale through verses, for instance, 'On Her Birthday', 'Ignite Minds With Flickers' and other poems:

...you have worlds to conquer,
and miles to go, my dear

you must rear the goose
and have the gold each day ('On Her Birthday', p-11)[9]

R. K. Singh is quite realistic in the two poems, 'I Am No Moses' and 'I Am No Jesus':

I am no Jesus
but I can feel the pains
of crucifixion ('I Am No Jesus', p-44)[10]

The poet creates realism and he no more wants to go to God or sing Psalms .In fact, it is through the medium of love that the poet finds a way to God. Like Osho's 'From Sambhog to Samadhi' , he takes us from sex to Nirvana:

The sky frightens with lightning and rain
raises neither fire nor quenches the earth

I've lost a chance to create despite ritual
end of the day and her parting with a kiss: ('Nirvana' p-77)[11]

It seems that R. K. Singh has been greatly influenced by the Buddhist philosophy. The present volume is a reflection of his Buddhist ideals which the poet tends to preach in an innovative manner, Even when talking about the body or the physical the poet does not sound vulgar. All these poems are written with good intentions and insight .He presents various forms of love in this volume as the loved, the spurned, as the winner or loser. The poet is sensuous and compact in his verses as he fuses in this volume love, sensuality and the meaning of life.

R.K. Singh's lyrical expressions are endowed withal the traits of any good and at the same time enjambed with philosophy. He is bold enough to present the expressions with sweetness of language. This volume is concise and many of the poems are written in the spirit of Haiku. Singh's style is cosmopolitan and prolific. The symbols that he employs are individual and graceful. To conclude, in *Sexless Solitude and Other Poems* one finds verses that depict disillusionment, despair, frustration and fury, along with verses of love for life in the spiritual, mental and physical form, and there are clarion calls for a release from this mundane world.

WORKS CITED

1. Singh, R.K. *Sexless Solitude and Other Poems*, Bareilly: Prakash Book Depot, 2009, p.1.
2. *Ibid.*, p.2.
3. *Ibid.*, p.7.
4. *Ibid.*, p.25.
5. *Ibid.*, p.26.
6. *Ibid.*, p.32.
7. *Ibid.*, p.61.
8. *Ibid.*, p.71.
9. *Ibid.*, p.11.
10. *Ibid.*, p.44.
11. *Ibid.*, p.77.

16

Haiku in English, Indian English Haiku and R. K. Singh

— ***Rajni Singh***

Haiku is one of the oldest forms of poetry yet the form has recently been discovered and embraced by writers around the world. It is believed that in 1970's haiku as a literary genre got highlighted internationally. Today, it is written in English as well as in several different languages and enjoyed widely in nearly 50 countries. But the actual credit for this haiku boom goes to Paul Louis who with the publication of his collection entitled *Haiku*, in the early 20th century, revived this genre. And since then the popularity and internationalization of haiku has kept on multiplying.

Haiku is short and light poetry with traditionally 5-7-5 sound syllables with a season word. Historically speaking, this poetic form had its roots in tanka, a kind of prayer/incantations to Gods by the Japanese. Tanka, with its 5-7-5-7-7 sound syllable count, its lofty ancestry and its shortness and ease for memorization, later became the favourite poetical form of the Japanese Imperial court. And from 9th to 12th centuries it reached the highest popularity and brilliance. However, in the 12th century a new form generated out of tanka, with the rival of an old Chinese form of linking tanka poems together in a novel way. The poem was 'split' in half, allowing one author to write the first three lines 5-7-5 and the concluding lines i.e. 7-7 part to be written by another, especially by men. This chain of writing did not stop there, again a new 5-7-5 was written as an answer to the previous 7-7 links and this genre was called 'renga' (meaning linked elegance). Renga became a fashionable form of poetry in the 14th century with two main styles: a serious, courtly style and the comic style, especially of the merchant class. Basho was a renga master of the comic style. This poetic form was not as simple to write as it appeared. Writing a good hokku i.e. the starting verse and haikai (any verse in a renga) was really a challenging task. Thus all could not meet the standards of a good hokku/ haikai. The quality of the renga tended to fluctuate with Buson and Issa and in the beginning of the 19th century M.Shiki declared renga officially dead and also ended the ongoing debate on hokku/ haikai by combining the two names into a new one- haiku.

Haiku is the smallest literary form with lot many rules and it is difficult for one to follow all the rules. Moreover, several of the rules are so contradictory with each other that there is no way to honour them all at once. Say, for example, the sound units of the three liners have a wide range of patterns-seventeen syllables in one line, seventeen syllables written in three lines, seventeen syllables written in three lines divided into 5-7-5, seventeen syllables written in a vertical (flush left or centred) line, less than seventeen syllables written in three lines as short- long- short, less than seventeen syllables written in three vertical lines as short- long- short and writing in one breath (which nearly covers 12-17 syllables). Second, the number of images and the kind of images which again do not follow any fixity- a haiku with two images that are only comparative when illuminated by the third image; a haiku with two images that are only associative when illuminated by the third image, two images that are only in contrast when illuminated by the third image and then the kind of images- images that evoke simple rustic seclusion/accepted poverty (sabi), images evoking classical elegant separateness (shubumi), images that evoke nostalgic romantic images/austere beauty(wabi),images from nature, images not from nature, season words (kigo), non-season words (muki), lofty / uplifting images. Third, the rules of punctuation- no punctuation to attain ambiguity, all normal sentence punctuation are also admissible- a colon (:) and full stop (.), a pause (;), three dots for something left unsaid, a comma for a slight pause, a dash for saying the same thing in other words, capitalizing the first word of every line or only the first word as well as the proper names according to English rules. Next, the rules of grammar- eliminating all the possible uses of gerunds and adverbs, little use of pronouns, ending the haiku with a noun, avoiding too many/all verbs and prepositions. Finally, the rules of rhetoric- avoiding rhymes/ bringing in rhymes by rhyming the last words in the first and third lines, using rhymes in other places within the haiku, using assonance and alliteration; and using puns and paradoxes to attain levels of meaning in haiku.

It is quite natural that with so many options, a beginner of haiku might get highly confused and find it difficult to start off with. But it is to be noted here that rules are not written in stone. Thus, it can be said that there is no one way to write a haiku, there is no one style or technique that is absolutely the best. Every writer can work out for herself. In fact, the varieties in style and technique of haiku provide enough freedom for the readers and writers of haiku to expose, expand and to investigate.

Today one can notice new trends emerging in haiku from several countries, including India as well. Now, there is no strict adherence to the old, traditional guidelines. Despite a small community of haiku writers in India, the haiku form has been widely experimented and written in several regional languages, including English and Hindi.

In India the traces of haiku can be found in the beginning of the 20th century. The Indian Nobel Laureate, Rabindra Nath Tagore, is probably considered to be the first haikuist of India. His collection of haiku like poems 'Fireflies' was published in English and Bengali. The names of Subramania Bharati, Prof. Satya Bhushan Verma and Prof. B.S. Agarwala are also familiar names in regional haiku in India. Among the Indian English haiku poets the few familiar names are- Dwarakanath H. Kabadi, N.V.Subbaraman, Angelee Deodhar, Kala Ramesh, K.Ramesh, Mujeeb Yar Jung, I.H.Rizvi, Urmila Kaul, D.C.Chambial, Kanwar Dinesh Singh, R.K.Singh Mahashwata Chaturvedi, etc. Yet, not many people are aware of haiku or its intricacies because of lack of literature and/or criticism in various languages in the Indian market.

Haiku writers from all over the country, even though small in number, have contributed their lot in promoting this poetic form in India and out of the many contributors writing in English R.K.Singh as a haikuist stands apart. R.K.Singh who has been known for economy of expression and brevity for the last three decades has drawn attention of readers to his haiku, first pubiished in trilogies *Every Stone Drop Pebble* (pub.1999) and *Peddling Dream* (pub.2003 in *Pacem in Terris*) and more recently in *The River Returns* (pub.2006). Abdul Rashid Bijapure seems right in his observation that "perhaps it is the single-minded journey of R.K. Singh to press for brevity in expression that leads him to devote his poetic energy to the three line haiku poems." Even Singh says " a haiku is terse, dynamic and complete poetry, rendering the vital energy, which animates not only an individual's small world but also the entire cosmos." For Singh it is rather a self- disciplining spiritual exercise marked by living momentness of a moment, imaging a moment:

After morning walk
the trio gossip each day
fresh revelation

Each day of our life is full of happenings and one such is captured here with all subtlety in the same fashion as a photographer clicks a moment.

The poem:

Ripe on the branches
mangoes fall one by one
end of the season

is highly sensuous in appeal. The reader gets an immediate image of a season. The ripeness of the mangoes can be seen and felt in the lines.

The lines:

The leaves sway
to fly like birds
free in the sky

evoke the image even before the eye blinks. Like the swaying of the leaves, the lines appear soft, light and rhythmic.

Singh's nature poems perfectly meet the traditional haiku standards:

Smell of Kamini
In front of my house excites:
hummingbirds mate

Or

The night queen fragrance
seeps from the window
my bedroom blooms

The naturalness of the lines instantly hits the sensory organs of the readers. The two poems:

Shining from the blade of grass
a drop on earth's breast:
tribute to sun

and

The mynahs
herald the day Clamouring
for moths

reflect the honesty of the poet in creating the images. There is no artificiality or imaginary renderings in these lines. With minutest details the poet constructs a striking image and allows space for reader to create his own image and interpretations.

Singh is not only a sharp watcher of the thinginess of the things in nature but is also a keen observer of complex human nature. Running away from reality is human nature and this hollowness of human beings is described in these poems with a tinge of irony:

She hides the mirror
with rose and lipstick
and keeps her fiction

and

He closes the eyes
expanding inner space
a short – cut tour

Some of his haiku appear as if speaking directly to the reader. To quote:

Among the white hairs
a solitary black one
keeps her hope alive

And

She reads my age in
the synthetic dark of moustache
and whitening chest

Singh's haiku have distinct local and Indian cultural flavour too:

Red oleander and
hibiscus calling morning
to Kali

The poet is unconventional in his form. He does not strictly abide by the traditional haiku rules. The adjective in the following poem depicts the unconventionality in the poet's style:

After prolonged heat wave
sky watery explosion
earth lovely doom

The use of the adjective 'lovely' with the noun 'doom' is highly contrastive.

The poet's experimentation with the syllabic pattern is again his break away from the rigid rules. Some of his poems are in 5-7-5 pattern, while the others are in 4-6-4, 3-5-3 and 4-7-4 patterns:

> No letters today
> addresses of his dead friends
> graying in diary

> Monsoon shower
> after a long heat wave
> monotony breaks

> My bedroom
> a maze of cobweb
> spiders breed

> Seeking good news
> I watch the lines on my palms
> taking new turns

This experimentation with the syllabic structure is actually due to the globalization of haiku and thus Singh alone is not to be blamed for it. In fact, it is to be noted here that the varied syllabic structures do not mar the haikuness of his haiku. His three liners, even though roped in different sound patterns/breathe, evoke the images explicitly.

In haiku there is no place for didacticism or philosophy. But Singh tries out even this trait in his poems. To cite-

> He sweeps yellow leaves
> or gathers years in a heap
> burns to merge with dust

The first line gives a clear picture of the persona who is engaged in a task of cleaning the garden. The second line is suggestive of aging or nearing of death or the autumn of one's life whereas the 'yellow leaves' of the first line suggests winter i.e. death. Thus both the lines focus the temporality of all existence, which further gets strengthened in the last line- 'burns to merge with dust'. The last line sounds philosophical and recalls to one's mind the Biblical line-'Thou cometh from dust and thou returneth to dust'. Moreover, the word 'burn' is again related to Hindu rites where the body is brought to the crematorium ground to burn on the funeral pyre. It seems that the poet was all set to bring in the epigrammatic terseness in this haiku. It is to be remembered here that haiku celebrates the beauty of the moment, the truth and minuteness of the moment with clear images rather than witty and layered meanings.

Similarly, the following haiku is highly philosophical in tone:

Long forgotten
the beginning and the end
exist in middles

Except for the three-liner haiku pattern, the lines do not fulfill any of the requirements of a haiku. Neither the reader gets an instant flash of the image nor does he come to a clear idea. He is only left with an option of reading between the lines. And if this is done to a haiku, it is then no haiku. The second line of the poem-'beginning and the end' is here, probably suggestive of the cycle of life and death. And the last line depicts the mediocrity of people in the present times. Man has forgotten the essence of his existence. He is only given to materiality and his comfort zone is his 'present', which he never wants to leave. This haiku is a poor one. In a book review R.K. Singh comments, "It often depresses me to read in the 'form' of haiku moral commands, philosophical teaching, sentimental reflections and didactic expressions. Haiku is not epigrammatic poetry or short saying; nor is it intellectualizing, romanticizing, or pedantry". The poet fails to create a haiku in those three lines; he fails to practice what he says.

Singh puts the first letter of his three liners in capital. Most of his haiku is expressed in a concise and crystallized form, in present tense with a seasonal word. The poems focus on "what is happening" at a particular moment with all its freshness and truth.

Challenging/experimenting with established/classical rules requires a lot of guts. Singh's experiments with the classical rules of haiku and the dexterity with which he handles his haiku are sufficient enough to define his poetic talent /craftsmanship.

WORKS CITED

1. Bijapure, Abdul Rashid. "The Poetry of R.K. Singh," *New Indian English Poetry: An Alternative Voice,* edited by I.K. Sharma, Jaipur: Book Enclave, 2004, p.161.

2. Singh, R. K. Book review. *Deuce: Haiku Poems* (New Delhi: K.K. Publishers and Distributors, 2001) in *Indian Book Chronicle*, vol. 28, no.4 April 2003, p. 5.

3. Mair, Catherine., Patricia Prime & R.K.Singh. *Every Stone Drop Pebble.* New Delhi: Bahri Publications, 1999.

4. Prime, Patricia. "Secrets Need Words: Critical Essay on the Haiku and Tanka of R.K. Singh," *New Indian English Poetry: An Alternative Voice* edited by I.K. Sharma, Jaipur: Book Enclave, 2004.

5. Kaul, Urmila. "Indian Haiku and *Peddling Dream*," *New Indian English Poetry: An Alternative Voice* edited by I.K. Sharma, Jaipur: Book Enclave, 2004.

6. Deodhar, Angelee. " Haiku: An Indian Perspective," http://www.haiku-hia.com

7. http:// tinywords.com

8. ahapoetry.com, Lynx

17

Form and Flow of R. K. Singh's Tanka and Haiku in *The River Returns*

—*Asha Viswas*

R. K. Singh's first collection of poems *My Silence* was published in 1985. Since then he has published eleven more books of poems. His latest is *Sexless Solitude and Other Poems* published from Bareilly in 2009. This means one collection every two years. *The River Returns* (Bareilly: Prakash Book Depot, 2009) is a collection of Tanka and Haiku. It would be relevant here to write briefly about these two forms in which Singh usually writes.

The Art of Tanka Composition

Born in Japan, Tanka is as old as 1300 years. From Japan it traveled to the West and has many lovers in English speaking countries. Tanka is much older than Haiku but younger to Waka. It was first practised in feudal Japan (Heian period) where it was a prerequisite for every courtier to write and appreciate aesthetically beautiful poems. Thus classical tanka reflected the refined tone of Japan's courts and its courtesans. The traditional classical tanka was used to exchange love notes between the lovers. The courtly lover, after spending a night with his lady love, sent a "thank you" note to her in the form of a tanka. The feeling and experience of the previous night was artistically written on a fan or on a stem of a blossom. A messenger delivered these love messages. While this "go between" waited, a tanka, in reply to the love note received, was composed and sent back. The tanka, sent as a relply, was not easy to be composed but the Japanese courtesans had learnt this art to please their lovers. The messages were written in a language which could be understood and appreciated only by the lover.

These morning love note became so famous that contests were held for reading and writing of the tanka, and Japanese emperors ordered the collection of these short love notes.

This traditional expression of passion has undergone great change in the present times. What has not changed is its number of syllables. In Japan it is still written in 31 syllabic units, 5-7-5-7-7. Tanka written in English does not follow this syllabic pattern and often uses less than 31 syllables. As far as the subject matter of modern tanka, specially the tanka written in English, is concerned, it can now be any human emotion expressed in simple language. Images are used to express human emotion. In his article " From Haiku to Tanka : Reversing Poetical History" Gerald St. Maur writes :

> In going beyond the experience of the moment, the tanka takes us from delight to fulfillment, from insight to comprehension, and psycho-organism to love; in general, from the spontaneous to the measured. To achieve this requires a fundamental shift in emphasis : from glimpse to gaze , from first sight to exploration, ... from awareness to perspective... to compose a tanka is to articulate reflectively... it takes us from the simple to the complex. More pointedly, it moves us from the poetry of the noun to the poetry of the verb; in weaving terms, from the thread to the tapestry; in botanical terms, from seed to plant, in chemical terms, from element to compound ; in painting terms, from sketch to picture; and in musical termsfrom chord to melody.[1]

Tanka, as a lyrical form, uses figurative language and is autobiographical in tone. It creates a balance between the self and the outside world. The outward phenomenon is used as a backdrop to express the inner world. Tanka is not rhymed, its one is elevated and it never becomes vulgar in themes.

Contents and Structure of Haiku

Haiku, in its present form, is only 300 years old but Hokku, the original form, is as old as the Mahayana Buddhism. Buddhism accepts the limitations of language owing to its human origin. Nagarjuna believed that language can refer only to those objects that are mortal. It fails to reach the truth of things. This conviction that metaphysical assertions cannot be made through ordinary language is accepted by Ch'an Buddhism. It was for this reason that Ch'an tradition invented new ways to use language that could help the seeker in his search for liberation.

One of the Ch'an masters Yun-men wen-yen(862-949) was known for his one word answers to questions. These short answers revealed his spontaneous reactions to questions, rather than well thought out, premeditated answers. In spite of their limitations, words are not completely useless. Language becomes transmuted by the attainment of realization. Dogen calls such enlightened words "dotoku". Yet another important thing in Ch'an Buddhism was the way they looked at nature. Dogen believed that mountains and rivers are 'sutras' or texts.[2] The entire world is a sacred text and nonsentient objects of nature can act as preachers of these sacred texts. This wordless preaching of nature cannot be heard with one's ears but with one's eyes.

Hokku retains both these features – the spirituality and deep understanding of nature. It focuses on the essence of an object or an event in nature without the intrusion of the poet that would distort the reality. The perception in hokku is an intuitive one and not an 'I'/ 'other', subject/object kind of process. Being rooted in Zen, Hokku is nonintellectual, has no faith in reason and words. It emphasizes all that is natural and concrete, It is also a pure experience of enlightenment (Satori).

From Hokku to Haiku has been a long journey. The early translators of haiku into English were R.H. Blyth and Harold G. Henderson. Blyth's four volumes of haiku were published in 1949 and Henderson's in 1959. Both these translators differ in their views about haiku. While Blyth believed that Zen is at the center of haiku, Henderson stated :

> Primarily, it (haiku) is a poem; and being a poem it is intended to express and to evoke emotion … it may be noted in passing that the use of 'ki'(season) is probably at the base of a charge that has been advanced that haiku are more concerned with nature than with human affairs. Such a statement is ridiculous.
>
> Haiku are more concerned with human emotions than with human acts, and natural phenomena are used to reflect human emotions… [3]

While Henderson believes that subjective human emotions are the most important part of a haiku, Blyth rules out subjectivity. In contemporary haiku even technology is accepted as a form of nature. Thus the meaning of nature is completely changed. While Blyth believes in the spiritual effect of nature, Pizzarelli plays with the word 'nature' and completely disassociates it from the outward phenomenon :

> To say that nature is all and all is nature,
> that the substance of this planet, the universe is of
> one nature is also to conclude that nothing is
> unnatural
> or artificial.[4]

Apart from their contradictory views about the content of a haiku, the modern practitioners of this form differ in their use of punctuation also. While some use minimal punctuation, others, imitating Ezra Pound and Company, use no punctuation at all. Thus each practitioner of haiku has become the arbiter of content and structure of his verse. There is no prescriptive critic now who can say this is/ not a haiku because it does not use/uses spirituality, has / has not nature, does not use/ uses punctuation.

R. K. Singh's Sensuous Tanka

In the light of this discussion of traditional and contemporary tanka and haiku, we can study R. K. Singh's collection of poems *The River Returns*. The title of the collection is taken from his haiku No. 347 – "Dancing/ a few muddied crocs:/the river returns". In his preface Singh confesses that he seeks to be "visual or sensuous" and has tried to express :

> natural concrete action or object or
> experiences from one's whole being , and
> does not'fake' poetic feelings or render
> fictitious or imaginative experience ...
> I have tried to evoke the essence of the
> moment in its sensory details as selflessly
> as possible. Even as I appear to speak
> directly, the subjective and the objective
> tend to mix up.[5]

The first section of the collection consists of 144 tanka. This section begins with spring season and ends with summer and dust storms. The poet is left "awaiting the wave/that will wash away empty hours/and endless longing." With spring comes love. Love (*kama*) is predominantly associated with the renewal of the world, the spring. The voluptuous spring time brings in the biological rite of the amorous play. Love is presented in its dual aspect – separation and union. The anonymous woman of the first few pages is seen waiting for the love tryst. Each of these early tanka is a visual of her different emotions. Her yearning for the lover is augmented by the song of the Koel (the basic emotion of love is aroused in tanka 1) . The promise of a love tryst makes her face glow with passion. (The basic emotion changes into passion in tanka 2). Tanka 3 presents her as a teasing wanton waxing and waning like the moon (the pleasure of feeling). From tanka 4 to tanka 10 her loneliness and sadness (the basic emotion of grief in separation) is depicted. The season of spring is simultaneously a source of misery and delight. Separated from her lover, the woman is presented as a conventional "Virahini" . She is delpressed, she weeps, she is afraid of going to bed alone and wants to die. In tanka 10 her loneliness is presented through an apt visual :

At the river
she folds her arms and legs
resting her head
upon the knees and sits
as an island

This love in separation ends by the 12th tanka. From tanka 15 love in union is presented in all its boldness. Singh revisits his favourite trope.

In tanka 13 we move from separation to union, "after three decades love waves/tense the flesh and rock the night". Singh surpasses others in the description of fragmented female anatomy. The reader is brought to the key hole to peep at the "erect nipples" (tanka 15), "foamy water... sting her vulva/a jelly fish passed/ through the crotch making her shy", (tanka 16), "nude dance.../ to match upstanding/ nipples under the blouse" (tanka 18).

As in conventional love-in-union, Singh's woman, too, is bashful :

When I wanted to change

seats my friend said she can
only if the door is locked
the light out and her mom
in another city (tanka 20)

She is also presented as a wanton who takes delight in the love play and the amatory art. In tanka 102 she "loves the etching on skin/ to enhance nudity".

The traditional tanka expressed the emotions of the lovers, specially their grief resulting from their separation, their desire for reunion, sadness caused by old age, unhappy present and absence of the lover. Singh's collection of tanka too presents this basic contrariety between pleasure and grief. Intense love fills the lover with fear. First, there is fear of rejection:

Roses await
sun and wind to clear
the baleful fog :
I fear she'll say no
to my love again (tanka 72)

A number of tanka depict night and nightmare. Darkness and light are archetypal symbols and denote the duality of flesh and spirit, female and male, unconscious and conscious, evil and good, *tamas* and *rajas* etc. In Singh there is only one tanka (No. 15) which shows the lovers together at night- "You and I alive/in cold winter night feeling/ warmth of your body..." In the rest of these short poems, night is the backdrop of fear, grief, loneliness, physical pain etc. In tanka 39 it is night that turns his dreams "to nightmare/again fear grips my soul/ I sense her presence around". In tanka 49 the lover's loneliness during night is vividly described. Thus :

My hand held out
in the dark remained empty:
no one reached it
to give joy of
the meeting hands

In the absence of the loved one, the lover is haunted by her memories. Each object of nature, specially the flowers and their fragrance, brings back her memories. In tanka 69 it is the "little petals to the ground/ echoing our first embrace". In tanka 138 " her letter smells/ the lotus she wore each time/meeting in the dark". The lotus image here is brought from Indian erotics where it was a representative of the force and energy inherent in the waters. Water was also regarded as a female substance and the lotus was associated with similar creative female principle. The lotus image in Singh does not have a tensive quality. It suggests only the erotic and sensuous and hence the smell of lotus causes the separated lover to grieve. Memories of the past (happy days) rise like ghosts and turn the heart into stone :

> Ghosts rise to mate
> in moonlight tear the tombs
> frighten with fingers
> rhino horns rock the center
> granite sensation (tanka 39)

This reminds us of Shelley's lines :

> Forget the dead, the past
> Oh yet there are ghosts,
> the memories that make
> the heart a tomb.

Besides this grief and pain that result from separation, we also find sadness in Singh on account of old age, asthma and insomnia. Tanka 58 shows him as " an insomniac/ weak with desires" while in No. 89 "wrinkles on the skin" remind him " of time's passage". In No 108 " asthmatic bouts haunt" him. In 119 he is again " down with stroke". Tanka 120 presents him as an old man thinking of death

> Aging he thinks of
> the ashes and the long trip
> ahead in spirit
> feels the earth he would
> become celebrating life

"Allergic asthma" recurs in No. 134. In No. 142 "dust storm and rain shatter/all hopes hanging by snapped wire".

Amid this scenario of separation and union of lovers hyphenated by hope for reunion and depression at separation, a few visuals of conjugal love come as a jarring note. The lover, who was heard singing the "body's song"(54), finds his voice "brown like autumn/ crushed in noisesI can't /understand..." (95). There is no love between them and they sleep with their "backs to each other" (87). In spite of being together, there is no understanding between them :

One thousand miles
travelling together
in tense silence
he and she contemplate
the next round of duel (tanka 111)

To escape the boredom of these scenes, one can come to such intense sensuous visuals as :

A cloud - eagle
curves to the haze
in the west
skimming the sail
on soundless sea (tanka 45)

Singh is capable of creating pure poetry where nature is left to itself but observed from a close angle. It is not a glance but a gaze.

R. K. Singh's Haiku for All Seasons

The second section of *The River Returns* consists of 372 haiku. The collection begins with a dash of bright colours — hibiscus, oleanders, rose, chrysanthemum, and ends with three visuals of rainbow. Here Singh gives us sequences and each sequence is related to a season. It is reminiscent of Bhojpuri cycles of seasons called " Barahmasa", the traditional folk poetry from eastern India that celebrates seasonal changes and diverse moods of nature. In Singh's haiku too this cycle begins with spring. In the vernal symbol there is a translucence of primary principles. Hibiscus, in the very first haiku, becomes a description of the male element: "Love tickles/with erect pistil/hibiscus," while oleander stands for the female element. This vernal union of male and female elements at the natural level reconciles union at human level. This depiction of flora also gives life to an interior landscape – there is a whole gamut of human emotions.

Even the winter season is not presented in its negative shade. We have a crystal pure visual of the snow covered hill :

Veiling her breasts
with the seasons first snows
the hill blushes

Singh tries to strike a balance between the personal and social concerns yet most of the times it is the personal that is privileged over the public. In this section also there is recurrence of old motifs – monotony of married life (49, 180, 181), shadow of old age (61), his loneliness and asthma (74, 90, 97, 114, 207, 208, 209). From haiku 150 to 200 there is love play and female body, sometimes covered:

Her shapely figure
in orange blouse and blue jeans
strained at the hips (22)

and sometimes bare :

Rain-soaked sun
sheds its sultry light :
her bare back

In his Preface Singh clearly says that he does not make any difference between haiku and senryu, so we cannot criticize his miniature poems for the absence of the 'satori' state of consciousness.

As an old practitioner of haiku, Singh no longer adheres to the 5-7-5 syllabic structure and makes minimal use of punctuation.

All lovers of tanka and haiku would love to read this collection.

WORKS CITED

1. Maur. Gerald St. "From Haiku to Tanka : Reversing Poetical History" , (TSA Newsletter, II : I , Spring 2001.)
2. Dogen Zenji, Shobagenzo (The Eye and Treasury of the True Law) Vols. Trans. Kosen Nishiyama (Tokyo: Nakayama Shobo,1986), Vol. I, p. 105.
3. Henderson, Harold G. *An Introduction to Haiku* (New York : Doubleday, 1958), pp. 2, 5.
4. Pizzarelli, Alan. *A Haiku Path* (New York : Haiku Society of America, 1994), p. 116.
5. Singh, R.K. *The River Returns* (Bareilly: Prakash Book Depot, 2006), pp. 1 –2.

18

Snapshots of Life in *The River Returns*

— Patricia Prime

All poetry is – or should be – written in love of the world. All poetry is in some sense erotic. The act of love, as opposed to lust, and the act of the imagination, as opposed to technological invention, occupy the same area of human consciousness. They are acts of mutuality and exchange, from which all participants derive value and understanding, and so are indispensable. Yet they are human endeavours too, and always contain the germ of their own impossibility and failure, which is the theme of many of the tanka and haiku contained in Ram Krishna Singh's *The River Returns*. *The River Returns* is divided into two parts, tanka and haiku.

At some point in his writing career Singh has taken note of the performance of language, learned to appreciate the subtleties of emphasis, tone, placement of words; of images called forth by carefully selected words. The level of diction is simple and consistent, especially considering that even though its imagery is natural, the poems are primarily made up of straightforward observations. Plain language, and repetition reinforce the simple nature of haiku and tanka, whilst simultaneously undercutting the philosophical or rational nature of the poems' construct. In this sense, the poems may look casual and simplistic whilst disguising the fact that they are heartfelt, both emotionally and intellectually, as we see in the following tanka:

Stains of dried dewy
tears on the eyelids tell of
the load on her mind:
clothed in spring the willow twigs
reveal the changed relation (*The River Returns*, p.4)

Living in dust smoke
and white darkness I know
I just flicker –

stand alone like a lighthouse
lost in the fog of seashore

This is what tanka is all about: a momentary embrace of the mystery inherent in the process of self-actualisation; a disguised direct address begging forgiveness for those tendencies towards insularity and over-intellectualisation. A celebration of the difficulties of selfhood, or whatever it is in us that calls us to a greater awareness of ourselves and the world of which we are a part, as described in the following tanka:

Standing at the edge
I long to float with waves and
wave with instant wind:
on the dream water's breast
I read tomorrow's wonder

An insomniac
weak with desires and prayers
hears the heartbeats
rising fast with dark hours
survives one more nightmare

In these two poems the poet casts around for some kind of relief, some sign of hope. The first tanka takes place at the moment when the poet, standing on the shore, allows his mind to wander over various thoughts. One of them is the longing "to float with waves", another is that he sees on "the water's breast" what the future has in store. In the second poem, Singh lies awake reviewing the day's events, surviving through the night to face yet another day. All these thoughts and more flash through the poet's mind. Yet neither the chattering of the mind, nor the thousands of thoughts that teem in his brain, can alter the fact that there on the foreshore, or awake at night, or in the midst of daily trauma, something of life's beauty can still be captured.

The following poem seems to come out of nowhere:

Drinking evening star
blue green patterns before eyes
no meditation
no god visits to forgive
the sinning soul in solitude

The poet may speak of not knowing how, or why, he has been forsaken. He wrote the poem. It speaks from the unconscious, the hidden recesses of the mind: the proverbial experience, the forgotten, the repressed. The poem seeks to bring precise expression to something previously unstated. In this respect, then, the tanka tells us "This is what is inside you. This is what it is all about".

For Singh, writing is an art of discovery. Some events, some people, are, for him, so charged with passionate complexity, that only the process of verbalising them allows him any measure of understanding. He writes about what he knows, getting it factually correct, then follows where the words and music lead. For example;

His first winter –
recalls swirling snowflakes
at Chaluka
inside the fibrehut
warmth of blue waves surging

There's a quantitive and geographic fact: "Chaluka", where the hard fact of "place" distinguishes the landscape and transforms it by art to a dreamlike state.

In the following tanka the action takes place on the war front:

From the border rings
he's stationed dangerously:
any moment war
may break out for their follies
he must kill and live ... to kill

The images of war suggest that the soldier's innocence is short-lived. It has the quality of a bad dream where the young man "must kill and live ... to kill", a plot that turns on the presence of evil, cruelty, and death. Thus the tanka assume a larger role – one of discovery of self, the responsibility they bring having thus embraced humanity in all its good and all its dirt and corruption. Knowing and having lived with ill health and in darkness, the poet can savour both the light and bitter experiences that life brings. So loneliness appears microscopic as one of life's problems:

Awaiting the wave
that'll wash away empty hours
and endless longing
in this dead silence at sea
I pull down chunks of sky

Life can either get better or worse. Life's flame can either be extinguished or kept ablaze for the greater responsibility that ensues.

In section two – Haiku – whatever the details of the short poem say about life and art can only be apprehended and expressed aslant; indirectly and, therefore, incompletely – the reader must fill in any gaps and make his/her own judgment. "Haiku moments" are everyday experiences. They are not "enlightened" in the ultimate sense of the word. They are, nevertheless, awakenings of a sort; moments in which the deeper nature of things is revealed, when one is reminded of the beauty and mystery that lie just beneath the surface of the seemingly mundane.

Haiku generally deal with everyday things – birds, flowers, the moon, nature. Yet they reveal these things to be mysterious and extraordinary. Haiku also tend to be contemplative and reflective – that is, the insights they contain and the experiences they describe are the fruits not of judgment but of quiet observation, not of self-seeking effort but of humble acceptance.

Allow me to quote just two haiku:

The lone hibiscus
waits for the sun to bloom:
morning's first offering

What a lovely haiku! In these three short lines we see the poet early in the morning, watching as the flower waits for the sun to arise, then we see that this is the first offering of the day made by a religious man.

In the well
studying her image
a woman

For me this conjures an image of a villager, who perhaps doesn't own a mirror, at the well drawing the day's water. She sees her reflection in the still water and looks at in wonder and admiration.

Because, like the original experience, the sum of the details are unspecific, as in "Without washing hands / he touches hibiscus for worship / her frowning glance", the reader is asked to make up his or her own mind about the haiku. What it means for the reader may be entirely different from the original thought of the poet. The death that is part of nature that we see in "Not sad to die / blooming after a day's rain –/ the mushroom", might cause us to ask: Are death and life the same thing in the context of the poem? Does Singh mean to express that the brevity of the mushroom's life is heightened by its refreshing wash of rain, even as we can be ecstatic in the midst of the thoughts of inevitable death and decay? In fact, the poem doesn't, I think, exclude this possibility and remains therefore true to itself.

Can art, either in writing or speech, driven to the level of the fabulous by intensity of desire, transcend mortality? Can it redeem or compensate for the indignities of ill health, physical labour or pain? These are themes that drive Singh's haiku. The eroticism of many of Singh's haiku have been previously remarked upon, but in this collection he puts a hard spin on traditional themes. The mortality, redemption and immortality of the poet seem to be uppermost in his mind, as in "Fearing allergies / he misses full moon party / savours white light".

In both the poems and in everyday reality, life is crumbling into dust. Indeed, in "The long night passes / sleeplessly I deep-breathe - / mosquitoes in bed", the poem seems to say all our lives are neither more nor less than "long nights" spent sleepless. In "the lone poet / watching his interview - / two minutes fame" there is the reprieve of "two minutes fame", against the final collapse and there's the possibility of, if not immortality, at least honour through art.

Singh's Prefactory Note to *The River Returns* includes the sentence: "In these selected tanka and haiku – at times providing sequences – I have tried to evoke the essence of the moment in its sensory details as selflessly as possible." Our world needs more of that awareness. We could all do with more tanka and haiku moments in our lives. We can discover these moments if we learn to live simply, sit quietly and observe with open eyes and hearts.

Perhaps dreams are all, as this collection seems to suggest: "A dead voice / calling up at dawn: / drowsy eyes". Perhaps the work done, no matter how mundane, or how grand, is the song and the dance, and the lines and scars we bear from it dignify. And perhaps poetry honours this wild dream of living.

WORK CITED

1. Singh, R.K. *The River Returns*, Bareilly: Prakash Book Depot, 2006.

19

Haiku and R. K. Singh: A Critical Analysis of *Peddling Dream*

— K. V. Dominic

As a poet, critic and editor, the immense contribution R. K. Singh has given to Indian English Literature and through it to World Literature is praiseworthy. Without any set norm or pattern, not concentrating particularly on any theme, without even naming the poems, but only numbering them, he goes on writing on all aspects of human life, on Nature and Universe, on abstract and concrete. As D. G. Rossetti and his Pre-Raphaelite Brotherhood have written vividly on the beauty of human body, R. K. Singh also praises the Creator, extolling the beauty of human body in many of his poems. Prof. Singh writes about it thus: “”don’t condemn me if I am not white” . . . “I love Him through the bodies He made” (p.i). I. K Sharma in his Foreword to R. K. Singh’s book *Sexless Solitude and Other Poems* compliments the poet aptly thus:

> Well-read in the important literary classics of India, well-trained in the use of English language, well-versed in modern western thoughts, Dr. Singh articulates his perceptions, his experiences, in a very unconventional way. Not at all shy of using words associated with sex , he puts them to different uses in his poems. It makes purists of literature believe that the poet is a shameless hawker of sex in the street of literature. His poems, they think, have soiled the white house (not the White House) of literature. Such persons in fact suffer from agoraphobia. (p. i)

Some poetasters and orthodox critics attacked Rossetti and his group calling them ‘Fleshly School of Poets’. Similarly we find such wrong-headed critics attacking R. K. Singh as a hawker of sex. In the ocean of the poems Singh has written, one can not accuse him of any obsession with sex, rather he touches that aspect also because sex is divine, sexual feelings are divine and sexual organs are divine.

I agree to the opinion of Dr Lyle Glazier of Bennington, Vermont, USA: "R. K. Singh writes with the directness of an overheard whisper, or a wind through trees, a ripple in a stream, or a cry in the street after dark" (qtd. in Krishna Srinivas). What Krishna Srinivas has written of genuine poets is quite true of R. K. Singh. In the words of Srinivas, "To the poet, the world is an extension of himself—his flesh, his blood, his bones. Poetical modernity is expressing its freedom of form, of structure, of imagery and idea" ("Foreword", p. i).

R. K. Singh is a poet specialised in economy of expression and brevity. *Every Stone Drop Pebble* (1999), *Peddling Dream* (2003) and *The River Returns* (2006) are his collections of haiku. *Every Stone Drop Pebble* contains fifty seven haiku, *Peddling Dream* has one hundred and ninety one haiku, and *The River Returns* bears two hundred and ninety five haiku. In addition to that there are one hundred and twenty nine haiku titled under *Some More Haiku*. There are also fifteen haiku sequences with the title *Some Haiku Sequences*. About R. K. Singh's haiku, Abdul Rashid Bijapure writes:

> Perhaps it is the single-minded journey of R. K. Singh to press for brevity in expression that leads him to devote his poetic energy to the three line Haiku poems. Even Singh says "a Haiku is terse, dynamic and complete poetry, rendering the vital energy, which animates not only an individual's small world but also the entire cosmos." For Singh it is rather a self-disciplining spiritual exercise marked by living momentness of a moment, imaging a moment.' (qtd. in Rajni Singh, p. 3).

In order to examine the haiku of R. K. Singh it is essential to reflect on this poetic form.

Haiku: Its features

Haiku originally is a Japanese form of poetry consisting of seventeen *moras* or *on*, in three metrical phrases of five, seven and five *moras* respectively. Haiku contain a *kigo*, or seasonal reference, and a *kireji* or verbal caesura, i.e., pause or break after each metrical phrase. In Japanese, haiku are printed in a single vertical line, while in English usually they appear in three lines. The famous verses of Japanese masters like Matsuo Basho, Yosa Buson, and Kobayashi Issa in the Edo-period (1600-1868) are properly referred to as *hokku. Hokku* was given the name Haiku by the Japanese writer Masaoka Shiki at the end of the 19th century.

There is no fixed format or subject matter for English haiku. The common features that are found in English haiku are the following:

1. Use of three (or fewer) lines of seventeen or fewer syllables
2. Use of lines as breath groups with number of syllables 5-7-5 or lesser in number
3. Use of a season word or *kigo*
4. Use of verbal caesura to bring out contrast or comparison
5. Use of caesura at the end of either the first or second line, but seldom at both
6. The three lines never make a complete or run-on sentence
7. Always written in the present tense of here and now
8. Limited use (or non-use) of personal pronouns
9. Use of common sentence syntax in both phrases
10. Use of sentence fragments
11. Writing about ordinary things in an ordinary way using ordinary language
12 Use of concrete images
13 Use no punctuation or normal sentence punctuation

While traditional Japanese haiku concentrate on Nature and humans in it, some modern haiku poets, in Japan, India and the West, take a broader range of subject matter suitable, including urban contexts. While traditional haiku avoided themes of sex and overt violence, contemporary haiku sometimes deal with them. In the words of Jane Reichhold:

> The fact that the smallest literary form—haiku—has the most rules never ceases to amaze and astound. The only real comfort one can find in this situation is the concept that this affords a wider range of rules from which a writer can pick and choose. You cannot follow all of the rules and several of them are so contradictory that there is no way to honor them

> both at once. You must always choose. In order to make a choice, you have to understand the reasons and methods. ("Haiku: How to Write Haiku")

There is no set syllabic pattern in the contemporary English haiku. Instead of the traditional 5-7-5 pattern, contemporary poets do not follow any pattern at all. R. K. Singh speaks on his haiku pattern thus:

> Now I do not adhere to the 5-7-5 syllables, nor do I make any difference between haiku and senryu. I just practise haiku in different beats (3-5-3; 4-6-4; 5-7-5) or free-form haiku, and when possible, expand its lyrical content to a tanka in five lines without restricting myself to 5-7-5-7-7 rhythm. As readers will bear me out, it is possible to convey so much within the 3- or 5-line span of the short-long-short or short-long-short-long-long flow of the haiku or tanka rhythm. It is also possible to elevate the quotidian experiences to the level of poetry, using the medium of haiku and tanka, provided one seeks to be visual or sensuous, or expresses natural concrete action or object, or experiences from ones whole being, and does not 'fake' poetic feelings or render fictitious or imaginative experiences. (Prefatory Note, p. 1)

The Haiku of R. K. Singh:

Singh's haiku collection entitled, *Peddling Dream* was originally published in *Pacem in Terris*, a trilogy collection, in 2003 and later republished in *Collected Poems 1974 – 2009*. Of the one hundred and ninety one haiku in *Peddling Dream,* none could be written off as silly or ordinary. Majority of haiku are on Nature, the magic of different seasons, how man goes hand in hand with Nature and reflections and echoes of Nature on man. The opening word of each of his haiku starts with a capital letter and there is often a caesura after the second line. For instance, the present haiku:

> 'A star shines bright
> beside the crescent moon:
> she fakes a smile'

The lines are quite suggestive. The very shape of the moon—crescent—reminds the reader of a smiling face. The moon is not happy at the presence of the bright star beside her because the star is more beautiful and brilliant than the moon. Hence the fake smile. No doubt the celestial moon is gentler than millions of moons on earth who turn their faces out of jealousy when such earthly stars appear before them. The punctuation mark of colon at the end of the second line is a connector of the first two lines to the third, with an additional function of explaining the third line.

In the haiku:

> 'Shaking hands
> couldn't part with the henna
> on her palms'

the poet speaks about the eternal relationships that cannot be parted with mere shake hands. Out of warmth of the shaking palms the henna got stained to the lover's palm. Naturally, like the henna, their love also will stick onto their hearts forever. The abstract idea of love and friendship is concretized well in this haiku. The next haiku, though seemingly funny, laughs at our lazy nature:

> 'Reluctant to climb
> the spiral staircase —
> bathing in kitchen'

Not willing to take pains, people are prone to lead low and average lives, just eating, sleeping and procreating. In the following haiku loneliness is measured to the sipping of coffee. The punctuation mark of dash at the end of the second line acts as a semantic marker of cause and effect: the third line is the effect of the first and second lines.

> 'Measures loneliness
> sip by sip
> at dining table'

Loneliness is something intolerable and hence the poet compares it to the sipping of a very hot coffee, eager to finish it soon and then leave the hall. The abstract idea of loneliness is visualized elegantly by the poet in the following haiku:

> 'Thick dust on leaves
> unwashed by rains for days —
> stagnant time'

This haiku speaks about the stark reality of drought which many parts of India face now. The drought, the poet believes, is man-made. Even though there has been continuous rain for several days, the dust on the leaves could not be washed out as the dust formation was very thick. The time is stagnant because there is no change in the nature. It is still hot summer, in spite of the rains. The rain cannot make any impact on nature. 'Thick dust on leaves' is a kigo phrase connoting the concrete image of the summer season. The punctuation mark of dash at the end of the second line is a very powerful semantic marker as it indicates that the first and second lines are the explanation of the third line.

'Chilly night
no soul on the road
guard at gate'

In the above haiku, the poem seems to be very considerate and humane. It is winter season; and night also. No human being is found outside the buildings, except the guard at gate. If people cannot go outside why should there be a guard at the gate? To guard against whom? Animals? The disregard and cruelty shown by the middle class and upper class to the working class is portrayed in this haiku. 'Chilly night,' 'no soul on the road' are kigo phrases standing for concrete images of winter season. In the following haiku:

'Welcoming the sun
dew drops on dry leaves—
an epitaph'

In the above haiku, the dew drops are longing for the appearance of the sun. They have been remaining as epitaph of the dry leaves throughout night, as lonely as in a cemetery. Hence they welcome the sun. The punctuation mark of dash at the end of the second line reveals that the first two lines are explanatory of the third line. Mark the beauty of the lines:

'A tiny spider
on the marigold sucking
its golden hue'

Unlike the conventional beautiful creatures in nature, a spider is portrayed by the poet, extolling the beauty of sucking golden hue from a marigold. R. K. Singh, like all great poets, believes that there is nothing ugly in this universe because God has created them. 'A tiny spider,' 'marigold' and 'golden hue' are kigo phrases standing for concrete images of the spring season. The haiku:

'A load of wood
on her frail back
autumn evening'

Here is a picture of a weak woman carrying a heavy load of wood on her frail back. This also is a regular sight in the villages of India. Winter is approaching and hence firewood has to be collected and stored for the season in autumn itself. The patriarchy has condemned women to do all the household works and even if they are sick and weak they are destined to do all such activities. It is their duty to look after the family. The poet seems to attack this evil trend. 'A load of wood on her frail back' is a concrete image of the autumn season, a usual sight at country sides.

'On a cycle
he sells bouquets and roses
peddling dreams'

In the above haiku a flower vendor is portrayed selling bouquets and roses on his cycle. The caesura after the second line brings out the contrast of ideas. Even though he is selling tokens of dreams and love, in his own life he has only unfulfilled dreams, and while he is selling such realities he is destined to have only fantasies, and that is what he does while peddling. The poet's humaneness and commitment to the society is reflected in these lines. The plight and futile dreams of the poor people are visualized in this beautiful haiku.

'The mirror is so small
I can't see the ocean
beyond my own look'

The above haiku proclaims that what we see, learn and understand is little. There is a vast ocean beyond, which is hidden to us. Our own ego hinders us from seeking the ocean of truth. We look at own reflection and feel content. The following haiku carries undercurrents of violence in religion:

'Silent Ram sheds
tears over the bodies burnt
in temple's name'

The statue of Ram, mute and helpless, sheds tears over the blood spilled and bodies burnt in His own name. As most of the terrorism is done in the name of God, and religious mafia dictates the world as such, this haiku is very relevant to the present century. An attack on the terrorists is found in the next haiku:

> 'Violence breeders
> climb power ladder —
> peace stings'

The terrorists, using power—military as well as religious and political—climb up the ladder to dictate the world and annihilate Peace; but Peace stings them like gnats. The caesura at the end of the second line followed by the dash brings out the antithesis of violence and peace. The terrorists are bound to climb down, and the poet believes that it is being happening in this world. The ultimate victory is that of Peace. Two abstract terms of "violence" and "peace" are beautifully concretized in this haiku. The following three liners in a very subtle way bring forth the crude realities of the world:

> 'Tears invisible
> on his water face
> Buddha meditates'

Here the statue of the Buddha is crying invisible to men. The caesura at the end of the second line gives an explanation of the final line. Due to rain, the Buddha's face is wet and hence none can identify the tears running through his cheeks. The Buddha can't but shed tears when he meditates on what is happening in this bloody world. The prophet of Ahimsa sees only blood and dead bodies—both human and non-human—around him. He shuts his eyes and cries over it. Here is a haiku that carries a grey shade:

> 'Through long shadows
> in the morning remembering
> gradual death'

The poet appears to be highly philosophical in the above haiku. He has been watching his own shadow throughout the morning. As morning grows on to noon, his shadow wanes, and it reminds him of the gradual advent of Death. Through the concrete image of shadows the poet explains the abstract idea of the advent of death in this haiku. On the contrary, the next three lines reflect the seven colours of rainbow:

> 'She snuggles up
> in my arms her dimples
> joy of heaven'

The above haiku portrays a love scene. The protagonist finds joy of heaven in the dimples of the lady love when she is cuddled up in his arms. As God is love, and sex is love, the sexual emotion and satisfaction bring heaven on earth. The haiku:

'A moving train —
confined in water bottle
rhythmic ripplets'

is a characteristic image of train journey in India. In summer, when the non-AC bogies of trains are just like furnaces, passengers are destined to drink bottles after bottles of water. The poet synthesizes the rhythm of the train with the rhythm of ripplets while drinking from the bottle. The scorching heat of summer is concretized in this haiku.

'Two toads croaking
in the drain celebrate
sudden shower'

How Nature celebrates the seasons is portrayed in the above haiku. The Creator's bounties are welcomed and greeted more merrily by non-human beings. The materialistic man fails to notice such beauties around him. 'Toads', 'croaking' and 'shower' are kigos of rainy season. In the following lines:

'Basking in the past
they grow backward and yet talk
about the future'

the poet reminds us about the futility of basking in the past. We will only grow backward if we are obsessed with the past achievements and glories. We have to look forward and plan our future. Mere talking about the future plans is not sufficient. The haiku below beautifully captures the mental state of the persona who is indecisive about the way he wants to spend his Sunday morning:

'Lingering in bed:
to go to church or pub —
Sunday morning'

It is Sunday morning. The persona is still lingering in bed with the dilemma: go to church for Sunday Mass or celebrate in a pub. He doesn't find much difference between the options. Rather he may choose the latter as it gives him much enjoyment. In this haiku, the poet seems to criticize the religious rituals and ceremonies devoid of real faith. It is useless to spend time in a church if one has no faith in such practices. The dash at the end of the second line is a semantic symbol, acting as an explanation of the third line. In the haiku:

'Moving shadows
in the silence of the room —
windows rattle'

an abstract thing is concretized in the above haiku. The huge shadows which got into the silent room through the narrow bars of the window rattle the bars. R. K. Singh's high imagination is visible here. The beauty it imparts is superb. The caesura and the dash at the end of the second line act as cause and effect of the lines before and after them. The haiku:

'Facing the sun
the lone flower
dying to bloom'

presents the pathetic sight of a lone flower longing to bloom, but destined to die. All the other flowers have died and fallen. The intolerable heat of the sun and the absence of water cause the flower to wither and die. 'Sun', 'flower', and 'bloom' are kigos of spring and summer.

'They take off again
their unthrown nets frighten fish—
water turns whiter'

Fishing is satisfying and pleasurable to the fishermen. But how it is frightening and shocking to fish and sea is portrayed in the above haiku. It is very mysterious why man is so cruel and unsympathetic to one of the meekest and most beautiful creatures—fish. He is sometimes sympathetic to his domestic animals but never to fish. Even the nature lovers have no love left to fish. The sea turns whiter and pale when the nets touch the surface. The sea is shocked at the atrocity of the fishermen. The dash at the end of the second line acts as a semantic marker of cause and effect. The haiku:

'Only two of us—
and a big house with roaming
rats and cockroaches'

is an attack on the wealthy peoples' craze of building mansions where only an old man and his wife live. Their children are employed abroad or in any remote cities. The house has become a status symbol to the Indians where they spend millions to compete with their neighbours. The palatial rooms where humans seldom tread have become haunting places for rats, cockroaches and spiders. The dash at the end of the first line expresses the effect of the idea of first line on the following lines. The concrete image in the haiku portrays the tragic fate of today's nuclear family.

'Chess of love:
checkmate before
playing the game'

In the above haiku, the poet compares love to a game of chess. Since the path of love is crooked and full of obstacles and hindrances, every step or movement meets with a checkmate. He who conquers checkmate comes out victorious in love. The colon at the end of the first line acts as definition or explanation of the first line as expressed in the following lines. Through the concrete image of the game of chess the poet has explained an abstract idea. The poet picks up a very sensitive issue in the following haiku:

'The holy Ganges
tolerates the city's garbage
even rape and death'

The pathetic situation of our rivers, especially holy rivers is portrayed in this haiku. It seems that the majority of the Indians believe that God has created rivers to dispose their garbage. Fully aware that it is the same water that they have to drink, they throw away their waste to the rivers. The holy river Ganges is destined to carry hundreds of dead bodies every day. The poor river has also to bear the screams of several rapes done on her lap. Even in the twenty first century, Indians are not a bit saved from the superstitions. Taking the Ganges as holy, they dispose the dead bodies in it so that the souls of the bodies will get Moksha. Religious leaders or religious mafia are to be blamed for cultivating such superstitions in the minds of the illiterate laymen and thus exploiting them through unnecessary rituals and ceremonies.

'Cloud over cloud
darken earth and hide stars:
dawn and dusk one'

Here is another tragic and appalling sight caused by indiscriminate industrialization. The cities are always overcast by the poisonous fumes of factories and vehicles. The sun, the moon and the stars are seldom visible. There is no difference between dawn and dusk. Rather it is always monotonous dusk. The poet, a social critic, invites our attention to this dangerous situation. The colon at the end of the second line is a semantic marker expressing cause and effect. Through concrete images the poet has pictured the horrible face of modern cities.

Like a magician with a magical wand, Prof. R. K. Singh has wielded these short lines of triplets with an enchanting effect. The readers are tempted to run their eyes over them again and again. It is the grand images which make his haiku splendid rather than the rhythm and music of words. Though alliteration and assonance are rare, the readers are bewitched by the grandeur of high imagination. Beyond any doubt, R. K. Singh haiku sensibility aligns him with the dexterous haiku writers of the world.

WORKS CITED

1. Reichhold, Jane. "Haiku: How to Haiku." Web. 10 Feb. 2010. <http://www.ahapoetry.com/HAIKU.HTM>.
2. Sharma, I. K. Foreword. *Sexless Solitude and Other Poems*. By R. K. Singh. Bareilly: Prakash Book Depot, 2009, pp. i-iii.
3. Singh, Rajni. "Haiku of R. K. Singh." *Muse India*. Issue 17, Jan-Feb 2008. Web. 10 Feb. 2010. <http://www.museindia.com/showfeature6.asp?id=818>
4. Singh, R. K. *Collected Poems 1974 – 2009*. Jaipur: Book Enclave, 2009. (haiku quoted in this paper are from this anthology)
5. ____ ______, Prefatory Note. *The River Returns: A Collection of Tanka and Haiku*. Bareilly: Prakash Book Depot, 2006.
6. Srinivas, Krishna. Foreword. *My Silence*. By R. K. Singh. Madras: Poets Press India, 1985.

20

Flashes from Flesh in R. K. Singh's *The River Returns*

— Sudhir K. Arora

Haiku, much contested Japanese term because of its various contradictory formats, is a 5-7-5 onji (syllables) verse. It is considered to be an offshoot of Tanka, (also known as waka or uta) a short poem of 31 onji or syllables in 5-7-5-7-7. Later, tanka gave way to a linked verse renga which formed a split. The first part (hokku) of 5-7-5 was written by one poet while the remaining (haikai) of 7-7 was written by another as a reply to the first part. The process continued. The form came into prominence in the last years of the 19th century. Basho (pseudonym of Matsuo Munefusa, 1644-94) and Kobayashi Issa (pseudonym of Kobayashi Nobuyuki, 1763-1828) were the gifted masters of this form. Their verses, which arc known and read as haiku today were referred to as hokku. It was the successful attempt of Masaoka Shiki who coined a new term haiku from hokku and haikai and made the three line verse of 5-7-5 independent from being a part of a longer chain of renga. Shiki's reform, which begun in 1892 resulted in its new independent poetic form. But, the change in division of 17 onji in the form of 5-7-5 and incorporation of kigo (a season word) remained out of his reach. Shiki's stand was taken by Kawaahigashi Hekigoto who took realism and the things related to daily life into focus.

Senryu and haiku seem to be the same because of the same criteria but in senryu, kigo (a season word) is not expected while in haiku, a kigo is a must. Senryu also takes human behaviour into a satirical focus from the viewpoints of poking fun.

Haiku has an advantage over English because of the Japanese language which is poly syllabic due to its pictorial script. It was introduced to the western world through translation which resulted in its different varieties. It was explored and investigated for further possibilities in terms of themes and techniques. To express life and its experiences in just three lines through images became a challenge which was accepted by the western practitioners who embraced it with love but modified its usual format of 5-7-5 into the format which suited them to clothe an experience from life.

R. K. Singh, a significant haiku bard who pays "minute attention to language, managing skill to achieve warmth and feeling with concision and pointedness" (Patricia Prime 21), has carved out "an imperishable apartment in the Glittering Mansion of Current Indian English Poetry" (Tiwari 30). *The River Returns* (2006) comprises 144 tanka and 371 haiku. The poet in R. K. Singh does not adhere to the set traditional pattern of tanka and haiku of 5-7-5-7-7 and 5-7-5 syllables respectively. He himself states his stand in Prefatory Note: "Now I do not adhere to the 5-7-5 syllables, nor do I make any difference between haiku and senryu. I just practice haiku in different beats (3-5-3, 4-6-4, 5-7-5) or free-form haiku, and when possible, expand its lyrical content to a tanka in five lines without restricting myself to 5-7-5-7-7 rhythm" (*The River Returns* 01). The traditional patterns confine the poet who feels uncomfortable and restricted to communicate his feelings. Hence, flexibility is always recommended to give more freedom to the poet who explores his space in a better way for his articulations. Recommending the new trends, Stephen Gill writes: "I suggest that the introduction of new trends into an old system should be welcomed with open arms. We know stagnant waters become breeding grounds for mosquitoes—anything that becomes stale will soon start to stink. It is in the interest of its health to let haiku breath in fresh air. No one should be afraid of change or experimentation. If haiku is alive today, it is largely due to its flexibility to allow new trends to be incorporated into it" (*Flashes* 8). R. K. Singh has successfully employed haiku and tanka for his poetic expressions in *The River Returns*. His skill in the use of haiku and tanka lies in elevating "the quotidian experiences to the level of poetry" (*The River Returns* 01). In this paper, my focus is on the flashes from flesh. These flashes provide pleasures—aesthetic as well as erotic—and I believe that they are a part of the quotidian experiences. I have attempted to justify the genius of R. K. Singh who, as a composer of haiku and tanka, succeeds not only in communicating such experiences but also in evoking them in the readers who are themselves sensuous to experience them.

The epigraph is a key to understand Singh's approach to haiku and tanka in *The River Returns*. The epigraph states: "No law can be sacred to me but that of my nature. Good and bad are but names very readily transferable to that or this; the only right is what is after my constitution; the only wrong what is against it. (Ralph Waldo Emerson, *Self-Reliance*). The epigraph makes it clear that the poet in R. K. Singh is going to communicate what he feels. He will feel no hesitation and no shame provided it comes from within. It depends on one's attitude to decide the criteria of right and wrong. Shakespeare in *Hamlet* states: "There is nothing either good or bad but thinking makes it so" (*Hamlet* 1141). No one can deny the religion of blood. It was D. H. Lawrence who articulated his love for the religion of blood that makes a human being alive. Everyone possesses the aesthetic sense but misses it somewhere because of shame or hesitation and so feels a void in him. Singh, who is an acknowledged poet of love and sex, has exploited the aesthetic and erotic experiences in *The River Returns*.

The title, *The River Returns*, is itself suggestive, as it creates an image on the mind of the reader, who sees a river returning to its usual course. It is the re-turn of the river which makes life worth-living and worth-enjoying. River signifies life and its return signifies return of life, energy, vigour amid deadliness and gloom.

Dancing
a few muddied crocs:
the river returns (*The River Returns,* p. 98)

It is love that makes life worth living. Who knows the magic of love better than R. K. Singh? It is the love in which he has a keen desire to merge his 'Self' so that he may explore himself and feel the ecstacy. Sample the tanka for Singh's philosophy of love:

Love is the efflux
from her body spreading
parabolic hue—
enlightens the self I merge
in her glowing presence (*The River Returns,* p. 10)

The poet in R. K. Singh possesses an exceptional aesthetic sense. At the river, he sees a female persona who is sitting with her folded arms and legs while her head is on her knees. She seems to be an island—an island that attracts. Mark R. K. Singh's scenery of such an island painted with poetic colour:

At the river
she folds her arms and legs
resting her head
upon the knees and sits
as an island (*The River Returns* , p. 5)

The coos of the Koel attract the female persona who associates herself with it and feels happy while hearing the voice of the unrealized bliss. The very association with koel makes her feel 'koel' in her, to the extent, that she becomes wet with the rain of love and delight. The poet has poeticized the female persona's association with koel. Sample the tanka:

She hears the voice
of unrealized bliss in
the coos of koel
at the window sill this evening
rains love and delight (*The River Returns* , p.3)

What makes R.K. Singh's poetry striking is its unique way of opening the doors of imagination. The scenes or pictures he creates offer multiple interpretations. He is an artist who paints the painting with visual words that have the unusual charm to provide the pleasures to the readers who interpret according to their whims. No meaning can be finalized from the painting hanging in his poetic gallery. Mark the excerpt for multiple versions that the readers search on repeated readings:

Before the foamy
water could sting her vulva
a jelly fish passed
through the crotch making her shy
the sea whispered a new song (*The River Returns* ,p. 6)

This tanka, though simple in appeal, carries various connotations. A reader with the aesthetic sense will create the new interpretations from it. The lines also reveal the fore-play before the sex act. The comment of Natshishi: "Currently Haiku may be accepted mainly because of its perceived exoticism. Superficial exoticism is a mere temporary pastime but deepened exoticism must bring something new and precious" (Natshishi 19) is quite true in the case of R. K. Singh who knows the value of eroticism and his poetic verse exhales eroticism which makes the readers feel intoxicated.

The Poet in R. K. Singh celebrates beauty and sex with the sense of worship as a woman is "the chief source of his creative afflatus; woman not as an imaginary angel but women in her all corporeal riches, eye, thighs, globular breasts" (Tiwari 3). It is he who makes the lover write haiku on the back of the beloved with the strands of watery hair.

Writing with strands of
watery hair on her back
a love haiku (*The River Returns*, p. 66)

The lover fondles with the beloved's breasts and writes a poem on her body.

Fondling her breasts
I incite a poem
on her body (*The River Returns*, p. 72)

The beloved is charming and bewitching. When the lover sees her, he feels sensation in his body.

Seeing her
a liquid sensation
between the thighs (*The River Returns*, p. 69)

The poet in Singh shoots the snap of the female persona challenging the moon. With her bulging breasts, she puts a challenge before the moon as she walks. She is herself a moon but thinks that her own breasts that are bobbing up and down are fairer than the moon.

With her breasts bobbing
up and down she challenges
the moon as she walks (*The River Returns*, p. 66)

Mark the following tanka which reveals the mental condition of the lover whose fingers search for the little pearl of blood in the forest of his beloved's hair. He calls hair forest, as he is lost like a man who forgets the path in the jungle. His fingers fondle the hair in hope of pearl that will show him a path that will lead him to the pinnacle of pleasure. Pearl of blood has the quality of stirring the hidden waters. Like D. H. Lawrence, he talks of the pearl of blood because it is the only thing that contains his restlessness.

In the forest of your hair
my finger searches
the little pearl of blood

that stirs the hidden waters
and contains my restlessness (*The River Returns*, p. 27)

The aesthetic sense is flowing in the veins of the poet who does not fail to praise the manicured fingers with which she peels the orange in an artistic manner. Sample the tanka for this aesthetic pleasure:

Peeling the orange
with manicured fingers:
she slits the rind from
top to bottom, separates
each section with artistry (*The River Returns*, p. 28)

Woman wish to be adored. If someone touches her in an impure manner, she becomes angry. She can be pleased only through love that culminates in the sacred sex, not through lust that culminates into rape. Here is a Haiku that presents the female persona in anger with the lover, who without washing hands, touches hibiscus for worship:

Without washing hands
he touches hibiscus for worship:
her frowning glance (*The River Returns*, p. 42)

She decorates her navel with the diamond that glitters and throws rays all around. The swinging diamond on her navel makes her sexually alluring to the extent that she seems to be an item bomb.

With glittering diamond
on the navel swinging
an item bomb (*The River Returns*, p. 96)

Further, the nose pin that the beloved wears attracts the lover so much that he sees a rainbow in it. The lover feels the tantalizing smell of food which has the rainbow variety to satisfy his hunger. The nose-pin that reflects the sensuous rays makes herself a delicious food that will fill his body and soul with the flashes of seven colours making him rich physically and spiritually.

Flashing a rainbow
at the dining table
her diamond nose-pin (*The River Returns*, p. 102)

The poet gives due significance to thighs and breasts in his erotic verses. "Thighs, regarded as the repository of warmth in Indian Erotics, occupy a major place in his sexual imagination" (Tiwari 4). Mark the sexual picture shot by Singh through his poetic camera:

Winter's chill—
sweating under the gown
her thighs and breasts (*The River Returns,* p. 71)

Here, the male persona in spite of being adult has the tendency to sleep on the thighs of his beloved. This is the place where he seeks rest. This is the motherly affection which he expects from his beloved who provides peace to his head. Mark the Haiku for such impression:

Her thighs—
resting place for his head
on bed (*The River Returns,* p. 71)

How candidly the poet expresses the childishness of man who in spite of being a man gets rest and feels secure in the lap of a woman who provides a sheltering shell for him!

Still a child—
embracing a breast
sleeps her man (*The River Returns,* p. 79)

The poet in Singh searches for the aesthetic pleasures even in the wet bodies of the bathing women. These women, when bathed, look fresh and their fair complexion begins to reflect to the extent that they vie with the full moon light that falls on their wet bodies making them more appealing and aesthetically satisfying. Sample the Haiku for such effect:

Wet bodies
of bathing women:
full moon night (*The River Returns,* p. 53)

The poet does not fail to trace out the titillating pleasures in day-today life. The power goes off and the result is that the female persona begins to feel summer heat which compels her to undo the hook of her bra.

The power goes off
suddenly summer heat chokes
in bed sleepless she turns
undoing a hook or two
of her tight bra (*The River Returns,* p. 19)

When there is power cut, it seems to the poet that it is playing with the female persona. The power cut is not the power cut but it becomes the male persona who is winking at her. Mark the haiku for poeticizing such an experience:

Winking at her
in the dark—
power cut (*The River Returns,* p. 98)

One power goes, the other comes. Darkness gives birth to the other power—sexual one.

Mark the following haiku for the poetic flash in the sexual act done on the sofa.

As the duo sit
lights go out—
sofa springs creaking (*The River Returns,* p. 48)

In the next haiku the male persona stands before the female persona who is like nude Venus to him. He is enthralled and excited to gaze the lady who looks seductive and ravishing. It is the genius of R.K. Singh to capture this universal experience in mere three lines.

He stands before
the nude Venus awaiting
her gown to drop (*The River Returns,* p. 44)

Now, the poet shoots the scene of two female lovers through his haiku that exhibits the landscape of Stone penis at Shinto shrine. The scene fills the two female lovers with pleasure and desire. It also has the hidden hint towards lesbianism. The stone penis that they lack makes them stare. Mark the female lover's staring at the huge stone penis which creates a longing in them:

Staring at the huge
Stone-penis at Shinto shrine—
two female lovers (*The River Returns,* p. 65)

R. K. Singh's haiku have layers within layers. He provides the space in three lines for exploration which leads the readers for further exploration. Mark the haiku for the multiple meanings:

Chanting mantra
with wine in one hand and
torch in other (*The River Returns,* p. 63)

This haiku though seems to be simple in expression is not so, as different readers trace meanings from it according to their imagination. The simple meaning that the haiku offers is that a man chants mantra with wine in one hand and a torch in other but such is not the case. The chanting of the mantra may be the male persona's cravings for spiritualism. The wine in his hand indicates that he is a hedonist and wants to enjoy life fully. Torch in hand shows the light—the light of knowledge and spiritualism that he wants to spread. This indicates that he wants to make a good adjustment in the two worlds—materialism and spiritualism. The readers may also read it from another angle. Mantra may be the songs of love that the lover sings to attract the beloved to him. The torch is suggestive of genital. This is the imaginative aesthetic beauty of Singh's haiku. In another haiku, the lover when he is alone prefers haiku to yoga and also wishes to enjoy life through scotch. "In the lone room / prefers haiku to yoga / drinking scotch" (*The River Returns,* p. 77)

Now, the poet focuses the erotic pleasures experienced by husband and wife—a relation that cannot be continued without sex—sex with adoration.

> The first night
> spots on the sheet:
> clothes wake up (*The River Returns,* p. 91)

This haiku takes the readers to the room where both husband and wife pass the first night. The very first line "The first night" creates a sensation in the mind that starts creating the picture of sex-act. The second line "spots on the sheet" makes the readers imagine virginity and loss of the same. The spots are not the spots to be washed but are desired on the sheet because of the belief in the integrity of the wife. Hence, these spots wake up the clothes. The husband feels proud of himself and his masculinity with the assumption that he succeeds in untying the virgin knot.

The two lovers share in each other's distress and misery. They wipe each other's tears and the action of wiping tears illustrates the intensity of their love. "Wiping tears / from each other's eyes / two souls in love" (*The River Returns,* p. 66). The young couple likes privacy which makes them share with and feel for each other. An example is: "A young couple / under the red umbrella / rejoicing privacy" (*The River Returns,* p. 59). Further, the husband gets the erotic pleasures when he sees his wife's *saree* which is hooked between her legs. Her lying on the bed in this posture magnetizes the husband who stares her body in this pose. "With her saree / hitched up between the legs / my wife in bed" (*The River Returns,* p. 48). Togetherness is the bonding agent that binds a husband and a wife or a lover or a beloved together. The main ingredient of this bonding agent is sex which is certainly a music that results from the rattling of their bones together. The flesh sings a song in the night and their sex activity brings them together. "Bones rattle to make / a song of flesh in the night – / togetherness" (*The River Returns* 73). They are the two peacocks who dance on a spree. This dancing together brings water—water of love in which both bath. "Two peacocks / on a dancing spree: / see water" (*The River Returns,* p. 98). Love and sex are correlated to enjoy relationship, particularly, the conjugal one. Sex is converted into rape when any partner is not willing. It is the possibility that the wife may leave her husband for forced sex. Sample the two haiku for forced sex which results in either her departure from husband's world or her threatening to move to daughter's room:

Fed up with my sex
she threatens to move
to our daughter's room (*The River Returns,* p. 70)

....

Leaves him alone
to escape daily rape
in bed his wife (*The River Returns,* p. 71)

R. K. Singh knows the magic that love brings in life. Love yields to the open arms. The rains fall from the sky to meet the earth. The meeting of rains with the earth symbolizes the philosophy of love.

The rains
cry to meet earth
fall from sky day and night
remind love always yields to arms
open (*The River Returns,* p. 37)

It is out of love that the poet sees the rainbow, which possesses seven colours, which colour life. Yamuna Bridge is not the Yamuna bridge; it becomes a symbol of love. It reflects the rainbow in the mirror of water. It is the bridge of relationship that joins two banks. The water of love that flows between the two hearts reflects the image of their relationship. "Reflects the rainbow / in the mirror of water—/Yamuna Bridge" (*The River Returns,* p. 102).

A few words about the technical aspects of R. K. Singh's Haiku and Tanka are worth- mentioning. One tanka and one haiku are being quoted for this purpose though a separate research paper is needed to explore the techniques. Mark the tanka or cinquain for the technical aspect.

At the river
she folds her arms and legs
resting her head
upon the knees and sits
as an island (*The River Returns,* p. 5)

Singh shoots first the sight of river, then a woman folding her arms, then her head, then her knees and at last her impression of an island. The camera first takes the wide view of the river and at last creates the impression of an island in the river. Island in the river, not in the sea—a marvelous image indeed! His camera takes the stills of woman in action—folding her arms , then folding her legs, then her head moving for rest and at last the place—knees where she will put her head. The images in lines are flowing seamlessly into one thought—the thought of island. It is written in elevated tone. In depiction, there is no vulgarity. However, he has employed gerunds, preposition and verbs which a tanka or haiku writer is expected to avoid. The poet in Singh knows it but uses them where they seem to be necessary. It does not matter if he has to sacrifice the traditional rules but he will not compromise with the quality of the haiku. He has used the liquid and simple words that make the tanka memorable and deep-imprinted on the mind. Now, one haiku for technical view point is analyzed here.

As the duo sit
lights go out—
sofa springs creaking (*The River Returns,* p. 48)

The haiku is in free form, as the poet likes to follow its traditional as well as modern form. The first line "As the duo sit" continues in the second line. If the poet had not used the word "as", it would not have been in continuation. Even without "as" the effect would have been the same. But, it seems that the poet knowingly is connecting the relation of the sitting of duo with the lights. Either the lights give them a chance for body –exploration or the word "as" reflect a chance happening. The punctuation at the end of second line makes the readers think for some moments for the consequence. But, in the first two lines, the poet has not mentioned sofa or the thing where they sit. The creaking of sofa spring indicates the sex-act in which the duo indulges. The word "creaking" creates an auditory image because of the darkness and the readers guess sex-act only through the creaking.

Generally a haiku ends with a noun but R. K. Singh gives variation and uses "creaking". He fills an ultimate experience in an unusual way with such words as produce sound. Creaking produces a particular feeling of sex-act which is the desired effect created in this haiku. Lyrical expression is flowing in the vein of this haiku and the poet has achieved it without using any rhyme.

Love and sex are correlated as both are essential for the exploration of the self. Sex is the background against which love shines colourfully. The poet in Singh attempts to attain the ecstasy of love through sex which is not lust for him but a thing to be adored, as it prepares the way for the final *nirvana* in the materialistic world. Man gets peace and calm of his mind when passions are spent. Passions must be properly channelised so that they may be turned into a driving force. *The River Returns* provides the erotic as well as aesthetic flashes to the readers who appreciate the poet for his skill in translating such experiences. R. S. Tiwari writes: "R.K. Singh's Erotic Muse strikes us with its openness, its seriousness, its candour and its eventual exaltation of Rati to a plane where the apparent glamour of the flesh merges into a Universal Principle of Creation" (Tiwari 19). The poet creates visual scenes before the readers who with the persona feel all such experiences. But, nowhere, the poet sounds obscene and vulgar. He is always fresh in appeal and no where he compromises with the emotional content. What he states in the prefatory note: "Even as I appear to speak directly, the subjective and the objective tend to mix up, hopefully, without compromising the emotional content, passion, vigour or freshness" (*The River Returns* 02) is true and quite applicable to *The River Returns*.

WORKS CITED

1. Gill, Stephen. "The Haiku I Write." *Flashes*. New Delhi: Imprint, 2007: 7-10. Print.
2. Kaul, Urmila. "Article on Haiku." *Poetcrit*. No. 8 Vol. XXI July 2008:19-30. Print.
3. Natsuishi, Ban'ya. "My Romance with Haiku.", *Poets International*. No. 8, Vol. 23. 2006: 18-19. Print.

4. Prime, Patricia. "Poetry of Moment." *Poets International.* No: 1 Vol.: 25 January 2008: 19-23.Print.
5. Shakespeare, William. "*Hamlet.*" *The Complete Works of Shakespeare.* London and Glasgow: Collins Clear Type Press, 1127-1170. Print.
6. Singh, R. K. *The River Returns.* Bareilly: Prakash Book Depot, 2006. Print.
7. Tiwari, R. S. "R. K. Singh's Commitment to Fleshly Reality." *Current Indian Creativity in English.* Jaipur: Book Enclave, 2003: 3-22. Print.
8. Tiwari, R. S. "Above the Earth's Green." *Current Indian Creativity in English.* Jaipur: Book Enclave, 2003: 23-39. Print.

21

The Magnetism of the Measured Syllables: R.K. Singh's Haiku and Tanka Sequences

— ***Rajni Singh***

Today Japanese poetry has transcended the barriers of regions and augmented as a vivid poetic form. It is being translated, imitated and even integrated into different cultures. Many poets writing regular poems at one time or another have experimented with haiku or haiku-related genres. Perhaps, it would not be wrong to say that the present time witnesses the flowering of English- language haiku worldwide with some Indian poets as active contributors, namely Mujib Yar Jung , Angelee Deodhar, K.Ramesh, Kala Ramesh, R.K.Singh, Mohd. Farhruddin, D.H.Kabadi, I.H.Rizvi, Narayana Rao, Maria Netto, Urmila Kaul, Radhey Shyam, D.C. Chambial, Kanwar Dinesh Singh and others. One notices more and more poets have been exploring haiku and haiku related arts such as haibun and linked verse forms.

R.K.Singh is one such Indian English haikuist who began his poetic career with writing long poems followed by short verses—haiku and tanka—and further went on to experiment with haiku and tanka sequences. Singh's *Every Stone Drop Pebble* (jointly with Catherine Mair and Patricia Prime,1999) and *Peddling Dream* (in English and Italian trilogy, *Pacem in Terris*,2003) and more recently *The River Returns* (a tanka and haiku collection,2006) are the three volumes of haiku and tanka that confirm Singh's dominating presence in English language haiku scene. Singh's haiku and tanka have appeared in such prestigious journals as *Lynx, Simply Haiku, Maimichi Daily News,Modern English Tanka, The Asahi Shimbun, Ko-, The Tanka Journal, Ginyu, Haiku Spirit, Presence, Winterspin, Mirror, At Last, Moonset, Frogpond, Tinywords* etc. and his reputation as a haikuist continues to grow. Probably, the shift in poetic form, from long poems to haiku and tanka, must have happened to the poet naturally because even in his long poems the poet "articulates his feelings and thoughts in measured syllables, eschewing unnecessary flamboyance of language or flights of fancy." It is this poetic talent which makes R.K.Singh a prolific writer of haiku and tanka. Singh's recent dabbling at haiku sequences is another feather in his cap. The poet takes delight in haiku and tanka sequences and has composed quite a number of sequences, some of which have appeared in *India Saijiki* (July 2006) and *Lynx* (vol. XIX: 2, vol.XXII:1, vol.XX:3, Vol.XVIII:3, etc).

Singh composes his sequences by gathering and threading the haiku pieces thematically. In fact, the poet adopts the same style of composition for his longer poems as well. I.K. Sharma, too, has pointed out this distinct feature of R.K. Singh's poetry in his "Introduction" to New Indian English Poetry: An Alternative Voice: "His art of making poem is not to make a poem but to make beads for a poem, which he later on would string together."

Singh's haiku sequence "Love-making" is threaded with eight haiku pieces. It is a sensual vignette about the beauty and freedom in a single moment of intimacy between lovers:

Love making
he melts into her
time stands still

Love making
the sound of orgasm:
Lao Tzu

[" A great sound is audible , and a great image is formless," said Lao Tzu.]

Making love
she tastes the salt upon
his shoulder

Candling in vein
leaves marks of teeth on her neck
utters holiness

Unclothing
the white night:
lips meeting lips

Writes with strands of
watery hair on her bare back
a love haiku

After the tumble
buried between the sheets
left over passion

She departs
leaving behind her clothes
over mine

The sequence captures the essence of physical contact. Each string appears a delicate bundle of joy and captures within it an emotion and a moment of utmost bliss. The carnal yearnings of the lovers are presented in such a way that they exhilarate all the senses. The poet focuses one moment in time and that time seems suspended leaving the reader to only imagine the before and after.

The next haiku sequence, 'Winter', is a loosely liked haiku sequence. But the verses have the sensory depth, often visual and auditory vividness of the genre:

Wintry winds
bangs the window tonight
my thoughts agitate

Midnight—
absent whispers
from her room

The sun shines
on the winter blooms:
our first rose

Morning sun
in the dewy lawn
blue roses
Meeting again
the fragrance of night queen
in our bedroom

Naphthalene smell
oozes from the sweater—
fourth December

Noisy parrots
returning to the tree:
sun set early

Each haiku of the sequence is terse, dynamic and complete poetry and focuses the 'momentness' of a moment: "what is happening" at a particular moment with all its freshness and truth. For the poet Nature becomes a tool to probe into human nature. The depiction of the inner turmoil through the turbulent winds in the first haiku is remarkable.

Singh's haiku is notable for rich and resilient images. The succinctness, objectiveness, concreteness, directness and simplicity of his short verses captivate the reader's heart and mind.

Like the haiku sequences, Singh's tanka sequences, too, hold the interest of the reader throughout, moving along smoothly. Tanka traditionally embodies the delights and tragedies of love. Singh's tanka retain most of the traditional elements such as the syllabic pattern of 5-7-5-7-7, kake kotoba, i.e., pivot words, engo, i.e., puns and seasonal or cultural allusions. The following tanka sequence bespeaks love:

Love

His message to meet
at moonrise among flowers
sparkles a secret
on her smiling face passion
glows with charming fervor

She is no moon yet
she drifts like the moon takes care
of him from the sky—
meets him for a short, waxing
leaves him for a long, waning

Before going to bed
she looks too sad to have
any sweet dream:
the lonely lamp glints no love
and no star peeps through the curtains

Yearning to meet him
she turns a silk-worm spinning

love- silk in cold night—
stands in a shade melting tears
like a candle , drop by drop
Stains of dried dewy
tears on the eyelids tell of
the load on her mind:
clothed in spring the willow twigs
reveal the changed relation

'Love: Tanka Sequence' is a string of five tanka which envisages the joys and pangs in separation and union. In the first tanka the beloved's yearning to meet her lover is expressed covertly. The immediacy with which the bereaved soul transforms into a passionate flower is again striking.

The next tanka starts with a straight declarative statement 'she is no moon'. The antithetical statement is quick enough to capture the attention of the reader and to behold her/him.

The tanka is entwined in rhythmical pattern- 'drifts', 'meets', 'leaves', 'short', 'long', 'waxing', and 'waning'. The passionately stumbling movement of the damsel which is compared with the waxing and waning of the moon has a 'clicking' effect.

The next three tanka, resonate a deep melancholic strain. They weave the story of a wronged forlorn woman who cannot endure the pangs of separation and betrayal. The tragedies of love are well reflected in the following lines: '... the lonely lamp glints no love/and no star peeps through the curtain'; '...she turns a silk-worm spinning/ love-silk in cold night—/stands in a shade melting tears/ like a candle , drop by drop'; '...clothed in spring the willow twigs/reveal the changed relation'. The poet presents the paradoxes of human relationship in a mature manner. He skillfully constructs the emotional dynamics of the lovers. The cry of the agonized soul reverberates beyond the lines.

The tanka sequence is a good sequence as each poem is fitted in its exact place with a beginning, middle and end. Each poem holds a precise place in the sequence and yet stands alone as a unitary, aesthetic whole— a complete poem. The haiku pieces function as pieces of a collage and play a vital role in moving the story forward. It is through the exact positioning of the verses that each poem gains meaning from its connection to the poem preceding and following it.

The sequence is also remarkable for its economy of words in delineating the feelings of the beloved. Every word counts for maximum impact and import as the poet takes utmost care to give full weight and measure to each sparsely worded reflection.

Writing poetry is not just the practice of a technique it is something more than that. In Cid Corman's words, "it is life... and if one worked at one's life, the poem would come of its own." And in Basho's words, "To make a poem about the pine, study the pine, Become the pine." Singh's poetry is never a churned out machine work, it emerges right from his soul. His haiku and tanka have the lucid gleam of the morning dew and liquid clearness of the limpid stream that runs glittering in open sunshine. His sequences are remarkable for their clarity, chiseled beauty and inevitable afflatus.

WORKS CITED

1. Mair, Catherine., Patricia Prime & R.K.Singh. *Every Stone Drop Pebble.* New Delhi: Bahri Publications, 1999.
2. Trumbell, Charles. "The American Haiku Movement Part I: Haiku in English," *Modern Haiku* Vol. 36.3 Autumn 2005.
3. Sharma, I.K. "Introduction" *New Indian English Poetry: An Alternative Voice,* Edited by I.K. Sharma, Jaipur: Book Enclave, 2004, p.11.
4. Marton, John. "The Way of Poetry: Part I of II- for Jeremy Seligson" in *Moonset, The Newspaper*, vol3. Issue2. Autumn/ winter 2007 Oregon: New York USA, p.16.
5. Singh, R.K. Book Review. *Deuce: Haiku Poems* (New Delhi: K.K. Publishers and Distributors, 2001) in Indian Book Chronicle, Vol.28, No.4 April 2003, p.5.
6. Tiwary, R.S. " "Secret of the First Menstrual Flow":R.K.Singh's Commitment to Fleshly Reality"' *New Indian English Poetry: An Alternative Voice,* Edited by I.K. Sharma, Jaipur: Book Enclave, 2004, p.89.
7. Reichhold, Werner, "Some Developments in the House of Tanka" in *Lynx* Vol.XIV: No.2.
8. http:// www.haiku-hia.com

9. http:// www.tinywords.com
10. http://www.ahapoetry.com/ahalynx/
11. http://indiasaijikiworlkhaiku.blogspot.com/2006/07/r-k-singh.html

Publications of R. K. Singh

1. *Savitri: A Spiritual Epic.* Bareilly: Prakash Book Depot, 1984, pages 164. (A critical study of Sri Aurobindo's epic Savitri).
2. *Krishna Srinivas: The Poet of Inner Aspiration.* Madras: Poets Press India, 1984, pages 30. (A monograph).
3. *My Silence.* Madras: Poets Press India, 1985, pages 44. (A collection of poems).
4. *Sound and Silence.* Madras: Poets Press India, 1986, pages 160. (A collection of critical articles on the poetry of Krishna Srinivas, edited with an introduction).
5. *Indian English Writing: 1981-1985: Experiments with Expression.* New Delhi:Bahri Publications Pvt Ltd., 1987, rept. 1991, pages 168. (A collection of critical articles, edited with an introduction).
6. *Memories Unmemoried.* Berhampur: Poetry Time Publications, 1988, pages 24. (A collection of poems).
7. *Music Must Sound.* Dhanbad: R.K.Singh, 1990 (A stenciled collection of poems).
8. *Flight of Phoenix.* Berhampur: Poetry Time Publications, 1990, pages 35. (A Collection of Poems).
9. *Recent Indian English Poets: Expressions and Beliefs*. New Delhi: Bahri Publications, 1992, pages 192. (A collection of critical articles edited with Introduction).
10. *Two Poets: R.K.Singh* (I DO NOT QUESTION) Ujjal Singh Bahri (THE GRAMMAR OF MY LIFE).New Delhi: Bahri Publications, 1994, pages 83. (edited two collections of poems, including my own, pp.44).
11. *My Silence and Other Selected Poems: 1974-1994.* Bareilly: Prakash Book Depot, 1996, pages 185. (A collection of poems, including earlier volumes).
12. *Anger in Action: Explorations of Anger in Indian Writing in English.* New Delhi: Bahri Publications, 1997, pages 238. (A collection of critical articles – edited with an Introduction).

13. *Above the Earth's Green.* Calcutta: Writers Workshop, 1997, pages 126. (A collection of poems).

14. *Psychic Knot : Search for Tolerance in Indian English Fiction.*

    New Delhi : Bahri Publications, 1998, pages 211. (A collection of critical articles – edited with an Introduction).

15. *New Zealand Literature : Some Recent Trends.* New Delhi : Bahri Publications, 1998, pages 138. (A collection of critical articles- edited with an Introduction).

16. *Every Stone Drop Pebble.* New Delhi : Bahri Publications, 1999, pages 70. (A collection of Haiku jointly with Catherine Mair and Patricia Prime).

17. *Cover to Cover: A Collection of Poems* (R K Singh : The Face in All Seasons, pp 43). New Delhi : Bahri Publications, 2002. (A Collection of Poems jointly with Ujjal Singh Bahri).

18. *Pacem in Terris.* Trento, Italy: Edizioni Universum, 2003. (A trilogy collection of poems in English and Italian, jointly with Myriam Pierri and Giovanni Campisi, including my haiku collection, Peddling Dream, pages 63-88)

19. *Sri Aurobindo's Savitri : Essays on Love, Life and Death.* Bareilly: Prakash Book Depot, 2005, pages 176.

20. *For a World Peace.* (jointly with Renza Agnelli and Danae G. Papastraton).Rocca di Caprileone(ME): Edizioni Universum, 2005, pages 28.

21. *Voices of the Present: Critical Essays on Some Indian English Poets.* Jaipur: Book Enclave, 2006, pages 267.

22. *The River Returns.* Bareilly: Prakash Book Depot, 2006, pages 86. (A collection of tanka and haiku

23. *Sexless Solitude and Other Poems.* Bareilly: Prakash Book Depot, 2009, pages 86.

24. *Sense and Silence: Collected Poems.* Jaipur: Yking Books. 2010. Pages 338. (All previously published collections of poems with some new poems, haiku, and tanka).

    (The list excludes books on ELT/ESP practices.)

E-BOOKS:

1. My Silence. August 21, 2006, pages 30. Price: $6.10 http://www.lulu.com/product/paperback/my-silence/446796
2. Memories Unmemoried. August 24, 2006, pages 16. Price: $6.07. http://www.lulu.com/product/paperback/memories-unmemoried/450960
3. Music Must Sound. August 21, 2006, pages 29. Price: $6.33 http://www.lulu.com/product/paperback/music-must-sound/446932
4. Flight of Phoenix. August 20, 2006, pages 25. Price: $6.25 http://www.lulu.com/product/paperback/flight-of-phoenix/446767
5. No Moist Secret and Elements Clack Silence. August 21, 2006, pages 37. Price: $7.68 http://www.lulu.com/product/paperback/no-moist-secret-elements-clack-silence/446799
6. The River Returns. August 24, 2006, pages 55. Price: $8.13 http://www.lulu.com/product/paperback/the-river-returns/450953
7. I'm No River. August 21, 2006, pages 34. Price: $7.60 http://www.lulu.com/product/paperback/im-no-river/446785
8. Views and Reviews. August 21, 2007, pages 95. Price: $9.13 http://www.lulu.com/product/paperback/views-and-reviews/1450257
9. Sexless Solitude and Other Poems. November 20, 2007, pages 15. Price: $ 18.50 http://www.lulu.com/product/paperback/sexless-solitude-and-other-poems/1927418
10. Selected Poems of R.K.Singh. December 17, 2009, pages 461. Price: $ 16.78 http://www.lulu.com/product/paperback/selected-poems-of-rksingh/6148277
11. Sexless Solitude and Other Poems: A Bilingual Collection: English-Greek. January 16, 2010, pages 129. Price: $ 10.82 http://www.lulu.com/product/paperback/sexless-solitude-and-other-poems-a-bilingual-collection-english—greek/6258509
12. R.K.Singh: Poems. Poetry Series. February 2010. http://www.poemhunter.com/r-k-singh/

13. Night's Rumblings and Other Poems Volume One: R.K.Singh. Text CD. Price: $ 17.95 http://poetrypoem.com/cgi-bin/index.pl?sitename=poetry710&item=poetry&password=
14. Sexless Solitude and Other Poems. Text CD. Price: $17.95 http://poetrypoem.com/cgi-bin/index.pl?sitename=poetry710&item=poetry&password=

POEMS PUBLISHED IN JOURNALS:

Poet (Madras, Skylark(Aligarh), Indian Literature (New Delhi), Journal of Indian Writing in English (Gulbarga), The Educatonal Journal (New Delhi), ELT Forum Journal of India (Bombay), ELT Forum Journal of English Studies (Tellicherry), Rajasthan Journal of English Studies (Amravati/Jaipur), Commonwealth Quarterly (Mysore), Kuensel (Bhutan), Indian and Foreign Review (New Delhi), Quill (New Delhu), Unilit (Secunderabad), The Century (New Delhi), Adam and Eve (Madras), The Third Eye (Calcutta), University Today (New Delhi), The Call Beyond (New Delhi), Samvedana (Mangalore), Youth Age (Pondicherry), Asparagus (Hyderabad), Poetry Time (Berhampur), Poesie (Berhampur), Bharat Protiva (Calcutta), Byword (New Delhi), Poetry (Aska/Berhampur), Art and Poetry Today (New Delhi), Poets International (Bangalore), Canopy (Bareilly), Rock Pebbles (Cuttack), New Literary Horizons (Amravati), Indian Book Chronicle (Jaipur), Poetcrit (Maranda), Kavita India (Muzaffarpur), Ocarina (Madras), Rachna India (New Delhi), Hesperus Review (Calcutta), Eureka (Porbandar), International Poetry (Colorado, USA), The Indian Writer (Madras), Broadsheet (Aligarh), Triveni (Guntur/Hyderabad), Kanora (Colombia), Noreal (Caen, France), Kaiser-e-Hind (Bombay), Manxa (Ciudad Real, Spain), Symphony (Cuttack), Creative Forum (New Delhi), Puck and Pluck (Florida), CER*BER*US (Florida), East and West Literary Quarterly (San Francisco), Poiesis (Bombay), Prophetic Voices (Novato, CA), International Poets (Madras), Young Poet (Tellicherry), Creative Inspiration (Queensland, Australia), FEM-LIT (Kendrapara), Forum (New Zealand), BAFA Newsletter (Maastricht, The Netherlands), Arts Dialogue (Apeldoorn, The Netherlands), Bridge in Making (Calcutta), Indian Literary Panorama (Bombay), Haritham (Kottayam), Friends in Touch (New Mexico,USA), Thirteen Poetry Magazine (New York), Fantasy (Allahabad), Fun (Allahabad), Amber (Dartmouth, Canada),

Twilight Ending (Milford, CT), Micropress Yates (Queensland, Australia), La Pierna Tierna (PA, USA), Timber Creek Review (NJ, USA), The Quest (Ranchi), The Brain Wave (Madras), Inner Voice (Gajapati, Orissa), Spin (Auckland, NZ), Hummingbird (Madison, USA), Hobo Poetry Magazine (NSW, Australia), Paper Wasp(Queensland, Australia), Micropress NZ (Nelson, NZ), Lilliput Review (PA, USA), Simply Words (GA, USA), Xizquil (Arizona, USA), Scoria (Chandigarh), Moongate de Homo Sentiens (NM, USA), Albatross (Constanta, Romania), At Last (Fife, Scotland), Azami (Osaka, Japan), Still (London), Vrabac/Sparrow (Samobor (Croatia), Piedmont Literary Review (NJ, USA), RAW NerVZ (QC, Canada), SlugFest, Ltd (SC, USA), Replica (Cuttack), Woodpecker (Jutripp, The Netherlands), Prijatelj (Tolmin, Slovenia), The Beachcomber (Nova Scotia, Canada), Haiku Novine/Haiku Shimbun (Yugoslavia), Valley Micropress (Upper Hutt, NZ), Poets Guild (Guwahati), Mirrors (Calgary, Canada), Cyber Literature (Patna), The Cascade (Cuttack), Words of Wisdom (Greensboro, NC, USA), The Poetry Chain (Trivandrum), The Haiku Quarterly (Swindon, UK), Kafla Intercontinental (Chandigarh), Poetry Today (Calcutta), LOTOS (Yugoslavia), The Green Valleys & Golden Fields Weekly (Dehradun), Green Apples (Tolmin, Slovenia), The Tanka Journal (Tokyo), The Mawaheb International (Canada), Shine (Thanjavur), Haiku Spirit (Ireland), Phegoz (Greece), Dasoku (USA), Hidden Oak (Philadelphia, USA), YoMiMoNo (Japan), Metverse Muse (Visakhapatnam), Ilakkia Ciragu (Tanjavur/Pottukkottai), Indo-Asian Literature (Delhi), Explorer (Sasaram), Voice of Calcutta (Calcutta), The Green Lotus (Bhubaneswar), Presence (Leeds, UK), Ko (Nagoya, Japan), Lynx (USA), Poesie India International (Bhubaneswar), Orfeu (Romania), Osvit (Yugoslavia), Asahi Shimbun (Japan), The Golden Vase (Bhubaneswar), Ginyu (Japan), The Prince of Poetry (Chennai), Mainichi Daily News (Japan), Bizz Buzz (Bangalore), Mandakini (Bareilly), Evergreen (Japan), Re-Markings (Agra), Fonto (Brazil), Culturelink (Croatia), Noon (Tokyo), Sri Aurobindo's Action (Pondicherry), Verse Universe (24 Parganas), Seva Bharati Journal of English Studies (Paschim Medinipur), 21st Century Cultural Discourse (Lucknow), Reflections (Bhagalpur), Kohinoor (Begusarai), Research (Patna), Pegasus (Agra), Keng-Shen Daily News (Taiwan), bear creek haiku (Boulder, USA), The World Poets Quarterly

(Chongqing, P.R.China), Magnapoets (Ontario, Canada), Kelaino (Athens, Greece), The Literary Paritantra (Systems) (Dayalbagh), Moonset Literary Newspaper (Oregon, USA), Poetry World (Chennai), Chairman Poetics (Taiwan), Concise Delight Magazine of Short Poetry (USA), Time Haiku (London), International Journal of English Language and Literature (Patna), Sarasvati (UK), Time Haiku (London), Obelisk (Tirana, Albania)

POEMS PUBLISHED ON-LINE:

Zimmerzine, indiaworld poetry, ahapoetry.com, Haiku Harvest, niederngasse, Hindustan.net, thinkers.net, uXu, asahi.com, snakeskin, EPN, poetry.com, poeticvoices.com Nightskye Magazine, poetsindia.com, cordite, MDN, widethinker.com, tinywords.com, Short Stuff/haikuhut.com, DHG, wordmachine1.com, haijinx.com, writers-zone.com, eternalartproductions.com, postpoems.com, I-ku Haiku, Aozora, tempslibre.org, catscratch.org, The Daily Poison, lit.org, Lei's Virtual Reality, todays-woman.net, allpoetry.com, writesight.com, Simply Haiku, Poetrybang.com, peacefromharmony.spb.ru, kdme.ca, poetrypoem.com, eroticaexpressions.net, darkervison.com, midnightedition.com, blogger.com, toosquare.com, celaine.com, museindia.com, dreamagic.com, blogspot.com, love-poem biz/blog, The Borzoi Reader, creativejunction.topsideword.com, literaryescape.com, authorsden.com, eliteskills.com, VLQ Poetry Forums, ilovepoetry.com, serenepoet.com,lovetime.ro,unknownwriters.net,bilingualmca.bravehost.com, strangehorizons.com, thejapaneseconnection.com, classicsnet.com, Kritya, Wangmaya, motherbird.com, shreve-lib.org, alittlepoetry.com, circleofpoets.com, The Web Poetry Corner, poetbay.com, brainmeta.com, poemhunter.com, postpoems.net, thewritersezine.com (T-Zero), WHCindia, The Pen & Quill, Voicesinthecrowd.net, poetices.com, lulu.com, poetry.net, terebess.hu/English/India.html, http://haiku.hu/interkezdo.html, poemsabout.com/poet/r-k-singh, findpoet.com, newageincorporated.com, redthreadhaikusangh, criticalpoet.com, writebay.com, Noon (Tokyo), Verse Universe, deviantart.com, gotpoetry.com, http://ezinearticles.com, http://multiply.com, www.myspace.com, www.livejournal.com

OTHER LINKS:

http://rksinghpoet.blogspot.com
http://rksingh.blogspot.com
http://profrksingh.blogspot.com
http:// rkeroticpoetry.blogspot.com
http://collectedpoemsofrksingh.blogspot.com
www.poetrypoem.com/poetry710
http//bilingualmca.bravehost.com/rksingh.html
http://poemhunter.com/r-k-singh/poet-79587
www.poemsabout.com/poet/r-k-singh
www.blogbud.com/rksingh
www.lit.org/blog/R.K.Singh
http://writebay.com/rksingh
http:/rksingh.wordpress.com
http://writers-network.com/member/rksingh
http://www.redroom.com/member/rksingh
http://www.scribd.com/profrksingh
http://ezinearticles.com/?expert=Ram_krishna_singh
http://profrksingh.multiply.com
http://indiasaijikiworlkhaiku.blogspot.com/2006/07r-k-singh.html

Index